MATCH OF THE DAY
BBC SPORT
ANNUAL 2006

CONTENTS

THE BEST PLAYERS IN THE WORLD

Who are the world's best players in each position? The MATCH OF THE DAY computer spits out the answers.

MAKING *MATCH OF THE DAY*

The team behind MATCH OF THE DAY explain how they get the show on the telly.

THE CRAZY CAREER OF WAYNE ROONEY

Wayne Rooney may be barely 20 but he's still the most exciting player in the Premiership.

WORLD CUP 2006

Are you ready for the biggest football tournament on the planet? Here's your guide to the 2006 World Cup.

BRITISH CHAMPIONS OF EUROPE

Check out this guide to all the Brits who have been crowned Kings Of Europe.

THE CHANGING FACE OF CHELSEA

Chelsea have come a long way in just ten years, but just how much has success cost them? We add it up!

PREMIERSHIP GUIDE

Your guide to all of this season's Premiership clubs and their star players.

MATCH OF THE DAY ANNUAL 2006

EDITOR Chris Hunt **ART DIRECTOR** David Houghton **DESIGNER** Alan Beeson **DESIGN CONSULTANTS** Cambridge Publishers Ltd **CONTRIBUTORS** Frank Gilbert, Luke Nicoli, Paul Robson, Andy Winter **DATA** Warner Leach Ltd **PHOTOGRAPHY** Action Images PLC **PUBLISHER** Terry Pratt A 'MILE AWAY CLUB' PRODUCTION

First published in Great Britain by Interact Publishing Ltd, PO Box 239, Ware SG9 9WX. Copyright Interact Publishing 2005. All rights reserved. No part of this publication may be reproduced, stored in a retrieval system or transmitted in any form without the prior permission of the publishers.

By arrangement with the BBC. BBC logo © BBC 1996. Match Of The Day logo © BBC 2004. The BBC logo and Match Of The Day logo are registered trademarks of the British Broadcasting Corporation and are used under licence. Printed & bound by Proost, Groupe CPI. **ISBN** 0 954 98191 X

Web: www.footballyearbook.co.uk

9 TO ONE

PORTSMOUTH STRIKER LOMANA LUALUA FACES NINE SEARCHING QUESTIONS!

YOUR CAREER HIGHLIGHT?

"Making my goalscoring debut for Colchester against Chesterfield was special. Playing for a great club like Newcastle United was also an honour and then there's playing in front of these wonderful fans at Pompey. But the best moment was captaining and representing my country at the African Nations Cup tournament last year."

YOUR CAREER LOWLIGHT?

"Getting sent off in that tournament against the hosts, when I was under extreme provocation from their players, and then reading reports by some people that I had colluded with Tunisia to help them through. It was complete nonsense!"

THE BEST PLAYER YOU'VE EVER FACED?

"There are many great defenders but there are two that stand out: Tony Adams and Martin Keown. I hardly got a sniff of the ball when I came up against those two."

WHO WOULD YOU BUY FOR POMPEY?

"It would have to be Ronaldo. I've admired him for a long time because he's one of those strikers who can get you off your seat. Not sure he'd leave Real Madrid for Pompey though!"

EVER BEEN THE VICTIM OF A WIND UP?

"When I was at Newcastle I went to get into my car after training and someone had moved it. And I still don't know who did it."

WHAT ON YOUR CAR CD PLAYER?

"I've got a Range Rover and I'm playing 'Only God Can Judge Me' by Tupac. I've also got a lot of gospel music in my car."

YOUR WORST DRESSED TEAM-MATE?

"Andy Griffin wears some bad gear, really funky stuff that doesn't suit him. Saying that, he's improved greatly since our days together at Newcastle."

ANY SUPERSTITIONS TO TALK ABOUT?

"The night before a game, I'll watch a Ronaldo, Maradona or Gazza video – the entertainers. Then on the day of the game I'll pray."

IF YOU'RE HAVING A 'MARE, WOULD YOU FEIGN INJURY TO GET YOURSELF SUBBED?

"No chance. I would just get my head down and try to get myself back into the game. Then, if I'm still playing really badly, I'm sure the manager will haul me off!"

TEN REASONS
WHY MICHAEL OWEN IS A GEORDIE!

WELCOME MICHAEL

1. He's got black and white running through his veins

2. He had a poster of Mickey Quinn on his wall as a child!

3. He has a tattoo of Tyne Bridge in a very private place!

4. He often plays golf in a pair of crocodile shoes given to him by his favourite actor, Jimmy Nail

5. His dad was an unpaid extra in *Byker Grove*.

6. His favourite kind of sweet may be called an Everton mint, but it's black and white all the way through

7. He's always been an active member of the Ant and Dec fan club

8. He'd kill time on the bench at Real Madrid reading Catherine Cookson novels

9. Although you'd have him down as a red wine man, he always been more than partial to a pint of Newcastle Brown!

10. He was never interested in signing for anyone else, honest!

THE CHANGING FACE OF PHIL NEVILLE

1995 This cheeky chappy is a star of the Manchester United youth team!

1997 Phil shows why was the life and soul of the England squad after Euro 96!

1998 A look of panic as Phil is dropped from the England squad before France 98.

1999 Phil celebrates qualifying for Euro 2000 . . . er, or is it his sister?

2000 Phil shares a joke at Euro 2000 – but the tournament wasn't all fun and games!

2003 Party time. Phil celebrates another successful year on the Old Trafford bench.

2005 Phil wonders why his brother hasn't arrived at Goodison Park for training!

JOHN TERRY of CHELSEA
faces THE MOTD TASTE TEST

WHAT'S THE MOST IMPORTANT THING IN YOUR HOUSE?

"It would have to be my Sky Plus. As a footballer I'm often away, either on Champions League duty or with England, so it's important I don't miss anything. I'm not really a lover of the soaps and I tend to record football programmes mostly as I like to study my own performances." ✓

WHAT OTHER TV SHOWS ARE YOU INTO?

"In terms of comedy, I like watching *Little Britain* but my all-time favourite programme is *The Sopranos* – that is must-watch television." ✓

WHAT DO YOU LIKE TO DO ON YOUR DAYS OFF?

"When I'm not relaxing, I like to go fishing or have a round of golf. I play off a handicap of 12 at the moment and I play left-handed, which might surprise a few people. I got the golf bug from Franco Zola and we used to play regularly when he was at Chelsea." ✓

HOW DO YOU PASS THE TIME ON LONG AWAY TRIPS?

"I was fortunate enough to get a PSP before they came out in the UK, so I've been playing that. On the coach I'll usually have a game of *Pro Evolution 5*, which I'm absolutely hooked on, and with the Bluetooth technology I can play against Joe Cole and give him a good hiding!" ✓

WHAT DESIGNER LABELS ARE YOU INTO?

"I prefer to wear something casual, so I'll go for Abercrombie and Fitch or Ralph Lauren. I possess a number of suits though and my favourite designer at the moment is William Hunt." ✓

WHAT RINGTONE DO YOU HAVE AT THE MOMENT?

"I change them like the wind. I had 'Signs' by Snoop Dogg on there for a while but I change them from one week to the next. In terms of music I like Jaheim and Usher, but also a lot of old school soul like Luther Vandross and Marvin Gaye." ✗

WHAT'S IN YOUR FRIDGE AT THE MOMENT?

"All healthy stuff – honest! It's full of salads, pasta meals, chicken and plenty of bottled water. You have to eat like that if you want to succeed at the highest level." ✓

✓ **John Terry has passed the Taste Test challenge!**

A LAUGH A MINUTE WITH ALAN & GARY!

WHAT WOULD YOU GET IF CHELSEA WERE RELEGATED?

40,000 MORE MAN. UNITED FANS!

A DAY IN THE LIFE OF ENGLAND'S OWEN HARGREAVES

The England international might have been born in Canada, but he's English through and through!

7am: Get up and have breakfast. Read the *Sud Deutsche Zeitung* while I tuck into my fleischsalat.

9am: Drive to training. There's no traffic on the autobahn. *Wunderbar!*

1pm: Lunch at the schnitzelhaus. I usually have currywurst, but today I order the jagerschnitzel for a change.

7pm: Meet the lads in the Hofbrauhaus for a quick Doppelbock. Hope they'll be showing the Bundesliga game on the big screen.

10pm: Kaffee und kuchen before bed – then it's time for Schlafen!

DID THEY REALLY SAY THAT?
A PUNDITS LIFE IS NEVER EASY

"I don't think anyone enjoyed it. Apart from the people who watched it." ALAN HANSEN

"If Plan A fails, they could always revert to Plan A." MARK LAWRENSON

"It's amazing what you can see through Sven's specs – I must get a pair." GARY LINEKER

"Systems can help you, but if you took the England players who took part in those three games and got the best coach in the world to work with them for a year, it wouldn't have made any difference. [on England's Euro 2000 performance] ALAN HANSEN

"That goal surprised most people, least of all myself." GARTH CROOKS

"David James has improved as a goalkeeper but the one thing he hasn't improved on is his judgement." ALAN HANSEN

"There won't be a dry house in the place." MARK LAWRENSON

"The *one* thing England have got is spirit, resolve, grit and determination." ALAN HANSEN

"It's a tense time for managers. They have to *exhume* confidence.'" GARY LINEKER

"Figo is as important to England as Beckham is." MARK LAWRENSON

"Martin Keown is up everybody's backsides." TREVOR BROOKING

"He can be as good as he wants to be, that's how good he can be." MARK LAWRENSON

"One word to describe it would be absolutely pathetic!" ALAN HANSEN

"It's like the Sea of Galilee – the two defenders just parted." MARK LAWRENSON

"He's got two great feet. Left foot, right foot, either side." ALAN HANSEN

"He must be the only man alive who can eat an apple through a tennis racket." [about Ronaldo] GARY LINEKER

"Michael Owen isn't the tallest of lads, but his height more than makes up for that." MARK LAWRENSON

"He's got a lot of forehead!" [about Sven Göran Eriksson] GARY LINEKER

"Gary Neville was palpable for the second goal!" MARK LAWRENSON

"He signals to the bench with his groin!" MARK BRIGHT

"They'll be playing 4-4-1-2." MARK LAWRENSON

"I saw him kick the bucket over there which suggests he's not going to be able to continue." TREVOR BROOKING

"It's slightly alarming the way Manchester United decapitated against Stuttgart." MARK LAWRENSON

MAKING MAT

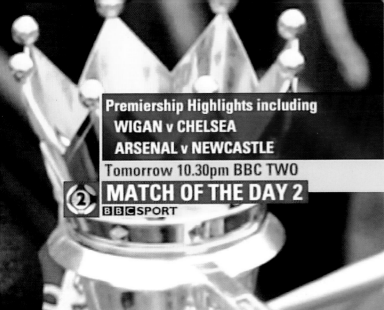

Premiership Highlights including
WIGAN v CHELSEA
ARSENAL v NEWCASTLE
Tomorrow 10.30pm BBC TWO
② **MATCH OF THE DAY 2**
BBC SPORT

CH OF THE DAY

How does Britain's best football TV show get on air every Saturday? Read on...

PUTTING TOGETHER A TELLY SHOW LIKE *MATCH OF THE DAY* each week takes a giant team of about 150 people. To find out a bit more about how the programme gets on air, we've asked three of them – a Producer, a Presenter and a Commentator – to tell us about their working week, culminating in Saturday's match day.

BUILDING UP TO THE NEW SEASON

PHIL BIGWOOD – THE EXECUTIVE PRODUCER: "There are two main parts to the way in which *Match Of The Day* runs – pre-season and during the season. Before a new season starts, myself and the editors have a meeting with the production team and the commentators to talk through programme principles, tweaks to requirements, and what changes we have made to the 'look' of the show. Changes to the show's sets and graphics can take months to perfect so there's a lot of planning in advance – for instance, plans for how the sets are going to look for the BBC's coverage of the World Cup actually started in the summer, a little under a year before a ball is even kicked in Germany. With that big meeting out of the way everyone is onboard and knows what is happening for the rest of the season."

THE WEEK LEADING UP TO A SHOW

PHIL BIGWOOD: "Once the season gets underway we tend to just have a small weekly get together with the editor, the director and the producer, running videos to ensure we're all on the same wavelength and to check if there are any changes to the norm. The production assistant will also ring all the commentators to check they are happy with arrangements on a weekly basis."

JOHN MOTSON – THE COMMENTATOR: "On a Tuesday we have a Football Focus head banging session at Television Centre. Then we have a much smaller meeting amongst those of us who were

DAVID MOYES
Manager, Everton

BBC SPORT

5 MAN U 5 | Shots Off Target: | EVE 5 MAN U 7 | Corners:

directly involved in *Match Of The Day* and we discuss the previous Saturday's programme, talk about any flaws that might need correcting and we just exchange a few views about the show and whether there were any lessons to be learned from the way certain things happened."

GARY LINEKER – THE PRESENTER:
"The majority of my work is done on matchdays, but it's obviously important that I keep up-to-date with all the news stories and transfers leading up to the Saturday. During the week I have conversations with the editor and producer to discuss any specifics and maybe we'll decide that I should do an interview with a player after a game, or maybe start the programme slightly differently. We also discuss the potential match running order."

JOHN MOTSON: "I get a rota about four or five weeks ahead, so I know roughly what match I am covering every Saturday. Research, background, and preparation are entirely down to me. This might involve going to see a team play in a midweek match if there is one available and it

certainly involves watching videos. In extreme cases, if I'm not familiar enough with the players, I would go to a training session."

FRIDAY

JOHN MOTSON: "During the week I would keep my eyes and ears open for any information that came through the newspapers or any other source and on Friday I would condense all that information on to what I call my commentary charts. I do them in different coloured pens – on one side I do the two teams and substitutes with little biographical notes alongside and on the back I put sequences and general themes about the game.

"What I try to do, by writing that down on a Friday, is to commit as much of that to memory as I can. Also on a Friday I would make various discreet phone calls to people at both clubs to see if I can establish who is in the squad and who is injured. Occasionally someone might mark your card and say there is a young substitute who might come on

for the first time, which alerts you to go and do some work on a player who you may never have seen before or even heard of."

SATURDAY MORNING

PHIL BIGWOOD: "Saturday is of course by far and away our busiest day. The pundit down to watch the early 12.45am kick-off, either Mark Lawrenson or Alan Hansen, gets in to watch that, while Gary Lineker and the other pundit tend to arrive about 1.30pm to 2.00pm. At 3pm, Gary, Alan and 'Lawro' settle down in the main production area to watch a live feed of all the Premiership matches kicking off at that time."

JOHN MOTSON: "On the day of the game I would expect to be at the ground three hours before the kick-off. If it's in London I drive. If it's in Newcastle I might fly. If it's Manchester I might jump on a train. I like to drive to games by myself because if I'm on my own in the car I can practice names and I can spend the time reminding myself of what the formation is going to be."

GARY LINEKER: "Typically I arrive at the BBC by early afternoon, usually 1.30ish, and often with some thoughts on scriptlines already prepared. Within our production office we have the ability to watch all live match feeds simultaneously, therefore once three o'clock arrives we will watch the games, looking for quirky shots for videotape sequences, discussing the ordering of matches, picking out

analysis themes and points for discussion, and generally enjoying the football like everyone else! BBC tea and biscuits are readily available to help the process."

JOHN MOTSON: "When I get to the ground I like to do things like check the commentary position. Have I got a good enough view? Am I on the halfway line? Is there a camera in the way? Then I like to read the programme, bump into one or two early arrivals like managers or coaches that might have a word for you, check fitness tests, possibly do an insert into *Football Focus*, maybe do something pre-match for *Score*, the BBC digital programme that Ray Stubbs presents.

"My next mandatory appearance is in the tunnel at two o'clock when the coaches come out of the dressing rooms with the official team sheets and hand them to the referee. That means I can tick off the players on my chart to see if I have got them right, and if there is a late change I've got some stickers and I have to get the pens out again and generally readjust my board."

PHIL BIGWOOD: "Sky get first pick of the weekend's games – they choose three to cover and then the BBC chooses three more. We send outdoor broadcast teams to our three matches, and again this is decided several weeks in advance, so very little is left to chance. Sky and the BBC share pictures for all the matches, but we send a commentator and floor manager to every game. The commentaries used in all the matches we show

BARCLAYS PREMIERSHIP			
Top	pld	+/-	pts
1 Charlton Athletic	1	+2	3
2 West Ham Utd	1	+2	3
3 Manchester Utd	1	+2	3
4 Tottenham Hotspur	1	+2	3
5 Aston Villa	1	0	1
6 Bolton Wanderers	1	0	1
7 Birmingham City	1	0	1
8 Fulham	1	0	1
9 Liverpool	1	0	1
10 Manchester City	1	0	1

BBC SPORT   bbc.co.uk/football

are recorded live – there are no voices dubbed on after the final whistle."

JOHN MOTSON: "When I've finished all my other jobs I would normally go up to the camera position where the commentary is set up for about half past two. The producer down in the van will have got his cameras working by then and we'll do a little rehearsal, usually based on what I'm going to say when the teams come out. When they do come out at five to three, I normally do an introduction of about 45 seconds. If my game doesn't amount to much in the evening that can always be dropped in the editing. But by and large that would be perhaps a feature in close up, a new player, somebody who wanted one goal for his hundred – that type of topical line."

KICK-OFF

JOHN MOTSON: "When they kick off I treat the match as a live game, whether it is recorded or not. For a regular *Match Of The Day* game I wouldn't have a co-commentator with me, because we only have that on a live match. I would look after all the replays and analysis myself.

"You've always got to be aware that something can happen in a game that has never happened

before – you do get the odd occasion where there is a refereeing incident, or where something happens with the crowd, or a strange substitution. You never take for granted that you've seen everything. By and large one of the challenging things about commentary is that you've always got to be on your guard against something unexpected and however much preparation that you do, something can still occur at a given time and you'll think 'my goodness, I've got to react to this and I haven't gone down this road before'. You've still got to leave your mind open for things you weren't anticipating."

HALF-TIME

JOHN MOTSON: "At half-time I would probably have a chat over the private microphone with the producer to see if we are on the right lines, to see if we missed anything. I would also keep my eyes open for substitutes when they come out for the second-half."

FULL-TIME

GARY LINEKER: "Once the games are over I sit down with the Editor to finalise the running order

and start scripting the whole show. This normally takes an hour or so. After this I'll then gets changed to do a BBC1 trail, which normally goes out at around 8pm. Following this we'll also record any short sound sequences that need doing. About 45 minutes before the programme, having finished in make-up, we'll start rehearsing, recording any other bits and pieces, and get ready for the show. The pundits join me on the set a few minutes before transmission and the whole show goes out live."

PHIL BIGWOOD: "After the final whistle has blown on all the games – around five o'clock – Gary and the show's producer will sit down and decide the order the games will be shown in on that night's broadcast. Although we pick three games to send OB teams to, it doesn't necessarily mean those games will be the three that we allocate the most time to. Sometimes we've picked games with very few goals while somewhere else it has ended 4-3 or 5-4. We have to be flexible enough to change our running schedules at quite short notice."

JOHN MOTSON: "At the end of the game all sorts of things can happen. Sometimes I might do a report for *Final Score* but more often than not I would stay in the commentary position and do a two-way chat with Ray Stubbs at about 5.25pm to go into the *Final Score* programme.

"While I'm doing that, interviews are being done on the other side of the ground. I don't do as many interviews as I used to but when I go back to the main side of the ground from the camera position I would go into a tea room, or maybe the boardroom if I could get in, just to see if there are any stories bubbling around that I can phone through to the *Match Of The Day* editor later.

"I would also speak to the producer who is actually editing the game, just to say 'don't forget that incident'. He might say to me 'what did you make of that, do we have to include it?' The only time I would do an overdub is if at the end of the game the video tape people had a separate replay of something that I hadn't seen at the time and they wanted different words to cover it, because it was from a different angle. But that is a technical thing really. When I call it, I call it as I see it. I've trained myself not to want to do redo anything, because I've learned through doing live football that you have to stand or fall by what you say at the time."

THE SHOW GOES ON AIR

PHIL BIGWOOD: "*Match Of The Day* always goes out live from Studio TC5 in Television Centre, in west London. All the material isn't normally ready until just before the show starts its transmission, so it has to be live! Everyone then stays until we are off air around midnight. The main match will get a 15-minute time slot, while the others get a minimum of five minutes, often around six or seven. We like to

ensure there's something in the show for fans of all the Premiership clubs playing that day."

GARY LINEKER: "I have a great relationship with Alan Hansen and 'Lawro'. We have a common interest in golf! During the show we all listen to the director and editor on talkback from the gallery at the same time as conducting a conversation – this helps us know where we're going next and how much time we have left on a section of chat."

JOHN MOTSON: "On the way home I would speak to the editor, just to see if there was anything he wants to raise about my match. There is a lot of two-way chat that goes on during the course of the evening and then eventually I finish up pretty exhausted at our local pub for a couple of pints and then I go home and watch the programme."

THE PROGRAMME ENDS

GARY LINEKER: "Once we're off air we tend to all re-convene in the production office to quickly talk through how things have gone. Hopefully all has gone well, the conversation is very brief and then we all head off home!"

PHIL BIGWOOD: "Producing *Match Of The Day* genuinely is a big team effort. If you include our three outside broadcast teams, there are around 150 people involved in a typical Saturday show – cameras, sound, VT editors, 'talent', producers, commentators, floor managers, graphics, vision mixers, engineering managers and many, many more."

JOHN MOTSON
"Commentary is challenging because you've always got to be on guard against the unexpected."

THE WORLD'S TOP 50

STRI

The MOTD computer spits out a list of the world's 50 best strikers!

OVER THE LAST 12 MONTHS WE'VE FOLLOWED 5,000 OF THE BEST PLAYERS IN world football to check on their form. Are they playing for teams that win? Do they make a difference to how goals are scored or conceded? We've turned the info into a chart for world's best strikers, midfielders, defenders and keepers. In doing this, we also show you where the player is ranked positionally in his domestic league (ie. 3rd best striker in the Premiership) and what their Overall World Ranking is (where they are ranked in the list of the world's best players, regardless of position).

To make the Top 50 Strikers chart you have to be scoring goals, making the attack more lethal, and taking part in winning performances. One of the key things we look at is a forward's strike rate – how many minutes it takes them to score a goal. Anything better than a goal every 200 minutes is a form striker. For example, **Andrei Shevchenko** of AC Milan averages a league goal every 132 minutes.

There are some famous faces who didn't make our list, so what happened? They either didn't play often enough through injury, suspension or by not being selected, or they didn't perform as well as other players in their position. Maybe they played in too many defeats and not enough wins. For example, **Michael Owen** scored the goals but didn't get enough starts for Real Madrid last season. His 13 league goals came at an impressive strike rate of one every 145 minutes but he barely featured in the Champions League and six goals for England wasn't enough to make up.

HOW DO WE PICK THE PLAYERS?

All our players are measured on appearances in important games for club and country. Do they start in the big games? Do they stay fit? Bookings and sending offs are also important – how often do they get suspended? For example, Gerrard was playing less than three out of four games for Liverpool last season and picked up three bookings in 900 minutes of Champions League action.

We count games played in league matches and not domestic cups where top players will be rested. Champions League games from the group stage on and UEFA Cup games after the qualifying rounds also count. We rate players only in competitive games played for their country, as international friendlies are increasingly used to experiment with fringe players.

Our rankings aren't based on opinions, only on facts: games played, goals scored by the side and the individual, goals conceded by the side when a player is on the pitch, the quality of the opposition and the results, and finally, whether a side does better or worse when the player is on the pitch.

---

1 ▲ Thierry Henry

Age: 27 • *Best striker in Premiership* • **Overall World Ranking: 5**

While Arsenal were forced to play second fiddle to Chelsea in the Premiership, Thierry Henry was again the league's most potent striker and a player Roman Abramovich would more than happily break the bank for. The Frenchmen netted 30 times in all competitions last season, the same total that fellow strikers Dennis Bergkamp, Robin van Persie and Jose Antonio Reyes scored between them.

Season 2004-05 record

National Team: France
Apps: 8 **Goals:** 1 **Cards:** 0 0

Club: Arsenal
Apps: 32 **Goals:** 25 **Cards:** 2 0
Strike rate: Goal every 113 mins
Mins played: 2826 **Ave mins:** 74

Europe: Champions League last 16
Apps: 8 **Goals:** 5 **Cards:** 1 0

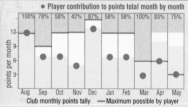

• Player contribution to points total month by month

| | 100% | 78% | 58% | 42% | 87% | 58% | 58% | 100% | 83% | 75% |

points per month

Aug Sep Oct Nov Dec Jan Feb Mar Apr May

Club monthly points tally — Maximum possible by player

UNDERSTANDING THE GRAPH

The figure at the top of the column shows what percentage of achievable points were won by the club each month. If the club got 9 points from a possible 12, then it would show 75%.

• Player contribution to points total month by month

| | 75% | 78% | 58% | 42% | 87% | 58% | 58% | 100% | 83% | 75% |

points per month

g Sep Nov Dec Jan Feb Mar Apr y

Club monthly points tally — Maximum possible by player

The red bar indicates the maximum number of points that the player's club could have got if they had won ALL the games that he played in. The May column shows the club could have won up to 6 points when the player was in the team.

The dark yellow bar show how many points the player's club won during the month. The August column here shows that the club won 9 points.

The light yellow bar stops at the maximum points the player's club could have won. The August column here shows the club could have won up to 12 points during the month.

The red spot indicates how many points the club actually won in games when the player was on the pitch. The May column shows that this player's club won three points when he played.

KERS

2 ▲ Dirk Kuijt

Age: 24 • *Best striker in Dutch League* • **Overall World Ranking: 7**

Dirk set the Dutch League alight last season. His 29 league goals made him the division's top scorer, while he helped fourth-placed Feyenoord score more goals than any other club. The 25-year-old was linked in the summer with a move to Liverpool, and although he's stayed in Holland, a host of other clubs are still courting the targetman, who has scored a total of 49 goals in just 68 games for 'De Kamaraden'.

Season 2004-05 record

National Team: Holland
Apps: 9 **Goals:** 2 **Cards:** 1 ⓞ

Club: Feyenoord
Apps: 34 **Goals:** 29 **Cards:** 0 ⓞ
Strike rate: Goal every 102 mins
Mins played: 2955 **Ave mins:** 87

Europe: UEFA Cup last 32
Apps: 7 **Goals:** 3 **Cards:** 0 ⓞ

● Player contribution to points total month by month

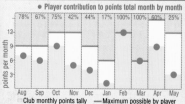

□ Club monthly points tally — Maximum possible by player

---

3 ▲ Samuel Eto'o

Age: 24 • *Best striker in Spanish League* • **Overall World Ranking: 9**

When you move to the Nou Camp it can take time to bed in as a striker, but the former Mallorca hitman had no such trouble last season, hitting the target 24 times as Barça won the Primera Liga title. This made him, along with Villarreal's Diego Forlan, the division's top scorer. The key to his success rate was his tremendous understanding with Ronaldinho, whose inch-perfect passes often fell perfectly for Eto'o's rapier-like speed.

Season 2004-05 record

National Team: Cameroon
Apps: 4 **Goals:** 1 **Cards:** 1 ⓞ

Club: Barcelona
Apps: 37 **Goals:** 24 **Cards:** 1 ⓞ
Strike rate: Goal every 130 mins
Mins played: 3118 **Ave mins:** 82

Europe: Champions League last 16
Apps: 7 **Goals:** 4 **Cards:** 0 ⓞ

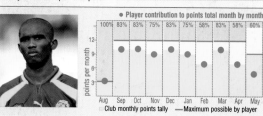

● Player contribution to points total month by month

□ Club monthly points tally — Maximum possible by player

---

4 ▲ Roy Makaay

Age: 30 • *Best striker in German League* • **Overall World Ranking: 12**

At 30, it had been said that the Dutchman's best days were behind him, but he again proved to be the talisman in the Munich side as they cruised to another Bundesliga and German Cup double. While Nuremburg's Marek Mintal finished the division's top scorer with 24 league goals, Makaay had the better ratio with 22 league goals in 33 games, taking his Bayern career tally to 45 league goals in 65 games.

Season 2004-05 record

National Team: Holland
Apps: 7 **Goals:** 0 **Cards:** 0 ⓞ

Club: Bayern Munich
Apps: 33 **Goals:** 22 **Cards:** 0 ⓞ
Strike rate: Goal every 129 mins
Mins played: 2836 **Ave mins:** 83

Europe: Champions League quarter-finals
Apps: 8 **Goals:** 7 **Cards:** 1 ⓞ

● Player contribution to points total month by month

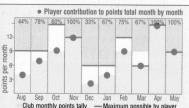

□ Club monthly points tally — Maximum possible by player

---

5 ▲ Ronaldo

Age: 28 • *2nd best striker in Spanish League* • **Overall World Ranking: 13**

The Brazilian marksman still attracts criticism for being unfit and overweight, yet he was ranked the second best striker in La Liga last season, netting 21 league goals as Madrid pushed Barça all the way to the title. He might be under more pressure this campaign, following the arrival of Robinho and Julio Baptista, but with Raul out of form, Ronaldo will again be looked upon as the club's number one striker.

Season 2004-05 record

National Team: Brazil
Apps: 8 **Goals:** 3 **Cards:** 1 ⓞ

Club: Real Madrid
Apps: 34 **Goals:** 21 **Cards:** 1 ⓞ
Strike rate: Goal every 133 mins
Mins played: 2790 **Ave mins:** 73

Europe: Champions League last 16
Apps: 10 **Goals:** 3 **Cards:** 0 ①

● Player contribution to points total month by month

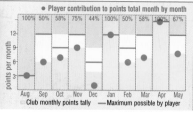

□ Club monthly points tally — Maximum possible by player

6 ▲ Ricardo Oliveira

Age: 25 • *3rd best striker in Spanish League* • **Overall World Ranking: 14**

Oliveira has not attracted too much attention outside of La Liga, but the Brazilian forward had a fantastic debut season with Real Betis last year, netting 22 league goals in 37 games. Having started with Santos, he made his name in Spain by helping Valencia to lift the championship title and the UEFA Cup, and much more is expected from the pacy 25-year-old this time around.

Season 2004-05 record

National Team: Brazil
Apps: 4 **Goals:** 3 **Cards:** 1 0

Club: Real Betis
Apps: 37 **Goals:** 22 **Cards:** 1 0
Strike rate: Goal every 149 mins
Mins played: 3279 **Ave mins:** 86

Europe: Did not play
Apps: 0 **Goals:** 0 **Cards:** 1 0

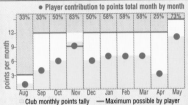

• Player contribution to points total month by month

	33%	33%	50%	83%	50%	58%	58%	58%	25%	73%

points per month

Aug Sep Oct Nov Dec Jan Feb Mar Apr May
Club monthly points tally — Maximum possible by player

8 ▲ Marcelinho

Age: 30 • *2nd best striker in German League* • **Overall World Ranking: 22**

The 30-year-old caught the headlines last season for a much-publicised punch-up with his skipper Arne Friedrich, but having netted 18 league goals in the season from an attacking midfield position, the incident was quickly glossed over by officials at the club. The Brazilian started the new campaign by dying his hair silver, which he feels will help bring him goals as he dreams of a Champions League place.

Season 2004-05 record

National Team: Brazil
Apps: 0 **Goals:** 0 **Cards:** 0 0

Club: Hertha Berlin
Apps: 32 **Goals:** 18 **Cards:** 7 0
Strike rate: Goal every 157 mins
Mins played: 2821 **Ave mins:** 83

Europe: Did not play
Apps: 0 **Goals:** 0 **Cards:** 0 0

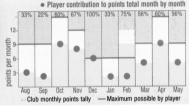
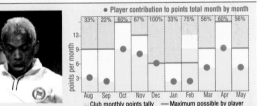

• Player contribution to points total month by month

	33%	22%	60%	67%	100%	33%	75%	56%	60%	56%

points per month

Aug Sep Oct Nov Dec Jan Feb Mar Apr May
Club monthly points tally — Maximum possible by player

7 ▲ Jan Vennegoor

Age: 26 • *2nd best striker in Dutch League* • **Overall World Ranking: 15**

The man with the longest name in footy (Jan Vennegoor of Hesselink) was also one of the most potent last season as his 19 league goals in 28 games helped fire PSV to the Dutch title. While he was not as successful in the Champions League, netting just once as the club reached the semi-final stage, his league tally was all the more impressive given that he was on the pitch for 2186 minutes, fewer than any striker in the top ten.

Season 2004-05 record

National Team: Holland
Apps: 1 **Goals:** 0 **Cards:** 1 0

Club: PSV Eindhoven
Apps: 28 **Goals:** 19 **Cards:** 2 0
Strike rate: Goal every 115 mins
Mins played: 2186 **Ave mins:** 64

Europe: Champions League semi-finals
Apps: 12 **Goals:** 3 **Cards:** 2 0

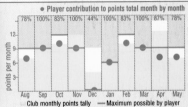

• Player contribution to points total month by month

	78%	100%	83%	100%	44%	100%	83%	100%	87%	78%

points per month

Aug Sep Oct Nov Dec Jan Feb Mar Apr May
Club monthly points tally — Maximum possible by player

9 ▲ Cristiano Lucarelli

Age: 29 • *Best striker in Italian League* • **Overall World Ranking: 26**

A natural goalscorer by definition, last season Cristiano Lucarelli netted a fantastic 19 league goals for his home-town side (13 more than the club's second-placed scorer), notching a further five in other competitions. Such was his remarkable run of form, he helped Livorno to an historic eighth place in the league, and despite interest from Torino, he has opted to stay with the club for another season.

Season 2004-05 record

National Team: Italy
Apps: 0 **Goals:** 0 **Cards:** 0 0

Club: Livorno
Apps: 35 **Goals:** 19 **Cards:** 7 0
Strike rate: Goal every 162 mins
Mins played: 3078 **Ave mins:** 81

Europe: Did not play
Apps: 0 **Goals:** 0 **Cards:** 0 0

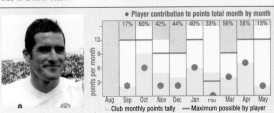

• Player contribution to points total month by month

	17%	60%	42%	44%	40%	33%	56%	58%	13%

points per month

Aug Sep Oct Nov Dec Jan Feb Mar Apr May
Club monthly points tally — Maximum possible by player

10 ▲ Salomon Kalou
Age: 19 • *3rd best striker in Dutch League* • **Overall World Ranking: 34**

While he featured for only 2318 minutes on the field for Feyenoord last season, Kalou proved to be the perfect foil for the club's leading striker Dirk Kuijt by scoring 20 goals. Small and quick, the 19-year-old younger brother of Ivory Coast and Auxerre front man Bonaventure Kalou (who himself spent six years at Feyenoord) had an incredible first full season and is attracting the attention of PSV and Ajax.

Season 2004-05 record
National Team: Ivory Coast
Apps: 0 **Goals:** 0 **Cards:** 0 0

Club: Feyenoord
Apps: 31 **Goals:** 20 **Cards:** 2 0
Strike rate: Goal every 116 mins
Mins played: 2318 **Ave mins:** 68

Europe: UEFA Cup last 32
Apps: 6 **Goals:** 4 **Cards:** 0 0

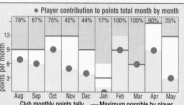

• Player contribution to points total month by month

	78%	67%	75%	42%	44%	17%	100%	100%	60%	25%

Aug Sep Oct Nov Dec Jan Feb Mar Apr May
▭ Club monthly points tally — Maximum possible by player

11 ▲ Dimitar Berbatov
Age: 24 • *3rd best striker in German League* • **Overall World Ranking: 43**

While he has been with Bayer Leverkusen for five seasons, the 24-year-old Bulgarian really came to the fore last season, netting five goals in ten Champions League fixtures and striking 20 times in the Bundesliga, as Leverkusen finished sixth in the table. He is ranked the 75th best player in the world here, but Berbatov's fifth-placed domestic ranking makes him one of Germany's most stand-out players.

Season 2004-05 record
National Team: Bulgaria
Apps: 6 **Goals:** 5 **Cards:** 2 0

Club: Bayer Leverkusen
Apps: 34 **Goals:** 20 **Cards:** 3 0
Strike rate: Goal every 151 mins
Mins played: 3013 **Ave mins:** 89

Europe: Champions League last 16
Apps: 10 **Goals:** 6 **Cards:** 0 0

• Player contribution to points total month by month

78%	11%	47%	58%	67%	100%	58%	44%	47%	78%

Aug Sep Oct Nov Dec Jan Feb Mar Apr May
▭ Club monthly points tally — Maximum possible by player

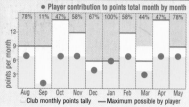

12 ▲ Adriano
Age: 23 • *2nd best striker in Italian League* • **Overall World Ranking: 48**

The Brazilian was subject of a supposed £35 million bid by Chelsea in the summer, having netted 16 times in Serie A last season and scoring a further seven goals in six Champions League fixtures. Having sold Christian Vieri to city rivals Milan, Inter have managed to keep hold of the 23-year-old, but another prolific season from this summer's Confederations Cup 'Player of the Tournament' could test their resolve.

Season 2004-05 record
National Team: Brazil
Apps: 9 **Goals:** 6 **Cards:** 1 0

Club: Inter Milan
Apps: 30 **Goals:** 16 **Cards:** 1 0
Strike rate: Goal every 142 mins
Mins played: 2278 **Ave mins:** 60

Europe: Champions League last 16
Apps: 8 **Goals:** 10 **Cards:** 0 1

• Player contribution to points total month by month

50%	47%	33%	78%	73%	53%	78%	75%	87%

Aug Sep Oct Nov Dec Jan Feb Mar Apr May
▭ Club monthly points tally — Maximum possible by player

13 ▲ Alberto Gilardino
Age: 23 • *3rd best striker in Italian League* • **Overall World Ranking: 51**

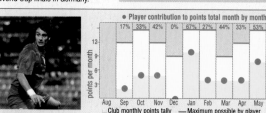

Seen as the bright young hope of the Azzuri, 23-year-old Gilardino joined Milan this summer in an £18 million move, following 46 goals in two seasons for Parma and finishing last season as Serie A's top marksman. Strong and powerful, Christian Vieri will have a job on his hands to outgun the former Italy Under-21 star, who is tipped to have a significant impact at the summer's World Cup finals in Germany.

Season 2004-05 record
National Team: Italy
Apps: 6 **Goals:** 2 **Cards:** 0 0

Club: Parma
Apps: 38 **Goals:** 22 **Cards:** 4 0
Strike rate: Goal every 151 mins
Mins played: 3325 **Ave mins:** 88

Europe: UEFA Cup semi-finals
Apps: 7 **Goals:** 1 **Cards:** 0 0

• Player contribution to points total month by month

17%	33%	42%	0%	67%	27%	44%	33%	53%

Aug Sep Oct Nov Dec Jan Feb Mar Apr May
▭ Club monthly points tally — Maximum possible by player

14 | Alessandro Del Piero

Age: 30 • *4th best striker in Italian League* • **Overall World Ranking: 52**

While he was only on the pitch for a total of 1941 minutes, Del Piero continues to shine for the 'Old Lady', netting 15 goals last season as Juvé clinched the Serie A title. Now 30, Del Piero is another who many believe is a spent force, but 'Sandro will be keen for another impressive season to cement a place in Italy's World Cup squad after his disappointing tournament in Japan and Korea in 2002.

Season 2004-05 record

National Team: Italy
Apps: 1 **Goals:** 1 **Cards:** 0 ▢

Club: Juventus
Apps: 30 **Goals:** 15 **Cards:** 2 ▢
Strike rate: Goal every 129 mins
Mins played: 1941 **Ave mins:** 51

Europe: Champions League quarter-finals
Apps: 10 **Goals:** 3 **Cards:** 1 ▢

● Player contribution to points total month by month

	Aug	Sep	Oct	Nov	Dec	Jan	Feb	Mar	Apr	May
		83%	100%	58%	78%	73%	47%	100%	58%	87%

points per month

☐ Club monthly points tally — Maximum possible by player

17

15 David Di Michele

Age: 29 • *5th best striker in Italian League* • **Overall World Ranking: 53**

Spawned from the same Lodigiani football school as Francesco Totti, the 28-year-old made his name in Serie B with Foggia and it was thought his temperamental nature always held him back from hitting the big time. That all changed last season as the deep-lying forward netted 15 league goals to help Udinese finish fourth in Serie A, while qualifying for the Champions League in the process.

Season 2004-05 record

National Team: Italy
Apps: 0 **Goals:** 0 **Cards:** 0 0

Club: Udinese
Apps: 37 **Goals:** 15 **Cards:** 4 0
Strike rate: Goal every 187 mins
Mins played: 2800 **Ave mins:** 74

Europe: Did not play
Apps: 0 **Goals:** 0 **Cards:** 0 0

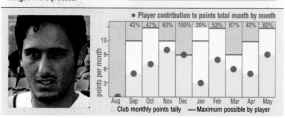

● Player contribution to points total month by month

42% 47% 83% 100% 20% 53% 67% 42% 60%

Aug Sep Oct Nov Dec Jan Feb Mar Apr May
□ Club monthly points tally — Maximum possible by player

---

16 Andriy Shevchenko

Age: 28 • *6th best striker in Italian League* • **Overall World Ranking: 55**

A 16th placed position will no doubt raise a number of eyebrows and while his Champions League exploits were not in question last season, the Ukrainian was less prolific in Serie A, netting 17 goals from 2251 minutes of football as Milan finished seven points behind Juventus in the championship. This did not stop Chelsea apparently bidding £60 million for a player many regard as the best striker in the world.

Season 2004-05 record

National Team: Ukraine
Apps: 7 **Goals:** 5 **Cards:** 0 0

Club: AC Milan
Apps: 29 **Goals:** 17 **Cards:** 2 0
Strike rate: Goal every 132 mins
Mins played: 2251 **Ave mins:** 59

Europe: Champions League final
Apps: 9 **Goals:** 5 **Cards:** 1 0

● Player contribution to points total month by month

58% 87% 67% 78% 47% 100% 100% 67% 25%

Aug Sep Oct Nov Dec Jan Feb Mar Apr May
□ Club monthly points tally — Maximum possible by player

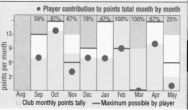

---

17 Eidur Gudjohnsen

Age: 26 • *2nd best striker in Premiership* • **Overall World Ranking: 56**

With José Mourinho opting to play 4-3-3 with one leading striker (Didier Drogba last season), Eidur Gudjohnsen did well to score 12 Premiership goals and 22 in all competitions from a withdrawn midfield position. With Hernan Crespo now at Stamford Bridge, maybe a switch back to 4-4-2 will help the Icelandic international, who has been a prolific performer in his five years at the club.

Season 2004-05 record

National Team: Iceland
Apps: 6 **Goals:** 5 **Cards:** 1 0

Club: Chelsea
Apps: 37 **Goals:** 12 **Cards:** 0 0
Strike rate: Goal every 208 mins
Mins played: 2494 **Ave mins:** 66

Europe: Champions League semi-finals
Apps: 11 **Goals:** 2 **Cards:** 0 0

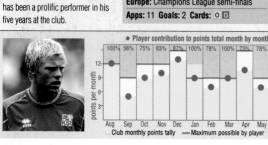

● Player contribution to points total month by month

100% 56% 75% 83% 87% 100% 78% 100% 73% 78%

Aug Sep Oct Nov Dec Jan Feb Mar Apr May
□ Club monthly points tally — Maximum possible by player

---

18 Blaise N'Kufo

Age: 30 • *4th best striker in Dutch League* • **Overall World Ranking: 58**

The Congolese-born striker with a Swiss passport hit the headlines last season, scoring twice in a 2-0 victory against Ajax, before ending the season with a 16-goal tally. The 30-year-old had played most of his football in Switzerland, enjoying a successful loan spell in Germany with Hannover, before making his mark in the Eredivisie where he initially linked up with Fulham's Collins John.

Season 2004-05 record

National Team: Switzerland
Apps: 0 **Goals:** 0 **Cards:** 0 0

Club: Twente
Apps: 32 **Goals:** 16 **Cards:** 2 0
Strike rate: Goal every 175 mins
Mins played: 2807 **Ave mins:** 83

Europe: Did not play
Apps: 0 **Goals:** 0 **Cards:** 0 0

● Player contribution to points total month by month

33% 22% 50% 25% 44% 67% 83% 100% 60% 44%

Aug Sep Oct Nov Dec Jan Feb Mar Apr May
□ Club monthly points tally — Maximum possible by player

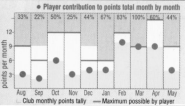

19 David Villa

Age: 23 • 4th best striker in Spanish League • Overall World Ranking: 61

With 15 league goals for Real Zaragoza, the 23-year-old marksman finished some ten goals behind Diego Forlan as the Primera Liga's leading scorer last season, and it was only a matter of time before he quit the club for pastures new. Manchester United were reportedly interested in the skilful goal-poacher, yet he opted to stay in Spain when he signed for Valencia in a £7 million deal in June 2005.

Season 2004-05 record

National Team: Spain
Apps: 0 **Goals:** 0 **Cards:** 0 0

Club: Real Zaragoza
Apps: 35 **Goals:** 15 **Cards:** 7 0
Strike rate: Goal every 187 mins
Mins played: 2806 **Ave mins:** 74

Europe: UEFA Cup last 16
Apps: 10 **Goals:** 3 **Cards:** 1 0

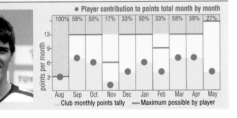

• Player contribution to points total month by month

	Aug	Sep	Oct	Nov	Dec	Jan	Feb	Mar	Apr	May
	100%	58%	50%	17%	33%	50%	33%	58%	58%	27%

☐ Club monthly points tally — Maximum possible by player

20 Luca Toni

Age: 28 • 7th best striker in Italian League • Overall World Ranking: 66

The 28-year-old netted 20 goals in 35 appearances for Palermo last season as the club surprisingly qualified for the UEFA Cup. Toni's form was put in some perspective, given Palermo's total of just 42 goals in 8 Serie A games, and it capped a remarkable season for a player who had gone from Serie B performer to Italian international. He signed a £6 million deal with Fiorentina this summer.

Season 2004-05 record

National Team: Italy
Apps: 9 **Goals:** 0 **Cards:** 0 0

Club: Palermo
Apps: 35 **Goals:** 20 **Cards:** 8 0
Strike rate: Goal every 156 mins
Mins played: 3125 **Ave mins:** 82

Europe: Did not play
Apps: 0 **Goals:** 0 **Cards:** 0 0

 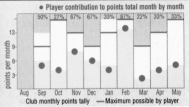

• Player contribution to points total month by month

	Aug	Sep	Oct	Nov	Dec	Jan	Feb	Mar	Apr	May
	50%	27%	67%	67%	33%	87%	22%	33%	33%	

☐ Club monthly points tally — Maximum possible by player

21 Vincenzo Montella

Age: 31 • 8th best striker in Italian League • Overall World Ranking: 70

Montella's prolific form continues with 21 goals last season and while he was ranked only eighth among his country's strikers, he has – along with fellow striker Francesco Totti – been Roma's leading light for the past five years with a ratio of one goal almost every two games. The 31-year-old has pledged his future to the club and is another keen to feature in the World Cup in Germany next summer.

Season 2004-05 record

National Team: Italy
Apps: 2 **Goals:** 0 **Cards:** 0 0

Club: Roma
Apps: 37 **Goals:** 21 **Cards:** 0 0
Strike rate: Goal every 142 mins
Mins played: 2991 **Ave mins:** 79

Europe: Champions League group stage
Apps: 2 **Goals:** 1 **Cards:** 0 0

• Player contribution to points total month by month

	Aug	Sep	Oct	Nov	Dec	Jan	Feb	Mar	Apr	May
	33%	53%	33%	78%	67%	33%	0%	8%	40%	

☐ Club monthly points tally — Maximum possible by player

22 Alexander Frei

Age: 25 • Best striker in French League • Overall World Ranking: 71

A charismatic two footed striker, Swiss international Frei gained notoriety in England when he allegedly spat at Steven Gerrard in a game between the two countries at Euro 2004. On a more positive note, he was ranked as the best player in the French League last season, having netted 20 league goals. His tally was one better than the previous campaign and his form helped Rennes to fourth spot in the table.

Season 2004-05 record

National Team: Switzerland
Apps: 4 **Goals:** 4 **Cards:** 0 0

Club: Rennes
Apps: 36 **Goals:** 20 **Cards:** 6 0
Strike rate: Goal every 151 mins
Mins played: 3014 **Ave mins:** 79

Europe: Did not play
Apps: 0 **Goals:** 0 **Cards:** 0 0

 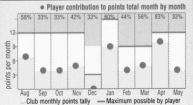

• Player contribution to points total month by month

	Aug	Sep	Oct	Nov	Dec	Jan	Feb	Mar	Apr	May
	58%	33%	33%	42%	33%	60%	44%	56%	83%	33%

☐ Club monthly points tally — Maximum possible by player

23 Klaas Jan Huntelaar

Age: 21 • *5th best striker in Dutch League* • **Overall World Ranking: 75**

Not a name you'd immediately put among the top 25 strikers in world football, yet the 22-year-old netted 17 goals as Heerenveen finished fifth in the table and secured a UEFA Cup spot. Having reached the last 32 of the competition last season, Huntelaar will be aiming to go further this time and will be buoyed by the arrival of strike partner Sebastiaan Steur from FC Volendam.

Season 2004-05 record

National Team: Holland
Apps: 0 **Goals:** 0 **Cards:** 2 [ ]

Club: Heerenveen
Apps: 31 **Goals:** 17 **Cards:** 2 [ ]
Strike rate: Goal every 146 mins
Mins played: 2480 **Ave mins:** 73

Europe: UEFA Cup last 32
Apps: 7 **Goals:** 3 **Cards:** 2 [ ]

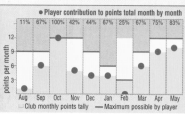

● Player contribution to points total month by month

| 11% | 67% | 100% | 42% | 44% | 67% | 25% | 67% | 75% | 83% |

☐ Club monthly points tally — Maximum possible by player

24 Jimmy-Fl. Hasselbaink

Age: 33 • *3rd best striker in Premiership* • **Overall World Ranking: 77**

Jimmy was forced to carry the Boro forward-line almost single-handed last season, following a lengthy injury to strike partner Mark Viduka. Few could doubt the Dutchman's commitment, however, having netted 13 times as Boro scraped into the UEFA Cup on the final day of the season. Has benefited from Stewart Downing's emergence on the left flank and will be looking to go even better this time out.

Season 2004-05 record

National Team: Holland
Apps: 0 **Goals:** 0 **Cards:** 0 [ ]

Club: Middlesbrough
Apps: 36 **Goals:** 13 **Cards:** 2 [ ]
Strike rate: Goal every 249 mins
Mins played: 3234 **Ave mins:** 85

Europe: UEFA Cup last 16
Apps: 7 **Goals:** 3 **Cards:** 0 [ ]

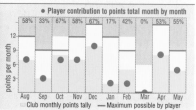

● Player contribution to points total month by month

| 58% | 33% | 67% | 58% | 67% | 17% | 42% | 0% | 53% | 55% |

☐ Club monthly points tally — Maximum possible by player

25 Wayne Rooney

Age: 19 • *4th best striker in Premiership* • **Overall World Ranking: 78**

While not the most prolific of strikers, there is no more explosive forward in world football than Rooney. His 17 goals in all competitions was still a fair return in a team that was clearly not at its best last season, but much more will be expected this season now that strike partner Ruud van Nistelrooy has recovered from injury. He will also be looking to play more games and this will only happen if he cuts his verbal tirade against referees.

Season 2004-05 record

National Team: England
Apps: 6 **Goals:** 0 **Cards:** 2 [ ]

Club: Manchester United
Apps: 29 **Goals:** 11 **Cards:** 7 [ ]
Strike rate: Goal every 198 mins
Mins played: 2181 **Ave mins:** 57

Europe: Champions League last 16
Apps: 6 **Goals:** 3 **Cards:** 0 [ ]

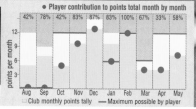

● Player contribution to points total month by month

| 42% | 78% | 42% | 83% | 87% | 83% | 100% | 67% | 33% | 58% |

☐ Club monthly points tally — Maximum possible by player

#	Name	National Team	Club	Europe
26	**Ailton** — Age: 31 • 4th best striker in Germany • Overall World Ranking: 83	Brazil — Caps: 0 Goals: 0 — Cards: 0	Schalke Games: 29 — Goals: 14 Cards: 1 — Strike rate: Goal every 159 mins — Mins played: 2229 Ave mins: 66	UEFA Cup Round of 32 — Games: 6 Goals: 1 Cards: 0
27	**Vincenzo Iaquinta** — Age: 25 • 9th best striker in Italy • Overall World Ranking: 85	Italy — Caps: 2 Goals: 0 — Cards: 0	Udinese Games: 31 — Goals: 13 Cards: 2 — Strike rate: Goal every 205 mins — Mins played: 2661 Ave mins: 70	UEFA Cup Round 1 — Games: 2 Goals: 0 Cards: 1
28	**Ronaldinho** — Age: 25 • 5th best striker in Spain • Overall World Ranking: 88	Brazil — Caps: 9 Goals: 6 — Cards: 1	Barcelona Games: 35 — Goals: 9 Cards: 5 — Strike rate: Goal every 340 mins — Mins played: 3068 Ave mins: 81	Champions League last 16 — Games: 7 Goals: 4 Cards: 1
29	**Zlatan Ibrahimovic** — Age: 23 • 10th best striker in Italy • Overall World Ranking: 92	Sweden — Caps: 7 Goals: 6 — Cards: 1	Juventus Games: 35 — Goals: 16 Cards: 4 — Strike rate: Goal every 172 mins — Mins played: 2757 Ave mins: 73	Champions League quarter-finals — Games: 10 Goals: 0 Cards: 2
30	**Francesco Flachi** — Age: 30 • 11th best striker in Italy • Overall World Ranking: 95	Italy — Caps: 0 Goals: 0 — Cards: 0	Sampdoria Games: 35 — Goals: 14 Cards: 6 — Strike rate: Goal every 216 mins — Mins played: 3037 Ave mins: 80	Did not play — Games: 0 Goals: 0 Cards: 0
31	**Delron Buckley** — Age: 27 • 5th best striker in Germany • Overall World Ranking: 98	South Africa — Caps: 7 Goals: 1 — Cards: 0	Arminia B Games: 29 — Goals: 15 Cards: 2 — Strike rate: Goal every 171 mins — Mins played: 2565 Ave mins: 75	Did not play — Games: 0 Goals: 0 Cards: 0
32	**Raul Tamudo** — Age: 27 • 6th best striker in Spain • Overall World Ranking: 100	Spain — Caps: 2 Goals: 2 — Cards: 0	Espanyol Games: 29 — Goals: 11 Cards: 7 — Strike rate: Goal every 229 mins — Mins played: 2523 Ave mins: 66	Did not play — Games: 0 Goals: 0 Cards: 0
33	**Fernando Torres** — Age: 21 • 7th best striker in Spain • Overall World Ranking: 105	Spain — Caps: 7 Goals: 6 — Cards: 0	Atl Madrid Games: 38 — Goals: 16 Cards: 5 — Strike rate: Goal every 211 mins — Mins played: 3390 Ave mins: 89	Did not play — Games: 0 Goals: 0 Cards: 0
34	**Edu** — Age: 26 • 8th best striker in Spain • Overall World Ranking: 107	Brazil — Caps: 8 Goals: 0 — Cards: 1	Real Betis Games: 32 — Goals: 11 Cards: 4 — Strike rate: Goal every 241 mins — Mins played: 2651 Ave mins: 70	Did not play — Games: 0 Goals: 0 Cards: 0
35	**Andriy Voronin** — Age: 25 • 6th best striker in Germany • Overall World Ranking: 109	Ukraine — Caps: 8 Goals: 1 — Cards: 1	B Leverkusen Games: 33 — Goals: 15 Cards: 2 — Strike rate: Goal every 143 mins — Mins played: 2148 Ave mins: 63	Champions League last 16 — Games: 6 Goals: 2 Cards: 2
36	**Jose Antonio Reyes** — Age: 21 • 5th best striker in Premiership • Overall World Ranking: 114	Spain — Caps: 6 Goals: 0 — Cards: 0	Arsenal Games: 30 — Goals: 9 Cards: 3 — Strike rate: Goal every 223 mins — Mins played: 2013 Ave mins: 53	Champions League last 16 — Games: 8 Goals: 1 Cards: 0
37	**Raul** — Age: 28 • 9th best striker in Spain • Overall World Ranking: 116	Spain — Caps: 8 Goals: 2 — Cards: 0	Real Madrid Games: 32 — Goals: 9 Cards: 1 — Strike rate: Goal every 285 mins — Mins played: 2565 Ave mins: 68	Champions League last 16 — Games: 10 Goals: 4 Cards: 0
38	**Arouna Kone** — Age: 21 • 6th best striker in Holland • Overall World Ranking: 118	Ivory Coast — Caps: 2 Goals: 0 — Cards: 0	Roda JC Kerk Games: 33 — Goals: 13 Cards: 3 — Strike rate: Goal every 222 mins — Mins played: 2893 Ave mins: 85	Did not play — Games: 0 Goals: 0 Cards: 0
39	**Jan Koller** — Age: 32 • 7th best striker in Germany • Overall World Ranking: 119	Czech Republic — Caps: 7 Goals: 6 — Cards: 0	B Dortmund Games: 30 — Goals: 15 Cards: 6 — Strike rate: Goal every 174 mins — Mins played: 2622 Ave mins: 77	Did not play — Games: 0 Goals: 0 Cards: 0
40	**Obafemi Martins** — Age: 20 • 12th best striker in Italy • Overall World Ranking: 120	Nigeria — Caps: 3 Goals: 2 — Cards: 0	Inter Milan Games: 31 — Goals: 11 Cards: 0 — Strike rate: Goal every 161 mins — Mins played: 1774 Ave mins: 47	Champions League quarter-finals — Games: 7 Goals: 5 Cards: 1
41	**Miroslav Klose** — Age: 27 • 8th best striker in Germany • Overall World Ranking: 135	Germany — Caps: 7 Goals: 4 — Cards: 0	W Bremen Games: 32 — Goals: 15 Cards: 7 — Strike rate: Goal every 160 mins — Mins played: 2410 Ave mins: 71	Champions League Last 16 — Games: 7 Goals: 2 Cards: 1
42	**Jermain Defoe** — Age: 22 • 6th best striker in Premiership • Overall World Ranking: 140	England — Caps: 11 Goals: 1 — Cards: 0	Tottenham Games: 35 — Goals: 13 Cards: 5 — Strike rate: Goal every 194 mins — Mins played: 2525 Ave mins: 66	Did not play — Games: 0 Goals: 0 Cards: 0
43	**Christian Vieri** — Age: 31 • 13th best striker in Italy • Overall World Ranking: 141	Italy — Caps: 2 Goals: 0 — Cards: 0	Inter Milan Games: 27 — Goals: 12 Cards: 2 — Strike rate: Goal every 143 mins — Mins played: 1724 Ave mins: 45	Champions League quarter-finals — Games: 6 Goals: 1 Cards: 0
44	**Diego Forlan** — Age: 26 • 10th best striker in Spain • Overall World Ranking: 145	Uruguay — Caps: 4 Goals: 1 — Cards: 0	Villarreal Games: 38 — Goals: 24 Cards: 5 — Strike rate: Goal every 125 mins — Mins played: 3006 Ave mins: 79	Did not play — Games: 0 Goals: 0 Cards: 0
45	**Claudio Pizarro** — Age: 26 • 9th best striker in Germany • Overall World Ranking: 151	Peru — Caps: 5 Goals: 0 — Cards: 1	Bayern Munich Games: 23 — Goals: 11 Cards: 2 — Strike rate: Goal every 155 mins — Mins played: 1708 Ave mins: 50	Champions League quarter-finals — Games: 7 Goals: 4 Cards: 0
46	**Riccardo Zampagna** — Age: 30 • 14th best striker in Italy • Overall World Ranking: 152	Italy — Caps: 0 Goals: 0 — Cards: 0	Messina Games: 28 — Goals: 12 Cards: 7 — Strike rate: Goal every 191 mins — Mins played: 2299 Ave mins: 61	Did not play — Games: 0 Goals: 0 Cards: 0
47	**Savio** — Age: 31 • 11th best striker in Spain • Overall World Ranking: 153	Brazil — Caps: 0 Goals: 0 — Cards: 0	Real Zaragoza Games: 36 — Goals: 10 Cards: 4 — Strike rate: Goal every 311 mins — Mins played: 3116 Ave mins: 82	UEFA Cup last 16 — Games: 10 Goals: 4 Cards: 1
48	**Matt Moussilou** — Age: 23 • 2th best striker in France • Overall World Ranking: 154	France — Caps: 0 Goals: 0 — Cards: 0	Lille Games: 34 — Goals: 13 Cards: 2 — Strike rate: Goal every 170 mins — Mins played: 2211 Ave mins: 58	UEFA Cup last 16 — Games: 10 Goals: 4 Cards: 0
49	**Dennis Bergkamp** — Age: 36 • 7th best striker in Premiership • Overall World Ranking: 158	Holland — Caps: 0 Goals: 0 — Cards: 0	Arsenal Games: 29 — Goals: 8 Cards: 1 — Strike rate: Goal every 240 mins — Mins played: 1920 Ave mins: 51	Champions League last 16 — Games: 4 Goals: 0 Cards: 1
50	**Robbie Fowler** — Age: 30 • 8th best striker in Premiership • Overall World Ranking: 159	England — Caps: 0 Goals: 0 — Cards: 0	Man City Games: 32 — Goals: 10 Cards: 3 — Strike rate: Goal every 251 mins — Mins played: 2515 Ave mins: 66	Did not play — Games: 0 Goals: 0 Cards: 0

THIERRY HENRY

ARSENAL & FRANCE

Do you know your football?

THINK YOU'RE A FOOTY KNOW-IT-ALL? TEST YOUR KNOWLEDGE ON THE FOUR QUIZ PAGES IN THIS ANNUAL. FILL IN YOUR ANSWERS ON PAGE 94 AND SEE HOW MANY YOU SCORED OUT OF 200!

NAME THE YEAR

Name the year these clubs are pictured lifting the Champions League trophy?

1. PORTO

2. MAN. UNITED

3. BARCELONA

4. AC MILAN

5. BAYERN MUNICH

ENGLAND WORD SEARCH

There are 35 recent England players hidden in the grid below. Can you spot them?

```
J A M E S N O R O O N E Y X E V D E D
O P Q R L M C O L E T U V Y L A E B C
H C H R A M S B E C K H A M T S F N C
N A A C A R R I C K N C O S G S O G A
S R R B U D E N E V I L L E S E E P R
O S G R E R D S N Q G B U T M L J E R
N O R F B H S O E F H E J E A L A F A
T N E G R E E N V J T O R T S K I N G
B P A U O S C O L A M P A R D I E S H
E L V A W A T O W E N A O Y A N G A E
A S E W N R I C K G A R D N E R D S R
T H S M I C A M P B E L L A J F D T D
T E R P L R I C H A R D S O N A U B I
I S B U T T F E Y O U I L A M E M V N
E K I N F E R D I N A N D G P J D A S
J E N T L R J O H S W R I G P E Y S M
E Y R O C R O U C H T E G P E N E T I
M E S B A Y O U N G A J E N F A R N T
Q V W R I G H T P H I L L I P S F E H
```

BEATTIE	CARRICK	GARDNER	JOHNSON	ROBINSON
BECKHAM	CARSON	GERRARD	KING	ROONEY
BRIDGE	COLE	GREEN	KNIGHT	SMITH
BROWN	CROUCH	HARGREAVES	LAMPARD	TERRY
BUTT	DEFOE	HESKEY	NEVILLE	VASSELL
CAMPBELL	DYER	JAMES	OWEN	WRIGHT-PHILLIPS
CARRAGHER	FERDINAND	JENAS	RICHARDSON	YOUNG

HOW MUCH CAN YOU REMEMBER ABOUT THE

2004-05 SEASON?

1. Who won the most England caps last season?

2. Which club used the most substitutes in the 2004-05 Premiership season?

3. Name the player who scored the winning penalty in the 2005 FA Cup Final?

4. Who took over as manager of Germany after Euro 2004?

5. Which club used the most players in the Premiership during the 2004-05 season?

6. Who was the Premiership's best penalty taker in 2004-05 and how many did he score?

7. Which club were Dutch Champions in 2004-05?

8. Which club had the most players red-carded in the Premiership last season?

9. Which team won the 2005 UEFA Cup?

10. Only three outfield players played every minute of every game in the last Premier campaign. Can you name them?

11. Who scored the most league goals for Chelsea last season?

12. Can you name the two clubs relegated from the Football League?

GUESS THE PUNDIT

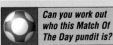
Can you work out who this Match Of The Day pundit is?

WHO PLAYS WHERE

Can you match the grounds with the clubs that play there?

1. PRENTON PARK
2. DEEPDALE
3. THE VALLEY
4. SINCIL BANK
5. ST MARY'S STADIUM
6. WITHDEAN STADIUM
7. VICARAGE ROAD
8. BRITANNIA STADIUM

A. LINCOLN CITY
B. SOUTHAMPTON
C. PRESTON
D. WATFORD
E. CHARLTON ATHLETIC
F. STOKE CITY
G. BRIGHTON
H. TRANMERE ROVERS

SUMMER SIGNINGS

These were summer signings in 2005, but can you name the clubs they came from?

1. EDGAR DAVIDS _____ to Tottenham

2. SHAUN WRIGHT-PHILLIPS _____ to Chelsea

3. PETER CROUCH _____ to Liverpool

4. CRAIG BELLAMY _____ to Blackburn

5. SANDER WESTERVELD _____ to Portsmouth

6. DARIUS VASSELL _____ to Man. City

THE CRAZY CAREER OF
WAYNE ROONEY

Barely 20 years old, WAYNE ROONEY is still the most exciting player in English football.

THERE'S NO DOUBTING THAT Wayne Rooney is the most exciting player English football has produced since Paul Gascoigne was at his peak in the late 1980s and early '90s. One look at his stunning performances for England at Euro 2004, or the brilliant brace he scored for Manchester United against Middlesbrough in last season's FA Cup, mark him out as a unique talent who could easily go on to rival the likes of Ronaldinho and Thierry Henry as the world's best player.

Wayne's rise has been truly meteoric, with less than nine years between him signing schoolboy terms at Everton as a nine-year-old in 1994 and his debut for England at the age of 17 in February 2003. Rooney's glamorous lifestyle today is a million miles from his humble beginnings on a Liverpool council estate and the days when he rode his BMX bike to training at Everton.

But the player has kept his feet on the ground and despite his celebrity status it's his need to be a winner that informs everything he does. Sometimes his desire for success boils over and it's that frustration when things don't go his way that have seen his aggressive on-pitch behaviour criticised. As Sir Alex Ferguson and Sven Göran Eriksson have been keen to point out though, Wayne is still a very young man and his temperament and self-discipline are sure to improve with age.

Although Wayne has achieved so much already, silverware has eluded him. Rest assured, the man they call 'Roonaldo' will be working his socks off to ensure Manchester United don't suffer another trophy-less season this year and will also be a vital part of the England squad hoping to compete in the summer's World Cup finals. In the meantime, we hope you enjoy our journey through Wayne's crazy career, which began in Croxteth, Merseyside in 1985…

OCTOBER 1994

BECOMING A BLUE

Everton scout Bob Pendleton spotted Wayne's potential as a future star when he saw him play, aged nine, for Copplehouse Under-10s, in the Walton & Kirkdale Junior League. Liverpool had also been sniffing around the talented youngster but Pendleton knew that Wayne was a true blue Everton fan who dreamt of playing at Goodison Park rather than Anfield. Pendleton took Wayne to meet Ray Hall, who was Director of Youth at the Everton Academy. After seeing Rooney perform brilliantly in just one training session, Hall agreed with Pendleton that he'd unearthed a real gem. Wayne was signed up on the spot and he wasn't even ten years old!

WAYNE SAID: *"I was approached by a Liverpool scout and invited to Melwood. I went along but after going there just once I got the call from Bob Pendleton. It was the call I had desperately wanted and that was it for me. I gave Liverpool a 'swerve' after that. As soon as Everton came in for me there was never a doubt in my mind."*

APRIL 2002

ON THE RISE

Wayne had stormed through the ranks at Everton and by the age of 15 was a vital member of the Toffees' Under-19 academy side that reached the final of the FA Youth Cup in 2001 (they lost a two-legged final 4-2 to Aston Villa). He was also making a name for himself at international level, debuting for the England Under-15 side against Scotland in November 2000, before being fast-tracked into the Under-17s to compete in the European Championship in Denmark in April and May 2002. England won bronze at the tournament, with 16-year-old Wayne netting a stunning hat-trick in a 4-1 third-place play-off victory against Spain.

WAYNE SAID: *"I want to play in Everton's first team because I've supported them all my life. They don't want to play me in too many games because that will have a detrimental effect. The games at that level are physical and I'll probably be introduced for 20 minute spells. When my chance comes I will have to take it."*

OCTOBER 2002

ARSENAL GUNNED DOWN

Reigning champions Arsenal went into their match on October 19, 2002 on the back of a 30-game unbeaten streak. With the scores stuck at 1-1 after 89 minutes, they looked certain to extend that run. Wayne, who'd made his Everton debut as sub against Southampton on August 17, had only been on the pitch for a few minutes when he unleashed a powerful, curling shot from 30 yards out that beat David Seaman. Aged just 16 years and 360 days, Wayne became the youngest player to score a Premiership goal and became popular so quickly that he was even named Young Sports Personality Of The Year four months later!

DAVID MOYES SAID: *"We were in the dressing room 15 minutes after the match ended and we could hear supporters still singing outside. It was a great experience. Wayne's goal was a great one. Sometimes we have criticised him for shooting when it's unrealistic, but his position gave him a chance to score and fortunately he did."*

FEBRUARY 2003

THREE LIONS ON HIS SHIRT

At 17 years and 111 days Wayne became the youngest England debutant in history when he came on as a second-half substitute in the friendly against Australia on February 12, 2003. The previous record, that of Clapham Rovers' James Prinsep (17 years and 253 days old), had stood since 1879! To celebrate the special occasion, Wayne's mum and dad hired a coach to bring family and friends down to London, a reward for the hard work they'd all put into helping Wayne's career over the years. Despite all the preparations it wasn't quite a perfect evening for Wayne and his family as England ran out 3-1 losers.

WAYNE SAID: *"My mum and dad were shocked at the call-up. There had been a lot of speculation and privately I did hope I would be named, but in all honesty I didn't really think I would. David Beckham spoke to me and gave me some good advice. I was nervous about meeting them all – I wondered what they would think of me."*

"It was a great feeling for me to score my first England goal, even better knowing it was in such an important game."

SEPTEMBER 2003

ON TARGET FOR ENGLAND

On September 6, 2003, at the age of 17 years and 317 days, Wayne became England's youngest ever goalscorer, beating the record set by Michael Owen. The Euro 2004 qualifier against Macedonia was only Wayne's third start for Sven Göran Eriksson's men and Wayne found it difficult to make an impression in the first half as the solid Macedonians hustled him out of the game. However, the introduction of Emile Heskey as a third England striker took some of the pressure off the Everton hitman and he made no mistake in the 53rd minute when unleashing a powerful drive past Macedonia's keeper from 25 yards out. England went on to win the game 2-1.

WAYNE SAID: *"It was a great feeling to score my first England goal – even better knowing it was in such an important game. If I'm honest then I have to say the result is more important to me than scoring because it was a vital win for us. It was a difficult game but once again all of the lads worked hard and showed a never-say-die spirit."*

JUNE 2004

ENGLAND'S EURO HERO

Wayne's brilliant performances for England at Euro 2004 in Portugal lit up the tournament. He scored four goals – two against Switzerland and another brace against Croatia – and looked set to fire England all the way to the final. Unfortunately, Wayne's participation was to end prematurely when he broke his foot following a challenge from Jorge Andrade in the 27th minute of England's quarter-final against the hosts. Sven Göran Eriksson's men eventually lost the game on penalties. Despite the injury, Wayne was England's top scorer in the tournament and had briefly been the youngest scorer in European Championship history.

SVEN GÖRAN ERIKSSON SAID: *"I can't say I know Wayne very well because he doesn't talk all that much. But he doesn't need to – he just goes out there and does it. Against France and Switzerland he was like a boy out on the school pitch. He was saying 'Give me the ball and let me enjoy myself'. He has no nerves."*

AUGUST 2004

OFF TO OLD TRAFFORD

After his impressive displays at Euro 2004, Everton slapped a £50 million price tag on Wayne. The 'Toffees' wanted to keep their most prized asset at Goodison Park, but with the club having debts of around £40 million it was only a matter of time before a big money offer broke their resolve. There were rumours every day concerning Wayne's future, with Chelsea, Real Madrid and Barcelona all said to be lining up huge bids. In the end, Wayne put in a transfer request, immediately bringing both Manchester United and Newcastle to the negotiating table. But it was the Old Trafford side who secured his signature in a £27 million deal on 31 August 2004.

SIR ALEX FERGUSON SAID: *"I'm very excited. We've signed the best young player this country has seen in the past 30 years. Everyone is delighted by Wayne's signing. Wayne is not the finished article yet, but he is a fantastic talent and he proved that at Euro 2004. He has marvellous potential."*

HAT-TRICK DEBUT

September 28, 2004 marked Wayne's first game since breaking his foot at Euro 2004, some 96 days previously. It was also his first match in the red of United. Sir Alex Ferguson had been tempted to play Wayne in the Premiership against Tottenham a few days earlier but had changed his mind. It was just as well for Spurs, really, as the 18-year-old striker started his United career with a bang, hitting a stunning hat-trick in the 17th, 28th and 55th minutes against Turkish side Fenerbahçe. The Champions League game ended up 6-2 to the Red Devils and Wayne's performance was universally hailed as one of the greatest debuts of all time.

SIR ALEX FERGUSON SAID: *"I've never seen a debut like it. That's why we signed him. We think he has great potential and it was a great start for him. As a coach, all I can try is to allow the boy to develop naturally without too much press and public attention and live as ordinary a life as he can."*

PAIN IN SPAIN

England's game against Spain on November 17, 2004 was marred not just by England's poor performance and the racist behaviour of the Madrid crowd, but also by a loss of discipline on Wayne's part that saw Sven Göran Eriksson sub him before half-time. Frustrated with poor service from the England midfield, Wayne made a series of reckless challenges and looked odds on for a red card before the England coach pulled him off. Unfortunately, the player let himself down again upon leaving the field, hurling away the black armband England players had been wearing in memory of Emlyn Hughes and refusing to shake hands with his replacement, Alan Smith.

SVEN GÖRAN ERIKSSON SAID: *"Wayne's young and he's learning and he was sorry in the dressing-room afterwards to Alan Smith and me. That's good. He needs to learn. I hope it will not happen any more. He's very young and it was his first time in a stadium like this. Normally he is very cool."*

CUP FINAL AGONY

Wayne had been the best player on the pitch in his first FA Cup final appearance but even his commanding display couldn't prevent United losing on penalties to bitter rivals Arsenal. The game had ended 0-0 after extra-time with Wayne coming closest to scoring, hitting the post with a fierce shot. Wayne stepped up and easily netted United's third penalty in the shoot-out but Paul Scholes' miss condemned United to a rare trophy-less season. Wayne did pick up one prize, though, his blistering volley against Middlesbrough in the FA Cup fifth round was named Goal Of The Season by *Match Of The Day*.

SIR ALEX FERGUSON SAID: *"You could toss a coin for Man Of The Match out of Wayne Rooney and Cristiano Ronaldo because they were great, the pair of them. There's a great future for those boys. The season's over now and we can reflect on what might have been as long as we like, but we have to look forward now."*

THE WORLD'S TOP 50

MIDF

The MOTD computer runs the footy stats and works out the world's 50 best midfielders!

OVER THE LAST 12 MONTHS WE'VE FOLLOWED 5,000 OF THE BEST PLAYERS in world football to check their form. Are they playing for teams that win? Do they make a difference to how goals are scored or conceded? We've turned the info into a chart for world's best strikers, midfielders, defenders and keepers. In doing this, we also show you where the player is ranked positionally in his domestic league (ie. 3rd best midfielder in the Premiership) and what their Overall World Ranking is (where they are ranked in the list of the world's best players, regardless of position).

The midfield is often key to a winning team. Here we measure not only how often a player's side scores when they play but also how often they concede. Both are important to top sides. Some midfield players protect the defence, others drive the attack and even score vital goals for the team – **Frank Lampard**'s 19 goals and 18 assists were crucial for Chelsea last season.

MIDFIELDERS WHO DIDN'T MAKE THE TOP 50

 There are some famous faces who didn't manage to make our Top 25 Midfielders chart – so what happened? They either didn't play often enough through injury, suspension or through not being selected, or maybe they didn't perform as well as other players in their position. Alternatively, they could have played in too many defeats and not enough wins.

 ZINEDINE ZIDANE: The ninth best midfielder in Spain, but with a worse Madrid record than Beckham he didn't make it into the chart. He also retired from international football, and Madrid didn't progress to the Champions League quarter-finals.

 STEVEN GERRARD: He made some inspirational performances in the Champions League but all Liverpool players struggled against a record of 14 league defeats – 12 when Gerrard was playing. He had a long spell out injured and the club surprisingly only scored a goal only every 80 minutes when he was on the pitch – Alonso, Hamann and Riise all had better midfield records.

 EDGAR DAVIDS: Barely featured for Inter Milan last year with only 14 games and eight other midfield players ahead of him in the pecking order. Five caps for Holland didn't make the difference.

CRISTIANO RONALDO: He started less than three out of four games for United and the team only scored a goal every 69 minutes when he played. The club average is a goal every 48 minutes.

UNDERSTANDING THE GRAPH

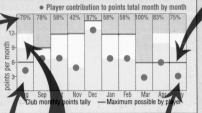

The figure at the top of the column shows what percentage of achievable points were won by the club each month. If the club got 9 points from a possible 12, then it would show 75%.

• Player contribution to points total month by month

The red bar indicates the maximum number of points that the player's club could have got if they had won ALL the games that he played in. The May column shows the club could have won up to 6 points when the player was in the team.

The dark yellow bar show how many points the player's club won during the month. The August column here shows that the club won 9 points.

The light yellow bar stops at the maximum points the player's club could have won. The August column here shows the club could have won up to 12 points during the month.

The red spot indicates how many points the club actually won in games when the player was on the pitch. The May column shows that this player's club won three points when he played.

1 ▲ Frank Lampard

Age: 27 • *Best midfielder in Premiership* • **Overall World Ranking:** 6

On the rare occasions that Chelsea are struggling they look to Frank Lampard. With 19 goals from midfield in all competitions and more assists than any other Premier player, he was top scorer, top provider, vice-captain and the ever-present heartbeat of Mourinho's title-winning side. Now he's firing his trademark edge-of-the-area goals in for England too and is a fixture in Eriksson's central midfield.

Season 2004-05 record

National Team: England
Apps: 9 **Goals:** 3 **Cards:** 0 0

Club: Chelsea
Apps: 38 **Goals:** 13 **Cards:** 6 0
Strike rate: Goal every 262 mins
Mins played: 3412 **Ave mins:** 90

Europe: Champions League semi-finals
Apps: 12 **Goals:** 4 **Cards:** 1 0

● Player contribution to points total month by month

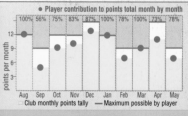

	Aug	Sep	Oct	Nov	Dec	Jan	Feb	Mar	Apr	May
%	100%	56%	75%	83%	87%	100%	78%	100%	73%	78%

points per month

☐ Club monthly points tally — Maximum possible by player

2 ▲ Claude Makelele

Age: 32 • *2nd best midfielder in Premiership* • **Overall World Ranking: 10**

If Frank Lampard is Chelsea's heart, Claude Makelele is the player who holds it all together. Under rated at Real Madrid, he became the last big money signing of Abramovich's first summer in London. Real immediately stopped winning titles, while Chelsea finally began to challenge for them. Makelele has an uncanny ability to break up opposition attacks on the edge of his own area and launch his own with clever, simple passes.

Season 2004-05 record

National Team: France
Apps: 1 **Goals:** 0 **Cards:** 1 1

Club: Chelsea
Apps: 36 **Goals:** 1 **Cards:** 6 0
Strike rate: Goal every 3238 mins
Mins played: 3238 **Ave mins:** 85

Europe: Champions League semi-finals
Apps: 10 **Goals:** 0 **Cards:** 1 0

• Player contribution to points total month by month

100% 56% 75% 83% 87% 100% 78% 100% 73% 78%

Aug Sep Oct Nov Dec Jan Feb Mar Apr May
☐ Club monthly points tally —— Maximum possible by player

3 ▲ Mark van Bommel

Age: 28 • *Best midfielder in Dutch League* • **Overall World Ranking: 17**

Mark van Bommel was the first name on Barcelona's transfer wish list this summer. He was fresh from steering PSV to the fourth title of his six seasons there – scoring 14 goals along the way – and reaching the Champions League semi-finals. Van Bommel is the top midfield talent in Holland with a reputation for striking screamers from a long way out – like the one he thumped past England from 36 yards in 2001.

Season 2004-05 record

National Team: Holland
Apps: 10 **Goals:** 2 **Cards:** 1 1

Club: PSV Eindhoven
Apps: 30 **Goals:** 14 **Cards:** 7 0
Strike rate: Goal every 188 mins
Mins played: 2631 **Ave mins:** 77

Europe: Champions League semi-finals
Apps: 14 **Goals:** 2 **Cards:** 2 0

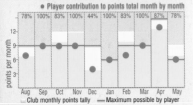

• Player contribution to points total month by month

78% 100% 83% 100% 44% 100% 83% 100% 87% 78%

Aug Sep Oct Nov Dec Jan Feb Mar Apr May
☐ Club monthly points tally —— Maximum possible by player

4 ▲ Ji-Sung Park

Age: 24 • *2nd best midfielder in Dutch League* • **Overall World Ranking:**

Alex Ferguson saw Ji-Sung Park terrorise AC Milan's defence over two legs in the Champions League semi-finals and picked him as Ryan Giggs' successor. Park hit the headlines scoring South Korea's winner to knock Portugal out of the 2002 World Cup. The Koreans' manager Guus Hiddink took Park with him to PSV and the tireless winger replaced Arjen Robben last season, scoring seven goals on the way to the title.

Season 2004-05 record

National Team: South Korea
Apps: 5 **Goals:** 1 **Cards:** 0 0

Club: PSV Eindhoven
Apps: 28 **Goals:** 7 **Cards:** 0 0
Strike rate: Goal every 339 mins
Mins played: 2375 **Ave mins:** 70

Europe: Champions League semi-finals
Apps: 13 **Goals:** 2 **Cards:** 3 1

• Player contribution to points total month by month

78% 100% 83% 100% 44% 100% 83% 100% 87% 78%

Aug Sep Oct Nov Dec Jan Feb Mar Apr May
☐ Club monthly points tally —— Maximum possible by player

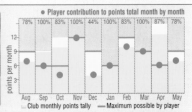

5 ▲ Anderson Deco

Age: 27 • *Best midfielder in Spanish League* • **Overall World Ranking: 31**

A UEFA Cup and Champions League winner in José Mourinho's Porto side in successive seasons, Deco was snapped up by Barcelona. The playmaker's partnership in central midfield with Xavi made for neat possession football and took Barça to the Spanish title. Deco traded his Brazilian heritage for Portugal after being granted dual citizenship in 2003 and scored the winner on his debut for his adopted country.

Season 2004-05 record

National Team: Portugal
Apps: 9 **Goals:** 1 **Cards:** 0 0

Club: Barcelona
Apps: 35 **Goals:** 7 **Cards:** 13 0
Strike rate: Goal every 434 mins
Mins played: 3038 **Ave mins:** 80

Europe: Champions League last 16
Apps: 7 **Goals:** 2 **Cards:** 0 0

• Player contribution to points total month by month

100% 83% 83% 75% 83% 75% 58% 83% 58% 60%

Aug Sep Oct Nov Dec Jan Feb Mar Apr May
☐ Club monthly points tally —— Maximum possible by player

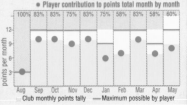

6 ▲ Phillip Cocu

Age: 34 • *3rd best midfielder in Dutch League* • **Overall World Ranking: 32**

Phillip Cocu seems to have done everything and played in every position for both club and country. Last season he left Barcelona after six years to rejoin PSV, the club where he enjoyed his early success. Adding his experience to a formidable midfield, PSV took the Dutch title and he was the outstanding player in a Champions League run culminating in two semi-final goals against Milan that nearly earned a final spot.

Season 2004-05 record

National Team: Holland
Apps: 5 **Goals:** 2 **Cards:** 0 0

Club: PSV Eindhoven
Apps: 29 **Goals:** 6 **Cards:** 4 1
Strike rate: Goal every 408mins
Mins played: 2448 **Ave mins:** 72

Europe: Champions League semi-finals
Apps: 13 **Goals:** 3 **Cards:** 2 0

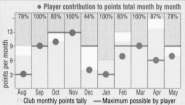

• Player contribution to points total month by month
78% 100% 83% 100% 44% 100% 83% 100% 87% 78%
Aug Sep Oct Nov Dec Jan Feb Mar Apr May
□ Club monthly points tally — Maximum possible by player

7 ▲ Mauro Camoranesi

Age: 28 • *Best midfielder in Italian League* • **Overall World Ranking: 33**

Old-fashioned wing play is the mark of Argentinian Mauro Camoranesi. He has the speed and footwork to leave his defender and the ability to finish it off with a fine cross. His dual nationality has led him to be capped by Italy and he has twice won the Serie A title with Juventus. Respected Italian coach Alberto Zaccheroni says: "He's quick, skilful, brave, has vision, and because of his low centre of gravity, he's a devil to stop."

Season 2004-05 record

National Team: Italy
Apps: 3 **Goals:** 0 **Cards:** 1 0

Club: Juventus
Apps: 36 **Goals:** 4 **Cards:** 6 0
Strike rate: Goal every 761 mins
Mins played: 3045 **Ave mins:** 80

Europe: Champions League quarter-finals
Apps: 9 **Goals:** 1 **Cards:** 3 0

• Player contribution to points total month by month
83% 100% 58% 78% 73% 47% 100% 58% 87%
Aug Sep Oct Nov Dec Jan Feb Mar Apr May
□ Club monthly points tally — Maximum possible by player

8 ▲ Gianluca Zambrotta

Age: 28 • *2nd best midfielder in Italian League* • **Overall World Ranking: 37**

Juventus and Gianluca Zambrotta have been together for three titles and nearly six years of success. The Italian winger can also play fullback and has done, for both club and country. He first came to the fore as a Bari player in 1999 when Italian manager Dino Zoff brought him into the national squad as an attacking right midfield option. Juventus won the scramble for his signature before he helped Italy to the Euro 2000 final.

Season 2004-05 record

National Team: Italy
Apps: 6 **Goals:** 0 **Cards:** 3 3

Club: Juventus
Apps: 36 **Goals:** 0 **Cards:** 3 0
Strike rate: None
Mins played: 3236 **Ave mins:** 85

Europe: Champions League quarter-finals
Apps: 12 **Goals:** 0 **Cards:** 2 0

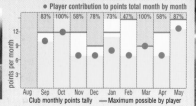

• Player contribution to points total month by month
83% 100% 58% 78% 73% 47% 100% 58% 87%
Aug Sep Oct Nov Dec Jan Feb Mar Apr May
□ Club monthly points tally — Maximum possible by player

Damien Duff

Age: 26 • *3rd best midfielder in Premiership* • **Overall World Ranking: 40**

The pacy winger was Chelsea's most consistent attacking threat last season. He played twice as much as Arjen Robben and looked more dangerous than Eidur Gudjohnsen. Duff scored ten goals and made seven assists. He is also one of the main reasons why the Republic of Ireland are ranked so high by FIFA. He disrupted defences in the 2002 World Cup and is the first name on Brian Kerr's team-sheet.

Season 2004-05 record

National Team: Rep of Ireland
Apps: 10 **Goals:** 0 **Cards:** 2 2

Club: Chelsea
Apps: 30 **Goals:** 6 **Cards:** 1 0
Strike rate: Goal every 399 mins
Mins played: 2396 **Ave mins:** 63

Europe: Champions League quarter-finals
Apps: 10 **Goals:** 2 **Cards:** 1 0

● Player contribution to points total month by month

	100%	56%	75%	83%	87%	100%	78%	100%	73%	78%
Aug	Sep	Oct	Nov	Dec	Jan	Feb	Mar	Apr	May

points per month

━ Club monthly points tally ─ Maximum possible by player

10 Johann Vogel

Age: 28 • *4th best midfielder in Dutch League* • **Overall World Ranking: 45**

AC Milan were so shocked at being outplayed by PSV in the Champions League semi-finals, they immediately signed the Dutch side's midfield dynamo Johann Vogel. The Swiss international captain doesn't always catch the eye and has only scored seven goals in 169 appearances but he is quietly effective, making crucial tackles, keeping possession with simple passes and working hard for the team.

Season 2004-05 record

National Team: Switzerland
Apps: 8 **Goals:** 0 **Cards:** 1 0

Club: PSV Eindhoven
Apps: 27 **Goals:** 1 **Cards:** 1 0
Strike rate: Goal every 1963 mins
Mins played: 1963 **Ave mins:** 58

Europe: Champions League semi-finals
Apps: 13 **Goals:** 0 **Cards:** 1 0

● Player contribution to points total month by month

	78%	100%	83%	100%	44%	100%	83%	100%	87%	78%
Aug	Sep	Oct	Nov	Dec	Jan	Feb	Mar	Apr	May

points per month
Club monthly points tally — Maximum possible by player

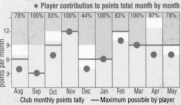

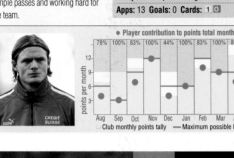

11 Xavi Hernandez

Age: 25 • *2nd best midfielder in Spanish League* • **Overall World Ranking: 47**

Everything seems to revolve around the small but busy Xavi Hernandez. Whether he's weaving his patterns in the blue and red of Barcelona or the red and gold of Spain, it's rare that a pass ever goes astray. Barcelona recognised his contribution to their first title for six years by extending his contract to 2010 this summer. England's players took note as Xavi gave them the run-around in a one-sided friendly in November 2004.

Season 2004-05 record

National Team: Spain
Apps: 7 **Goals:** 1 **Cards:** 1 1

Club: Barcelona
Apps: 36 **Goals:** 3 **Cards:** 4 0
Strike rate: Goal every 1046 mins
Mins played: 3139 **Ave mins:** 83

Europe: Champions League last 16
Apps: 8 **Goals:** 0 **Cards:** 1 0

● Player contribution to points total month by month

	100%	83%	83%	75%	83%	75%	58%	83%	58%	60%
Aug	Sep	Oct	Nov	Dec	Jan	Feb	Mar	Apr	May

points per month
Club monthly points tally — Maximum possible by player

12 Bart Goor

Age: 32 • *5th best midfielder in Dutch League* • **Overall World Ranking: 57**

Belgian Bart Goor has rejoined his former club Anderlecht after publicly falling out with his previous side Feyenoord. He adds pace and skill on the left to any side and captained a high-scoring Feyenoord to fourth place in the Dutch league last season. Goor scored seven goals himself and helped striker Dirk Kuijt to become the top scorer in the big European divisions. He also captained Belgian until a recent sending off.

Season 2004-05 record

National Team: Belgium
Apps: 3 **Goals:** 0 **Cards:** 2 2

Club: Feyenoord
Apps: 34 **Goals:** 7 **Cards:** 1 0
Strike rate: Goal every 416 mins
Mins played: 2912 **Ave mins:** 86

Europe: UEFA Cup 1ast 32
Apps: 7 **Goals:** 3 **Cards:** 2 0

● Player contribution to points total month by month

	78%	67%	75%	42%	44%	17%	100%	100%	60%	25%
Aug	Sep	Oct	Nov	Dec	Jan	Feb	Mar	Apr	May

points per month
Club monthly points tally — Maximum possible by player

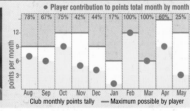
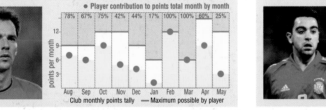

13 Emerson

Age: 29 • *3rd best midfielder in Italian League* • **Overall World Ranking: 72**

Patrick Vieira's midfield partner at Juventus is Emerson and the club's manager Fabio Capelli claims he now has the "best midfield duo" in the world. Emerson joined Juvé from Roma in 2004 and steered them to the title. He has all the midfield talents – playmaker, dribbler and ball-winner – and was the captain of Brazil's 2002 World Cup team until dislocating his shoulder, leaving Cafu to captain the side to their triumph.

Season 2004-05 record

National Team: Brazil
Apps: 3 **Goals:** 1 **Cards:** 1 0

Club: Juventus
Apps: 33 **Goals:** 1 **Cards:** 1 0
Strike rate: Goal every 2785 mins
Mins played: 2785 **Ave mins:** 73

Europe: Champions League quarter-finals
Apps: 11 **Goals:** 1 **Cards:** 1 0

● Player contribution to points total month by month

	83%	100%	58%	78%	73%	47%	100%	58%	87%
Aug	Sep	Oct	Nov	Dec	Jan	Feb	Mar	Apr	May

points per month
Club monthly points tally — Maximum possible by player

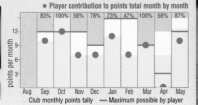

14 Ricardo Kaká

Age: 23 • *4th best midfielder in Italian League* • **Overall World Ranking: 74**

Kaká is widely seen as the most creative midfield player in world football and was voted player of the season in the Brazilian championship when just 20. Now the playmaker in AC Milan's midfield, only Maldini played more outfield games for them in a season where they ended runners-up in the Champions League and Serie A. The Brazilian team are favourites for the coming World Cup, and Kaká is one reason why.

Season 2004-05 record

National Team: Brazil
Apps: 4 **Goals:** 3 **Cards:** 1 0

Club: AC Milan
Apps: 36 **Goals:** 7 **Cards:** 5 0
Strike rate: Goal every 417 mins
Mins played: 2917 **Ave mins:** 77

Europe: Champions League final
Apps: 12 **Goals:** 2 **Cards:** 1 0

● Player contribution to points total month by month

| | 58% | 87% | 67% | 78% | 47% | 100% | 100% | 67% | 25% |

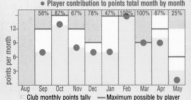

Club monthly points tally — Maximum possible by player

15 Juan Riquelme

Age: 27 • *3rd best midfielder in Spanish League* • **Overall World Ranking: 76**

Everton's rude awakening to the demands of the Champions League came courtesy of Juan Riquelme. He plays for Villarreal (nicknamed the 'Yellow Submarines') on loan from Barcelona and provided the ammunition last season that took them to third in La Liga and transformed Diego Forlan from United failure to top striker in Spain. Now he is also playmaker to the Argentinian midfield.

Season 2004-05 record

National Team: Argentina
Apps: 6 **Goals:** 1 **Cards:** 0 0

Club: Villarreal
Apps: 35 **Goals:** 15 **Cards:** 5 0
Strike rate: Goal every 208 mins
Mins played: 3117 **Ave mins:** 82

Europe: UEFA Cup quarter-finals
Apps: 9 **Goals:** 2 **Cards:** 2 1

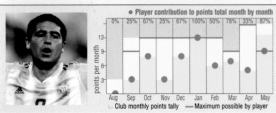

● Player contribution to points total month by month

| 0% | 25% | 67% | 25% | 67% | 100% | 50% | 78% | 33% | 87% |

Club monthly points tally — Maximum possible by player

16 Romeo Castelen

Age: 22 • *6th best midfielder in Dutch League* • **Overall World Ranking: 80**

The pacy right winger has made his mark in Dutch football after just one year at Feyenoord, following a transfer from the struggling Den Haag team. Castelen hit ten goals as Feyenoord became the highest scorers in European football ahead of PSV and Arsenal. He forced his way into Marco van Basten's young Dutch squad, receiving eight caps, and impressed against Ashley Cole in a friendly at Villa Park last February.

Season 2004-05 record

National Team: Holland
Apps: 8 **Goals:** 1 **Cards:** 2 0

Club: Feyenoord
Apps: 30 **Goals:** 10 **Cards:** 2 0
Strike rate: Goal every 244 mins
Mins played: 2442 **Ave mins:** 72

Europe: UEFA Cup last 32
Apps: 7 **Goals:** 0 **Cards:** 2 0

● Player contribution to points total month by month

| 78% | 67% | 75% | 42% | 44% | 17% | 100% | 100% | 60% | 25% |

Club monthly points tally — Maximum possible by player

17 Gilberto

Age: 28 • *Best midfielder in German League* • **Overall World Ranking: 81**

Two Brazilians are the key to Hertha Berlin's move up the Bundesliga from mid-table also-rans to within a point of a Champions League spot: the striker Marcelinho and the midfield defender Gilberto. Gilberto scored six goals and combined with Yildiray Basturk and Nico Kovac, giving Hertha the best midfield in Germany. His efforts were rewarded with a call-up to Brazil's squad for the Confederations Cup in the summer.

Season 2004-05 record

National Team: Brazil
Apps: 0 **Goals:** 0 **Cards:** 2 0

Club: Hertha Berlin
Apps: 33 **Goals:** 6 **Cards:** 2 0
Strike rate: Goal every 481 mins
Mins played: 2888 **Ave mins:** 85

Europe: Did not play
Apps: 0 **Goals:** 0 **Cards:** 2 0

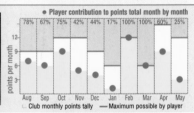

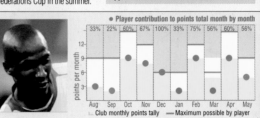

● Player contribution to points total month by month

| 33% | 22% | 60% | 67% | 100% | 33% | 75% | 56% | 60% | 56% |

Club monthly points tally — Maximum possible by player

18 Javier Zanetti

Age: 31 • *5th best midfielder in Italian League* • **Overall World Ranking: 82**

Versatility is the word associated with Javier Zanetti. The Argentinian has played in almost every position at Inter Milan since he joined the club ten years ago. The right-footed star has even appeared on the left wing and is currently used in the Argentina national side to protect the defence. He plays more games for Inter than his colleagues and is seen as one of Serie A's 'gentlemen', winning the league's Fair Play award last season.

Season 2004-05 record

National Team: Argentina
Apps: 9 **Goals:** 1 **Cards:** 1 0

Club: Inter Milan
Apps: 35 **Goals:** 0 **Cards:** 1 0
Strike rate: None
Mins played: 3010 **Ave mins:** 79

Europe: Champions League quarter-finals
Apps: 10 **Goals:** 0 **Cards:** 0 0

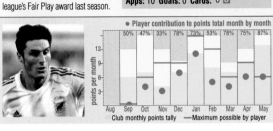

● Player contribution to points total month by month

20 Gio. Van Bronckhorst

Age: 30 • *4h best midfielder in Spanish League* • **Overall World Ranking: 90**

A success at Rangers but a bit-part player with Arsene Wenger's Arsenal, Giovanni van Bronckhorst first moved to Barcelona on loan in 2003. There, the left back moved into midfield and so impressed that the Catalan club signed him. Last season Deco and Xavi joined him as midfield regulars as Barça won the Spanish La Liga title. 'Gio' is also a regular in the Dutch side with eight caps in the last 12 months.

Season 2004-05 record

National Team: Holland
Apps: 9 **Goals:** 0 **Cards:** 2 0

Club: Barcelona
Apps: 30 **Goals:** 4 **Cards:** 2 0
Strike rate: Goal every 619 mins
Mins played: 2477 **Ave mins:** 65

Europe: Champions League last 16
Apps: 8 **Goals:** 0 **Cards:** 2 0

● Player contribution to points total month by month

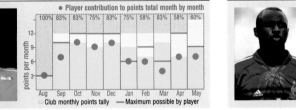

Club monthly points tally — Maximum possible by player

19 Patrick Vieira

Age: 29 • *4th best midfielder in Premiership* • **Overall World Ranking: 84**

Juvé prised Vieira away from Arsenal as the man to help them retain the Serie A title. Arsene Wenger had plucked Vieira out of AC Milan reserves as his first signing when he became Arsenal manager. The player was the driving force behind the London club's recent successes. He has won over 80 caps for France and excels as ball-winner, passer and scorer of important goals, but it is his competitive spirit that marks him out.

Season 2004-05 record

National Team: France
Apps: 8 **Goals:** 0 **Cards:** 4 4

Club: Arsenal
Apps: 32 **Goals:** 6 **Cards:** 9 0
Strike rate: Goal every 466 mins
Mins played: 2794 **Ave mins:** 74

Europe: Champions League last 16
Apps: 6 **Goals:** 0 **Cards:** 3 1

● Player contribution to points total month by month

Club monthly points tally — Maximum possible by player

21 Roy Keane

Age: 33 • *5th best midfielder in Premiership* • **Overall World Ranking: 91**

The abrasive United captain is the ultimate competitor. Alex Ferguson rates Roy Keane as the best player he's ever worked with and both men seem similarly driven. When signed from Brian Clough's Nottingham Forest 'Keano' covered every blade on the pitch, now he relies more on his incredible ability to read the game and keep possession. And he's back in the Irish team after angrily quitting on the eve of World Cup 2002.

Season 2004-05 record

National Team: Rep of Ireland
Apps: 6 **Goals:** 0 **Cards:** 2 0

Club: Man Utd
Apps: 31 **Goals:** 1 **Cards:** 2 0
Strike rate: Goal every 2610 mins
Mins played: 2610 **Ave mins:** 69

Europe: Champions League last 16
Apps: 6 **Goals:** 0 **Cards:** 2 0

● Player contribution to points total month by month

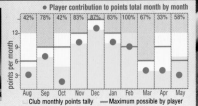

Club monthly points tally — Maximum possible by player

22 Sanchez Joaquin

▲ **Age: 24** • *5th best midfielder in Spanish League* • **Overall World Ranking: 93**

An all round midfield player, Sanchez Joaquin is able to play in the centre or on the wing. He began his professional career at Real Betis in 1999 and helped the club to promotion to the Spanish Primeira Liga in 2001. The following season he earned a UEFA Cup spot and last season he appeared in all 38 league games as they came fourth. His loyalty has earned him a regular place in Spain's international side.

Season 2004-05 record

National Team: Spain
Apps: 7 **Goals:** 2 **Cards:** 2 0

Club: Real Betis
Apps: 38 **Goals:** 5 **Cards:** 2 0
Strike rate: Goal every 650 mins
Mins played: 3249 **Ave mins:** 86

Europe: Did not play
Apps: 0 **Goals:** 0 **Cards:** 2 0

• **Player contribution to points total month by month**

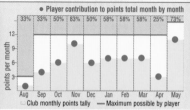

☐ Club monthly points tally — Maximum possible by player

---

23 Pavel Nedved

▲ **Age: 32** • *6th best midfielder in Italian League* • **Overall World Ranking: 94**

Pavel Nedved's contribution to Serie A and the Czech international side was recognised in 2003 when he was voted European Player of the Year. The former Czech captain took his team to No.2 in the FIFA Rankings before retiring from international football after Euro 2004. Juventus immediately benefited, winning the Serie A title. Nedved has pace, vision and a powerful shot and can inspire his sides to astonishing feats.

Season 2004-05 record

National Team: Czech Republic
Apps: 0 **Goals:** 0 **Cards:** 0 0

Club: Juventus
Apps: 27 **Goals:** 8 **Cards:** 7 0
Strike rate: Goal every 297 mins
Mins played: 2379 **Ave mins:** 63

Europe: Champions League quarter-finals
Apps: 10 **Goals:** 3 **Cards:** 1 0

• **Player contribution to points total month by month**

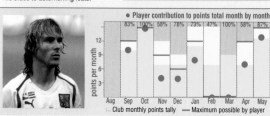

☐ Club monthly points tally — Maximum possible by player

---

24 Ryan Giggs

▲ **Age: 31** • *6th best midfielder in Premiership* • **Overall World Ranking: 99**

Ryan Giggs broke into the United side at just 17 and immediately started dismantling defences. Fourteen years on the nippy Welsh winger is still doing it – only now he is captain of Wales and has Premiership and Champions League titles to his name. There is supposed to be no finer sight in football than Giggs running hard at defenders, and his 'wonder goal' against Arsenal is viewed as one of the best ever.

Season 2004-05 record

National Team: Wales
Apps: 3 **Goals:** 0 **Cards:** 0 0

Club: Man Utd
Apps: 32 **Goals:** 6 **Cards:** 3 0
Strike rate: Goal every 387 mins
Mins played: 2321 **Ave mins:** 61

Europe: Champions League last 16
Apps: 6 **Goals:** 2 **Cards:** 0 0

• **Player contribution to points total month by month**

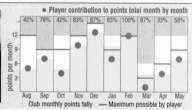

☐ Club monthly points tally — Maximum possible by player

---

25 David Beckham

▲ **Age: 30** • *6th best midfielder in Spanish League* • **Overall World Ranking: 102**

The most famous face in world sport (with a lifestyle and sponsorship deals to match) David Beckham has refused to be distracted from the game he loves. The "best crosser of a ball" has always worked hard on his game and England's captain has had to use that determination to win over Real Madrid's demanding fans. He succeeded and last year eclipsed Luis Figo and Zinedine Zidane to be Real's most influential midfielder.

Season 2004-05 record

National Team: England
Apps: 9 **Goals:** 3 **Cards:** 3 0

Club: Real Madrid
Apps: 30 **Goals:** 4 **Cards:** 1 0
Strike rate: Goal every 608 mins
Mins played: 2432 **Ave mins:** 64

Europe: Champions League last 16
Apps: 8 **Goals:** 0 **Cards:** 1 0

• **Player contribution to points total month by month**

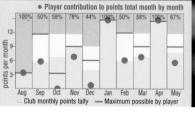

☐ Club monthly points tally — Maximum possible by player

Maximum possible by player

36

#	Name	Player Info	National/Club	Stats	Europe
26 ▲	**David Garcia**	Age: 24 • 7h best midfielder in Spain • Overall World Ranking: 104	National Team: Spain / Caps: 0 Goals: 0 / Cards: 0	Club: Espanyol Games: 34 / Goals: 0 Cards: 4 Strike rate: - / Mins played: 2955 Ave mins: 78	Europe: Did not play / Games: - Goals: 0 Cards: 0
27 ▲	**Nico Kovac**	Age: 33 • 2nd best midfielder in Germany • Overall World Ranking: 106	National Team: Croatia / Caps: 9 Goals: 2 / Cards: 1	Club: Hertha Berlin Games: 30 / Goals: 4 Cards: 11 Strike rate: Goal every 638 mins / Mins played: 2553 Ave mins: 75	Europe: Did not play / Games: - Goals: 0 Cards: 0
28 ▲	**Esteban Cambiasso**	Age: 24 • 7th best midfielder in Italy • Overall World Ranking: 102	National Team: Argentina / Caps: 6 Goals: 0 / Cards: 1	Club: Inter Milan Games: 30 / Goals: 2 Cards: 7 Strike rate: Goal every 1290 mins / Mins played: 2580 Ave mins: 68	Europe: Champions League quarter-finals / Games: 10 Goals: 0 Cards: 1
29 ▲	**Rodriguez Maxi**	Age: 24 • 8th best midfielder in Spain • Overall World Ranking: 111	National Team: Argentina / Caps: 4 Goals: 0 / Cards: 1	Club: Espanyol Games: 37 / Goals: 15 Cards: 3 Strike rate: Goal every 199 mins / Mins played: 2985 Ave mins: 79	Europe: Did not play / Games: - Goals: 0 Cards: 0
30 ▲	**David Marcelo Pizarro**	Age: 25 • 8th best midfielder in Italy • Overall World Ranking: 112	National Team: Chile / Caps: 8 Goals: 0 / Cards: 0	Club: Udinese Games: 34 / Goals: 2 Cards: 3 Strike rate: Goal every 1427 mins / Mins played: 2854 Ave mins: 75	Europe: Did not play / Games: - Goals: 0 Cards: 1
31 ▲	**Michael Essien**	Age: 22 • Best midfielder in France • Overall World Ranking: 113	National Team: Ghana / Caps: 6 Goals: 2 / Cards: 2	Club: Lyon Games: 37 / Goals: 4 Cards: 12 Strike rate: Goal every 799 mins / Mins played: 3194 Ave mins: 84	Europe: Champions League quarter-finals / Games: 10 Goals: 5 Cards: 0
32 ▲	**Zinedine Zidane**	Age: 33 • 9th best midfielder in Spain • Overall World Ranking: 115	National Team: France / Caps: 0 Goals: 0 / Cards: 0	Club: Real Madrid Games: 29 / Goals: 6 Cards: 5 Strike rate: Goal every 390 mins / Mins played: 2340 Ave mins: 62	Europe: Champions League last 16 / Games: 10 Goals: 0 Cards: 1
33 ▲	**Cesc Fabregas**	Age: 18 • 7th best midfielder in Premiership • Overall World Ranking: 121	National Team: Spain / Caps: 0 Goals: 0 / Cards: 0	Club: Arsenal Games: 33 / Goals: 1 Cards: 4 Strike rate: Goal every 2118 mins / Mins played: 2118 Ave mins: 56	Europe: Champions League last 16 / Games: 5 Goals: 1 Cards: 1
34 ▲	**Robert Pires**	Age: 31 • 8th best midfielder in Premiership • Overall World Ranking: 124	National Team: France / Caps: 5 Goals: 0 / Cards: 0	Club: Arsenal Games: 33 / Goals: 14 Cards: 2 Strike rate: Goal every 165 mins / Mins played: 2316 Ave mins: 61	Europe: Champions League last 16 / Games: 8 Goals: 1 Cards: 0
35 ▲	**Florent Malouda**	Age: 25 • 2nd best midfielder in France • Overall World Ranking: 130	National Team: France / Caps: 4 Goals: 1 / Cards: 0	Club: Lyon Games: 37 / Goals: 5 Cards: 0 Strike rate: Goal every 599 mins / Mins played: 2996 Ave mins: 79	Europe: Champions League quarter-finals / Games: 10 Goals: 3 Cards: 1
36 ▲	**Clarence Seedorf**	Age: 29 • 9th best midfielder in Italy • Overall World Ranking: 132	National Team: Holland / Caps: 0 Goals: 0 / Cards: 0	Club: AC Milan Games: 33 / Goals: 5 Cards: 5 Strike rate: Goal every 472 mins / Mins played: 2362 Ave mins: 62	Europe: Champions League final / Games: 12 Goals: 1 Cards: 1
37 ▲	**Arjen Robben**	Age: 21 • 9th best midfielder in Premiership • Overall World Ranking: 133	National Team: Holland / Caps: 3 Goals: 2 / Cards: 0	Club: Chelsea Games: 18 / Goals: 7 Cards: 5 Strike rate: Goal every 179 mins / Mins played: 1255 Ave mins: 33	Europe: Champions League semi-finals / Games: 5 Goals: 1 Cards: 0
38 ▲	**Paul Scholes**	Age: 30 • 10th best midfielder in Premiership • Overall World Ranking: 139	National Team: England / Caps: 0 Goals: 0 / Cards: 0	Club: Man Utd Games: 33 / Goals: 9 Cards: 5 Strike rate: Goal every 290 mins / Mins played: 2606 Ave mins: 69	Europe: Champions League last 16 / Games: 7 Goals: 0 Cards: 2
39 ▲	**Michael Ballack**	Age: 28 • 3rd best midfielder in Germany • Overall World Ranking: 143	National Team: Germany / Caps: 8 Goals: 4 / Cards: 1	Club: Bayern Munich Games: 27 / Goals: 13 Cards: 7 Strike rate: Goal every 184 mins / Mins played: 2395 Ave mins: 70	Europe: Champions League quarter-finals / Games: 9 Goals: 2 Cards: 2
40 ▲	**Maxwell**	Age: 23 • 7th best midfielder in Holland • Overall World Ranking: 144	National Team: Brazil / Caps: 0 Goals: 0 / Cards: 0	Club: Ajax Games: 29 / Goals: 3 Cards: 2 Strike rate: Goal every 840 mins / Mins played: 2521 Ave mins: 74	Europe: UEFA Cup round of 32 / Games: 6 Goals: 1 Cards: 0
41 ▲	**Cardoso Tiago**	Age: 24 • 11th best midfielder in Premiership • Overall World Ranking: 148	National Team: Portugal / Caps: 7 Goals: 0 / Cards: 1	Club: Chelsea Games: 34 / Goals: 4 Cards: 4 Strike rate: Goal every 493 mins / Mins played: 1970 Ave mins: 52	Europe: Champions League semi-finals / Games: 11 Goals: 0 Cards: 1
42 ▲	**Yildiray Basturk**	Age: 26 • 4th best midfielder in Germany • Overall World Ranking: 149	National Team: Turkey / Caps: 4 Goals: 1 / Cards: 1	Club: Hertha Berlin Games: 25 / Goals: 7 Cards: 3 Strike rate: Goal every 295 mins / Mins played: 2064 Ave mins: 61	Europe: Did not play / Games: - Goals: 0 Cards: 0
43 ▲	**Levan Kobiashvili**	Age: 27 • 5th best midfielder in Germany • Overall World Ranking: 150	National Team: Georgia / Caps: 7 Goals: 2 / Cards: 0	Club: Schalke Games: 32 / Goals: 3 Cards: 9 Strike rate: Goal every 951 mins / Mins played: 2854 Ave mins: 84	Europe: UEFA Cup round of 32 / Games: 6 Goals: 2 Cards: 0
44 ▲	**Shaun Wright-Phillips**	Age: 23 • 12th best midfielder in Premiership • Overall World Ranking: 155	National Team: England / Caps: 7 Goals: 1 / Cards: 0	Club: Man City Games: 34 / Goals: 10 Cards: 4 Strike rate: Goal every 300 mins / Mins played: 2998 Ave mins: 79	Europe: Did not play / Games: - Goals: 0 Cards: 0
45 ▲	**Andrea Pirlo**	Age: 26 • 10th best midfielder in Italy • Overall World Ranking: 157	National Team: Italy / Caps: 5 Goals: 2 / Cards: 0	Club: AC Milan Games: 30 / Goals: 4 Cards: 4 Strike rate: Goal every 574 mins / Mins played: 2296 Ave mins: 60	Europe: Champions League final / Games: 11 Goals: 1 Cards: 0
46 ▲	**Boudewijn Zenden**	Age: 28 • 13th best midfielder in Premiership • Overall World Ranking: 160	National Team: Holland / Caps: 1 Goals: 0 / Cards: 0	Club: Middlesbrough Games: 36 / Goals: 5 Cards: 8 Strike rate: Goal every 611 mins / Mins played: 3055 Ave mins: 80	Europe: UEFA Cup last 16 / Games: 10 Goals: 3 Cards: 1
47 ▲	**Mahamadou Diarra**	Age: 24 • 3rd best midfielder in France • Overall World Ranking: 161	National Team: Mali / Caps: 5 Goals: 1 / Cards: 1	Club: Lyon Games: 34 / Goals: 2 Cards: 5 Strike rate: Goal every 1465 mins / Mins played: 2930 Ave mins: 77	Europe: Champions League quarter-finals / Games: 9 Goals: 2 Cards: 2
48 ▲	**Antonio Ito**	Age: 30 • 10th best midfielder in Spain • Overall World Ranking: 162	National Team: Spain / Caps: 0 Goals: 0 / Cards: 0	Club: Espanyol Games: 31 / Goals: 0 Cards: 11 Strike rate: - / Mins played: 2699 Ave mins: 71	Europe: Did not play / Games: - Goals: 0 Cards: 0
49 ▲	**Johan Micoud**	Age: 31 • 6th best midfielder in Germany • Overall World Ranking: 165	National Team: France / Caps: 0 Goals: 0 / Cards: 0	Club: W Bremen Games: 33 / Goals: 8 Cards: 4 Strike rate: Goal every 361 mins / Mins played: 2891 Ave mins: 85	Europe: Champions League last 16 / Games: 8 Goals: 1 Cards: 2
50 ▲	**Carlos Gurpegui**	Age: 24 • 11th best midfielder in Spain • Overall World Ranking: 168	National Team: Spain / Caps: 0 Goals: 0 / Cards: 0	Club: Athl Bilbao Games: 33 / Goals: 4 Cards: 7 Strike rate: Goal every 728 mins / Mins played: 2911 Ave mins: 77	Europe: UEFA Cup round of 32 / Games: 8 Goals: 3 Cards: 1

MATCH OF THE DAY
MICHAEL ESSIEN
CHELSEA & GHANA

FOOTBALL CHALLENGE QUIZ 2

Do you know your football?

THINK YOU'RE A FOOTY KNOW-IT-ALL? TEST YOUR KNOWLEDGE ON THE FOUR QUIZ PAGES IN THIS ANNUAL. FILL IN THE ANSWERS ON PAGE 94 AND SEE HOW MANY YOU SCORED OUT OF 200!

CUP WINNERS

The teams below are all celebrating a cup win – but do you know what they've won?

1 MAN. UNITED 2000

2 LIVERPOOL 2001

3 EVERTON 1995

4 JUVENTUS 1996

5 BLACKBURN 2002

ENGLAND QUIZ

How much do you know about the history of the England football team? Here are 12 tough-tackling questions to test your knowledge!

1. Who did England play in the first international match in 1872?
2. Which country was responsible for England's first ever World Cup defeat in the finals of 1950?
3. Who is the England team's record goalscorer?
4. Geoff Hurst scored three goals in the 1966 World Cup Final. Who scored England's other goal?
5. Who was England's manager at the 1970 World Cup finals?
6. Who knocked England out of the World Cup in 1990?
7. Who was England captain at Euro 2000?
8. Who were Sven-Göran Eriksson's first opponents after he took over as England manager?
9. Who scored a hat-trick in England's 5-1 victory over Germany in 2001?
10. Who has made the most appearances for England?
11. Which England player was the tournament's top goalscorer at Euro 2004?
12. Who was England's captain for the game against the USA in the summer?

HOW MUCH CAN YOU REMEMBER ABOUT THE 2004-05 SEASON?

1. How many league goals did David Beckham score for Real Madrid in 2004-05?
2. Who did Harry Redknapp replace as Southampton manager last season?
3. Who was the first signing by Graeme Souness as Newcastle United manager?
4. Name the stadium where Manchester City played their home games last season?
5. Who scored the most league goals for Sunderland in last season's table-topping campaign?
6. Who started last season as West Brom manager?
7. Who was Blackburn's first choice goalkeeper?
8. Who was voted 2005 PFA Player Of The Year?
9. Who won promotion to the Premiership in the play-offs?
10. Who were 2005 French champions?
11. Name the club who finished bottom of the Premiership last season?
12. Who made the most appearances in goal for Manchester United last season – Roy Carroll or Tim Howard?

GUESS THE PUNDIT

Can you work out who this Match Of The Day pundit is?

WHO PLAYED WHERE?

Can you match the clubs with their former grounds?

1. SUNDERLAND	A. BURNDEN PARK
2. BOLTON WANDERERS	B. VICTORIA GROUND
3. SOUTHAMPTON	C. ELM PARK
4. DERBY COUNTY	D. ROKER PARK
5. STOKE CITY	E. BANK STREET
6. READING	F. AYRESOME PARK
7. MIDDLESBROUGH	G. THE BASEBALL GROUND
8. MANCHESTER UNITED	H. THE DELL

MISSING WINNERS

Name the four players missing from Liverpool's starting XI who won the 2005 Champions League.

?
STEVE FINNAN
DJIMI TRAORE
?
JAMIE CARRAGHER
JOHN ARNE RIISE
?
JAVIER LUIS GARCIA
XABI ALONSO
?
MILAN BAROS

WORLD CUP

IT SEEMS LIKE YESTERDAY that Brazil lifted the World Cup in Japan, but with the 2006 World Cup now just months away, fans are already on the edge of their seats in anticipation, and with Germany among the most passionate football nations on the planet, next summer's tournament looks set to be the best ever.

Host to some of Europe's grandest stadiums, the Germans have been renovating and rebuilding their football arenas in preparation for the biggest World Cup yet. And on June 9, 2006, the best 32 nations in world football will be ready for the big kick-off, with the home nation backing Jurgen Klinsmann and his national team to lift the trophy again, as they did the last time Germany were World Cup hosts in 1974.

Although not at the top of their game at the moment, it is never possible to rule Germany out of the equation – and with home advantage to help them, will it be a German World Cup victory again?

In the words of *Match Of The Day* presenter and former England legend Gary Lineker, "Football is a game with 22 men – and in the end Germany always win". While that's not really true, football fans could be forgiven for mistaking it to be so! The methodical, machine-like efficiency of the German team has helped them to become the second-most successful nation in World Cup history, with only Brazil boasting more title wins!

COUNTRY	
Official name: Bundesrepublik Deutschland	
Continent: Europe	
Capital: Berlin	
Major cities: Hamburg, Munich, Cologne, Essen, Frankfurt, Dortmund, Stuttgart, Düsseldorf, Leipzig	
Neighbouring countries: France, Luxembourg, Holland, Belgium, Denmark, Poland, Czech Republic, Austria, Switzerland	
Neighbouring seas: North Sea, Baltic Sea	
Surface area: 357,021 km²	
Population: 82.4 million	
Average age: 41 years	
Life expectancy: 78 years	
Currency: Euro	
Official languages: German	
Motto: "Unity and justice and freedom" (Einigkeit und Recht und Freiheit).	

FOOTBALL

Federation: Deutscher Fussball-Bund

Founded: 1900

Joined FIFA: 1904

Confederation: UEFA

Honours: World Cup 1954, 1974, 1990; European Champions 1972, 1980, 1996* (* all except 1996 won as West Germany)

HAMBURG

Stadium: Hamburg Stadium **Capacity:** 51,055	
Club: Hamburger SV **City population:** 1.7 million	

Hamburg's new World Cup stadium was opened in September 2000. The old Volksparkstadion was demolished, the pitch rotated and the stands were rebuilt to accommodate a stadium suitable for the World Cup.

FIXTURES

JUNE 10: C1 v C2 (8pm)
JUNE 15: A4 v A2 (2pm)
JUNE 19: H4 v H2 (8pm)
JUNE 22: E4 v E1 (3pm)
JUNE 30: Quarter-final 2 (8pm)

HANOVER

Stadium: Niedersachsenstadion **Capacity:** 44,652	
Club: Hannover 96 **City population:** 525,000	

The Niedersachsenstadion was completed in 1954. It has been home to Hannover 96 since 1959 and it was among the venues used for the 1974 World Cup. In preparation for 2006 a major reconstruction programme was started in 2003.

FIXTURES

JUNE 12: E1 v E2 (2pm)
JUNE 16: D1 v D3 (8pm)
JUNE 20: A2 v A3 (3pm)
JUNE 23: G2 v G3 (3pm)
JUNE 27: Second Round (8pm)

BERLIN

Built for the 1936 Olympics, the stadium went through a major renovation for the World Cup, the newly remodelled ground opening on July 31, 2004. It is often called 'the German Wembley'.

Stadium: Olympiastadion **Capacity:** 74,176	
Club: Hertha Berlin **City population:** 3.39 million	

FIXTURES

JUNE 12: F1 v F2 (8pm)
JUNE 15: B4 v B2 (8pm)
JUNE 20: A4 v A1 (3pm)
JUNE 23: H2 v H3 (8pm)
JUNE 30: Quarter-final 1 (4pm)
JULY 9: 2006 Final (7pm)

GELSENKIRCHEN

Stadium: Arena AufSchalke **Capacity:** 53,804	
Club: FC Schalke 04 **City population:** 278,000	

One of the most modern stadiums in Europe, the AufSchalke Arena is situated next to Schalke's old Parkstadion and was officially opened in August 2001. Built at a cost of €192m, it also played host to the 2004 Champions League Final.

FIXTURES

JUNE 9: A3 v A4 (8pm)
JUNE 12: E3 v E4 (5pm)
JUNE 16: C1 v C3 (2pm)
JUNE 21: D4 v D1 (8pm)
JULY 1: Quarter-final 3 (4pm)

DORTMUND

Stadium: Westfalenstadion **Capacity:** 66,981	
Club: Borussia Dortmund **City population:** 590,000	

Known as the Bundesliga's opera-house, the Westfalenstadion was built for the 1974 World Cup and was host to the 2001 UEFA Cup Final. In preparation for the World Cup the four stands were joined at the corners.

FIXTURES

JUNE 10: B3 v B4 (5pm)
JUNE 14: A1 v A3 (8pm)
JUNE 19: G4 v G2 (2pm)
JUNE 27: F4 v F1 (8pm)
JULY 4: Semi-final 1 (8pm)

HAMBURG

HANOVER

GELSENKIRCHEN

DORTMUND

COLOGNE

FRANKFURT

KAISERSLAUTERN

STUTTGART

2006

With Germany 2006 just a few months away, here's your chance to learn a little bit more about where it's being staged!

FIFA WORLD CUP
GERMANY
2006

BERLIN

LEIPZIG

NUREMBERG

MUNICH

LEIPZIG

Stadium: Zentralstadion **Capacity:** 44,199
Club: VfB Leipzig **City population:** 494,000

With a capacity of 100,000 this was once the largest stadium in Germany, but in 2004 a smaller arena was built within the walls of the old stadium. Although the German FA was founded in Leipzig, no local team currently plays in Bundesliga 1 or 2.

FIXTURES
JUNE 11: C3 v C4 (2pm)
JUNE 14: H1 v H2 (2pm)
JUNE 18: G1 v G3 (8pm)
JUNE 21: D2 v D3 (8pm)
JUNE 24: Second Round (8pm)

COLOGNE

Stadium: Volksparkstadion **Capacity:** 51,055
Club: Hamburger SV **City Population:** 1.7 million

Hamburg's World Cup stadium was opened in September 2000. The old Volksparkstadion was demolished, the pitch rotated and the stands were rebuilt to accommodate a stadium suitable for the World Cup.

FIXTURES
JUNE 11: D3 v D4 (8pm)
JUNE 17: E4 v E2 (8pm)
JUNE 20: B4 V B1 (8pm)
JUNE 23: G4 v G1 (3pm)
JUNE 26: Second Round (8pm)

FRANKFURT

Stadium: Waldstadion **Capacity:** 48,132
Club: Eintracht Frankfurt **City population:** 650,000

Built in the 1920s the old Waldstadion staged the opening ceremony of the 1974 World Cup, the 1980 UEFA Cup Final and the 1966 World Title fight between Muhammad Ali and Karl Mildenberger. The rebuilt arena opened in 2005 and features a retractable roof.

FIXTURES
JUNE 10: B1 v B2 (2pm)
JUNE 13: G3 v G4 (8pm)
JUNE 17: D4 v D2 (2pm)
JUNE 21: C4 v C1 (3pm)
JULY 1: Quarter-final 4 (8pm)

KAISERSLAUTERN

Stadium: Fritz-Walter-Stadion **Capacity:** 41,170
Club: FC Kaiserslautern **City Population:** 100,000

Nicknamed 'Betzenberg' because it is built on the Betzenberg mountain, Fritz-Walter-Stadion takes its official name from the Captain of the German 1954 World Cup winning team. It has been extensively reconstructed for 2006.

FIXTURES
JUNE 13: F3 v F4 (2pm)
JUNE 17: E1 v E3 (5pm)
JUNE 20: B2 v B3 (8pm)
JUNE 23: H4 v H1 (8pm)
JUNE 26: Second Round (4pm)

GERMANY

NUREMBERG

Stadium: Franken-Stadion **Capacity:** 41,926
Club: 1 FC Nürnberg **City population:** 490,000

Built in the late 1920s on the future Nazi party rally grounds, the Municipal Stadium was renamed the Franken-Stadion after major refurbishment in the 1990s. Further rebuilding for 2006 involves lowering the pitch. It was the venue for the 1967 European Cup Final.

FIXTURES
JUNE 11: D1 v D2 (5pm)
JUNE 15: B1 v B3 (5pm)
JUNE 18: F4 v F2 (5pm)
JUNE 22: E2 v E3 (3pm)
JUNE 25: Second Round (8pm)

STUTTGART

Stadium: Gottlieb-Daimler-Stadion **Capacity:** 54,267
Clubs: VfB Stuttgart **City population:** 590,000

Built in 1933, the Neckar-Stadion was renamed the Gottlieb-Daimler-Stadion in 1993. It was the venue for Germany's first international games after both the war and German reunification.

FIXTURES
JUNE 13: G1 v G2 (5pm)
JUNE 16: C4 v C2 (5pm)
JUNE19: H1 v H3 (5pm)
JUNE 22: F2 v F3 (8pm)
JUNE 25: Second Round (4pm)
JULY 8: 3rd place match (8pm)

MUNICH

Stadium: Allianz Arena **Capacity:** 66,016 **Clubs:** Bayern Munich & Munich 1860 **City population:** 1.3 million

After a local referendum, plans to renovate the Olympiastadion were shelved in favour of a purpose built stadium on a new site, the cost split between the city's two Bundesliga clubs.

FIXTURES
JUNE 9: A1 v A2 (5pm)
JUNE 14: H3 v H4 (5pm)
JUNE 18: F1 v F3 (2pm)
JUNE 21: C2 v C3 (3pm)
JUNE 24: Second Round (4pm)
JULY 5: Semi-final 2 (8pm)

GROUP A

| TEAM A1 |
| TEAM A2 |
| TEAM A3 |
| TEAM A4 |

FIXTURES

JUN 9: MATCH 1: **A1 V A2** (5PM), MUNICH — v
JUN 9: MATCH 2: **A3 v A4** (8PM), GELSENKIRCHEN — v
JUN 14: MATCH 17: **A1 v A3** (8PM), DORTMUND — v
JUN 15: MATCH 18: **A4 v A2** (2PM), HAMBURG — v
JUN 20: MATCH 33: **A4 v A1** (3PM), BERLIN — v
JUN 20: MATCH 34: **A2 v A3** (3PM), HANOVER — v

FINAL GROUP TABLE

	P	W	D	L	F	A	Pts
1							
2							
3							
4							

GROUP B

| TEAM B1 |
| TEAM B2 |
| TEAM B3 |
| TEAM B4 |

FIXTURES

JUN 10: MATCH 3: **B1 v B2** (2PM), FRANKFURT — v
JUN 10: MATCH 4: **B3 v B4** (5PM), DORTMUND — v
JUN 15: MATCH 19: **B1 v B3** (5PM), NUREMBERG — v
JUN 15: MATCH 20: **B4 v B2** (8PM), BERLIN — v
JUN 20: MATCH 35: **B4 v B1** (8PM), COLOGNE — v
JUN 20: MATCH 36: **B2 v B3** (8PM), KAISERSLAUTERN — v

FINAL GROUP TABLE

	P	W	D	L	F	A	Pts
1							
2							
3							
4							

GROUP C

| TEAM C1 |
| TEAM C2 |
| TEAM C3 |
| TEAM C4 |

FIXTURES

JUN 10: MATCH 5: **C1 v C2** (8PM), HAMBURG — v
JUN 11: MATCH 6: **C3 v C4** (2PM), LEIPZIG — v
JUN 16: MATCH 21: **C1 v C3** (2PM), GELSENKIRCHEN — v
JUN 16: MATCH 22: **C4 v C2** (5PM), STUTTGART — v
JUN 16: MATCH 22: **C4 v C2** (5PM), STUTTGART — v
JUN 21: MATCH 38: **C2 v C3** (3PM), MUNICH — v

FINAL GROUP TABLE

	P	W	D	L	F	A	Pts
1							
2							
3							
4							

GROUP D

| TEAM D1 |
| TEAM D2 |
| TEAM D3 |
| TEAM D4 |

FIXTURES

JUN 11: MATCH 7: **D1 v D2** (5PM), NUREMBERG — v
JUN 11: MATCH 8: **D3 v D4** (8PM), COLOGNE — v
JUN 16: MATCH 23: **D1 v D3** (8PM), HANOVER — v
JUN 17: MATCH 24: **D4 v D2** (2PM), FRANKFURT — v
JUN 21: MATCH 39: **D4 v D1** (8PM), GELSENKIRCHEN — v
JUN 21: MATCH 40: **D2 v D3** (8PM), LEIPZIG — v

FINAL GROUP TABLE

	P	W	D	L	F	A	Pts
1							
2							
3							
4							

GROUP E

| TEAM E1 |
| TEAM E2 |
| TEAM E3 |
| TEAM E4 |

FIXTURES

JUN 12: MATCH 9: **E1 v E2** (2PM), HANOVER — v
JUN 12: MATCH 10: **E3 v E4** (5PM), GELSENKIRCHEN — v
JUN 17: MATCH 25: **E1 v E3** (5PM), KAISERSLAUTERN — v
JUN 17: MATCH 26: **E4 v E2** (8PM), COLOGNE — v
JUN 22: MATCH 41: **E4 v E1** (3PM), HAMBURG — v
JUN 22: MATCH 42: **E2 v E3** (3PM), NUREMBERG — v

FINAL GROUP TABLE

	P	W	D	L	F	A	Pts
1							
2							
3							
4							

GROUP F

| TEAM F1 |
| TEAM F2 |
| TEAM F3 |
| TEAM F4 |

FIXTURES

JUN 12: MATCH 11: **F1 v F2** (8PM), BERLIN — v
JUN 13: MATCH 12: **F3 v F4** (2PM), KAISERSLAUTERN — v
JUN 18: MATCH 27: **F1 v F3** (2PM), MUNICH — v
JUN 18: MATCH 28: **F4 v F2** (5PM), NUREMBERG — v
JUN 22: MATCH 43: **F4 v F1** (8PM), DORTMUND — v
JUN 22: MATCH 44: **F2 v F3** (8PM), STUTTGART — v

FINAL GROUP TABLE

	P	W	D	L	F	A	Pts
1							
2							
3							
4							

GROUP G

| TEAM G1 |
| TEAM G2 |
| TEAM G3 |
| TEAM G4 |

FIXTURES

JUN 13: MATCH 13: **G1 v G2** (5PM), STUTTGART — v
JUN 13: MATCH 14: **G3 v G4** (8PM), FRANKFURT — v
JUN 18: MATCH 29: **G1 v G3** (8PM), LEIPZIG — v
JUN 19: MATCH 30: **G4 v G2** (2PM), DORTMUND — v
JUN 23: MATCH 45: **G4 v G1** (3PM), COLOGNE — v
JUN 23: MATCH 46: **G2 v G3** (3PM), HANOVER — v

FINAL GROUP TABLE

	P	W	D	L	F	A	Pts
1							
2							
3							
4							

GROUP H

| TEAM H1 |
| TEAM H2 |
| TEAM H3 |
| TEAM H4 |

FIXTURES

JUN 14: MATCH 15: **H1 v H2** (2PM), LEIPZIG — v
JUN 14: MATCH 16: **H3 v H4** (5PM), MUNICH — v
JUN19: MATCH 31: **H1 v H3** (5PM), STUTTGART — v
JUN 19: MATCH 32: **H4 v H2** (8PM), HAMBURG — v
JUN 23: MATCH 47: **H4 v H1** (8PM), KAISERSLAUTERN — v
JUN 23: MATCH 48: **H2 v H3** (8PM), BERLIN — v

FINAL GROUP TABLE

	P	W	D	L	F	A	Pts
1							
2							
3							
4							

MATCH 49 JUNE 24 **1A v 2B** (4PM), MUNICH

WINNER OF GROUP A
v
RUNNER-UP OF GROUP B

MATCH 50 JUNE 24 **1C v 2D** (8PM), LEIPZIG

WINNER OF GROUP C
v
RUNNER-UP OF GROUP D

MATCH 51 JUNE 25 **1B v 2A** (4PM), STUTTGART

WINNER OF GROUP B
v
RUNNER-UP OF GROUP A

MATCH 52 JUNE 25 **1D v 2C** (8PM), NUREMBERG

WINNER OF GROUP D
v
RUNNER-UP OF GROUP C

MATCH 53 JUNE 26 **E1 v 2F** (4PM), KAISERSLAUTERN

WINNER OF GROUP E
v
RUNNER-UP OF GROUP F

MATCH 54 JUNE 26 **1G v 2H** (8PM), COLOGNE

WINNER OF GROUP G
v
RUNNER-UP OF GROUP H

MATCH 55 JUNE 27 **1F v 2E** (4PM), DORTMUND

WINNER OF GROUP F
v
RUNNER-UP OF GROUP E

MATCH 56 JUNE 27 **1H v 2G** (8PM), HANOVER

WINNER OF GROUP H
v
WINNER OF GROUP G

THE WORLD CUP DRAW IS HAPPENING IN LEIPZIG ON DECEMBER 9, 2005. IF YOU FILL IN THE TEAM NAMES AFTER THE DRAW YOU WILL KNOW THE FIXTURES FOR THE FIRST PHASE OF THE TOURNAMENT. THEN WATCH MATCH OF THE DAY'S COVERAGE OF THE COMPETITION, FILLING IN THE RESULTS AS YOU GO.

QUARTER-FINALS

MATCH 57 JUNE 30   QTR-FINAL 1 (4PM), BERLIN

WINNER OF MATCH 49
v
WINNER OF MATCH 50

MATCH 58 JUNE 30   QTR-FINAL 2 (8PM), HAMBURG

WINNER OF MATCH 53
v
WINNER OF MATCH 54

MATCH 59 JULY 1   QTR-FINAL 3 (4PM), GELSENKIRCHEN

WINNER OF MATCH 51
v
WINNER OF MATCH 52

MATCH 60 JULY 1   QTR-FINAL 4 (8PM), FRANKFURT

WINNER OF MATCH 55
v
WINNER OF MATCH 56

SEMI FINALS

MATCH 61 JULY 4   SEMI FINAL 1 (8PM), DORTMUND

WINNER OF QUARTER-FINAL 1
v
WINNER OF QUARTER-FINAL 2

MATCH 62 JULY 5   SEMI FINAL 2 (8PM), MUNICH

WINNER OF QUARTER-FINAL 3
v
WINNER OF QUARTER-FINAL 4

FINAL

MATCH 64 JULY 9   FINAL (7PM), BERLIN

Italy WINNER OF SEMI-FINAL 1   2
v
France WINNER OF SEMI-FINAL 2   1

THIRD PLACE PLAY-OFF

MATCH 63 JULY 8   THIRD PLACE (8PM), STUTTGART

LOSER OF SEMI-FINAL 1
v
LOSER OF SEMI-FINAL 2

43

THE WORLD'S TOP 50

DEFE

The MOTD computer spits out a list of the 50 best defenders in the world!

OVER THE LAST 12 MONTHS WE'VE FOLLOWED 5,000 OF THE BEST PLAYERS in world football to check on their form. Are they playing for teams that win? When they play, do they make a difference to how goals are scored or conceded? We've turned the info into a chart for world's best strikers, midfielders, defenders and keepers. In doing this, we also show you where the player is ranked positionally in his domestic league (ie. 3rd best defender in the Premiership) and what their Overall World Ranking is (where they are ranked in the list of the world's best players, regardless of position).

To be a top defender your first job is to stop the opposition scoring. We work out how often their international and club sides concede when they are playing, we count their clean sheets and we check that their team wins when they play. For example, Real Madrid concede a goal every 115 minutes when **Roberto Carlos** is playing and one every 70 minutes when he doesn't.

THE WORLD'S TOP 100 PLAYERS: COUNTRY BY COUNTRY

While working out the Top 50 players in every position, our MOTD computer also compiled a chart of the Top 100 Players in the world, regardless of position – which has given every player an Overall World Ranking in addition to their positional ranking and their ranking within their own domestic league. Brazil and Italy have the most players in our Top 100. Both countries have 16 players. France are third with 11 players.

	Top Countries	No. of players
1	BRAZIL	16
=	ITALY	16
3	FRANCE	11
4	SPAIN	10
=	HOLLAND	10
6	ENGLAND	7
7	ARGENTINA	5
8	PORTUGAL	3

UNDERSTANDING THE GRAPH

The figure at the top of the column shows what percentage of achievable points were won by the club each month. If the club got 9 points from a possible 12, then it would show 75%.

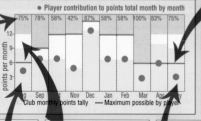

The red bar indicates the maximum number of points that the player's club could have got if they had won ALL the games that he played in. The May column shows the club could have won up to 6 points when the player was in the team.

The dark yellow bar show how many points the player's club won during the month. The August column here shows that the club won 9 points.

The light yellow bar stops at the maximum points the player's club could have won. The August column here shows the club could have won up to 12 points during the month.

The red spot indicates how many points the club actually won in games when the player was on the pitch. The May column shows that this player's club won three points when he played.

44

1 ▲ John Terry

Age: 24 • *Best defender in Premiership* • **Overall World Ranking: 2**

John Terry led his Chelsea defence to astonishing records last season, conceding the fewest goals ever in a Premiership season. Time and time again Terry was the rock on which opposition attacks came to grief. England are blessed with a number of world class centre halves but Terry's form meant he got the call when Rio Ferdinand was banned for Euro 2004 and when Sol Campbell was injured. Now he's in the side on merit.

Season 2004-05 record

National Team: England
Apps: 8 Goals conceded: 4 Cards: 0 0

Club: Chelsea
Apps: 36 Goals conceded: 13 Cards: 7 0
Concede rate: Goal every 249 mins
Mins played: 3240 Ave mins: 85

Europe: Champions League semi-finals
Apps: 11 Goals conceded: 13 Cards: 0 0

● **Player contribution to points total month by month**

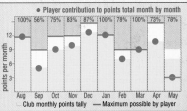

	100%	56%	75%	83%	87%	100%	78%	100%	73%	78%
	Aug	Sep	Oct	Nov	Dec	Jan	Feb	Mar	Apr	May

points per month

☐ Club monthly points tally ── Maximum possible by player

2 Paulo Ferreira

Age: 26 • *2nd best defender in Premiership* • **Overall World Ranking: 3**

Already a Champions League winner with Porto, Ferreira followed José Mourinho to Chelsea for £13 million. He continued to build on a reputation, which included being voted best right back in Europe in 2004, and his pace and hard work made him a regular choice in a Chelsea squad full of defensive options. A broken foot cut short his debut season but now he's back to his best for Portugal and Chelsea.

Season 2004-05 record

National Team: Portugal
Apps: 8 **Goals conceded:** 6 **Cards:** 0

Club: Chelsea
Apps: 29 **Goals conceded:** 10 **Cards:** 2
Concede rate: Goal every 261 mins
Mins played: 2610 **Ave mins:** 69

Europe: Champions League last 16
Apps: 7 **Goals conceded:** 7 **Cards:** 1

● Player contribution to points total month by month

100% 56% 75% 83% 87% 100% 78% 100% 73% 78%

points per month

Aug Sep Oct Nov Dec Jan Feb Mar Apr May
☐ Club monthly points tally — Maximum possible by player

3 William Gallas

Age: 27 • *3rd best defender in Premiership* • **Overall World Ranking: 4**

You can't move for inspired defenders at Chelsea but most rival managers would pick out William Gallas if they had a choice. The French international prefers to play at centre-back but his versatility means he can cover either full-back position – and he regularly does so. He has strength to go with his speed and reliably gets a foot in to tackle opponents. France have used him at full-back and centre back.

Season 2004-05 record

National Team: France
Apps: 10 **Goals conceded:** 4 **Cards:** 0

Club: Chelsea
Apps: 28 **Goals conceded:** 10 **Cards:** 1
Concede rate: Goal every 245 mins
Mins played: 2445 **Ave mins:** 64

Europe: Champions League semi-finals
Apps: 12 **Goals conceded:** 13 **Cards:** 2

● Player contribution to points total month by month

100% 56% 75% 83% 87% 100% 78% 100% 73% 78%

points per month

Aug Sep Oct Nov Dec Jan Feb Mar Apr May
☐ Club monthly points tally — Maximum possible by player

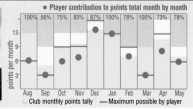

4 Young-Pyo Lee

Age: 28 • *Best defender in Dutch League* • **Overall World Ranking: 16**

PSV Eindhoven benefited from its South Korean connection last season, the growing stature of Ji-Sung Park and Young-Pyo Lee being two of the main reasons they took the Dutch title and reached the Champions League semis. Former Korean manager Guus Hiddick brought left back Lee with him from the successful Korean World Cup team, before Spurs signed PSV's most consistent defender.

Season 2004-05 record

National Team: South Korea
Apps: 0 **Goals conceded:** 0 **Cards:** 0

Club: PSV Eindhoven
Apps: 6 **Goals conceded:** 4 **Cards:** 1
Concede rate: Goal every 174 mins
Mins played: 2790 **Ave mins:** 82

Europe: Champions League semi-finals
Apps: 14 **Goals conceded:** 15 **Cards:** 1

● Player contribution to points total month by month

78% 100% 83% 100% 44% 100% 83% 100% 87% 78%

points per month

Aug Sep Oct Nov Dec Jan Feb Mar Apr May
☐ Club monthly points tally — Maximum possible by player

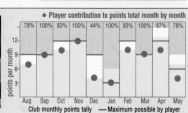

5 Fabio Cannavaro

Age: 31 • *Best defender in Italian League* • **Overall World Ranking: 18**

Italy has a reputation for top-quality defending and Fabio Cannavaro is probably the finest central defender in Serie A today. No surprise then that he captains the Italian international side and helped Juventus to the title last season. He's strong in the air despite his lack of inches, as Liverpool found out in the Champions League quarter finals, and his timing and anticipation make him among the best around.

Season 2004-05 record

National Team: Italy
Apps: 5 **Goals conceded:** 3 **Cards:** 1

Club: Juventus
Apps: 38 **Goals conceded:** 24 **Cards:** 2
Concede rate: Goal every 139 mins
Mins played: 3333 **Ave mins:** 88

Europe: Champions League quarter-finals
Apps: 9 **Goals conceded:** 4 **Cards:** 2

● Player contribution to points total month by month

83% 100% 58% 78% 73% 47% 100% 58% 87%

points per month

Aug Sep Oct Nov Dec Jan Feb Mar Apr May
☐ Club monthly points tally — Maximum possible by player

6 ▲ Wilfred Bouma

Age: 27 • *2nd best defender in Dutch League* • **Overall World Ranking: 19**

Wilfred Bouma is the powerful centre half behind Dutch title winners PSV. He has also been the stand out defender for Holland in recent tournaments. When Bouma was on the pitch for PSV they were only conceding a goal every 190 minutes on average – a Defensive Rating only bettered by three Chelsea defenders last season. Initially a striker, and then a fullback, Bouma can score useful goals – nine in one season.

Season 2004-05 record

National Team: Holland
Apps: 6 **Goals conceded:** 2 **Cards:** 0 0

Club: PSV Eindhoven
Apps: 28 **Goals conceded:** 13 **Cards:** 3 0
Concede rate: Goal every 190 mins
Mins played: 2475 **Ave mins:** 73

Europe: Champions League semi-finals
Apps: 14 **Goals conceded:** 13 **Cards:** 0 0

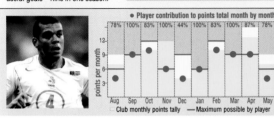

● Player contribution to points total month by month

78% 100% 83% 100% 44% 100% 83% 100% 87% 78%

Aug Sep Oct Nov Dec Jan Feb Mar Apr May
☐ Club monthly points tally — Maximum possible by player

7 ▲ Lilian Thuram

Age: 33 • *2nd best defender in Italian League* • **Overall World Ranking: 23**

Alongside Marcel Desailly, Raymond Blanc and Bixente Lizarazu, Lilian Thuram formed the top defence in world football, winning France the 1998 World Cup and Euro 2000. Thuram hit his first two international goals for France in the World Cup semi-final against Croatia. He joined Juventus for £23 million – then a record for a defender. Playing full-back and centre half, he has helped Juvé to three titles in four seasons.

Season 2004-05 record

National Team: France
Apps: 0 **Goals conceded:** 0 **Cards:** 0 0

Club: Juventus
Apps: 37 **Goals conceded:** 26 **Cards:** 5 0
Concede rate: Goal every 128 mins
Mins played: 3330 **Ave mins:** 88

Europe: Champions League quarter-finals
Apps: 11 **Goals conceded:** 6 **Cards:** 2 0

● Player contribution to points total month by month

83% 100% 58% 78% 73% 47% 100% 58% 87%

Aug Sep Oct Nov Dec Jan Feb Mar Apr May
☐ Club monthly points tally — Maximum possible by player

8 ▲ Anthony Reveillere

Age: 25 • *Best defender in French League* • **Overall World Ranking: 24**

Lyon's defence is in the top three in Europe and at the heart of this side is the young talent of Anthony Reveillere – just breaking into the French national team. He started his career at Rennes where he was once dropped by new coach Vahid Halilhodzic who caught him playing computer games just before a match. The fullback moved to Valencia and is now one of the few French talents regularly on view at champions Lyon.

Season 2004-05 record

National Team: France
Apps: 2 **Goals conceded:** 1 **Cards:** 0 0

Club: Lyon
Apps: 33 **Goals conceded:** 16 **Cards:** 9 0
Concede rate: Goal every 185 mins
Mins played: 2962 **Ave mins:** 78

Europe: Champions League quarter-finals
Apps: 8 **Goals conceded:** 10 **Cards:** 0 0

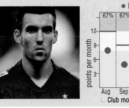

● Player contribution to points total month by month

67% 67% 83% 83% 33% 75% 67% 67% 58% 83%

Aug Sep Oct Nov Dec Jan Feb Mar Apr May
☐ Club monthly points tally — Maximum possible by player

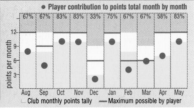

9 ▲ Cris

Age: 28 • *2nd best defender in French League* • **Overall World Ranking: 29**

Lyon already had three French titles in the bag when they signed Cris from Bayer Leverkusen. The Brazilian centre-back immediately slotted into the side and helped secure a fourth title, conceding only 22 goals on the way. He scored against Manchester United in the Champions League as Lyon topped their Group last season but they lost to PSV on penalties in the quarter finals. He has been capped once for Brazil.

Season 2004-05 record

National Team: Brazil
Apps: 0 **Goals conceded:** 0 **Cards:** 0 0

Club: Lyon
Apps: 33 **Goals conceded:** 17 **Cards:** 4 0
Concede rate: Goal every 175 mins
Mins played: 2970 **Ave mins:** 78

Europe: Champions League quarter-finals
Apps: 9 **Goals conceded:** 12 **Cards:** 2 0

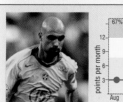

● Player contribution to points total month by month

67% 67% 83% 83% 33% 75% 67% 67% 58% 83%

Aug Sep Oct Nov Dec Jan Feb Mar Apr May
☐ Club monthly points tally — Maximum possible by player

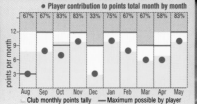

10 ▲ Alessandro Nesta

Age: 29 • *3rd best defender in Italian League* • **Overall World Ranking: 30**

Alessandro Nesta oozes defensive class and elegance. With his long legs tackling seems effortless, while his positional sense makes defending look easy. He won many youth honours while with Lazio's academy and now he is at AC Milan in a peerless back line alongside Paolo Maldini, Cafu and Jaap Stam. One of Pele's 'Greatest Living Footballers', last year Nesta narrowly missed Serie A and Champions League honours.

Season 2004-05 record

National Team: Italy
Apps: 5 **Goals conceded:** 7 **Cards:** 1 0

Club: AC Milan
Apps: 29 **Goals conceded:** 16 **Cards:** 6 2
Concede rate: Goal every 159 mins
Mins played: 2547 **Ave mins:** 67

Europe: Champions League final
Apps: 11 **Goals conceded:** 9 **Cards:** 2 0

● Player contribution to points total month by month

	58%	87%	67%	78%	47%	100%	100%	67%	25%
Aug	Sep	Oct	Nov	Dec	Jan	Feb	Mar	Apr	May

Club monthly points tally — Maximum possible by player

48

11 Rio Ferdinand

▲ Age: 26 • *4th best defender in Premiership* • **Overall World Ranking: 36**

Ferdinand became the world's most expensive defender when Manchester United broke the bank, paying Leeds £30 million for him after the 2002 World Cup. He has since earned the wrath of the FA by missing a drugs test and angered United fans before finally committing his future to them in August. But when he is on the pitch, defending for United or England, he is an unruffled defender, attracting the ball like a magnet.

Season 2004-05 record

National Team: England
Apps: 5 **Goals conceded:** 1 **Cards:** 0 0

Club: Man Utd
Apps: 31 **Goals conceded:** 20 **Cards:** 3 0
Concede rate: Goal every 140 mins
Mins played: 2790 **Ave mins:** 73

Europe: Champions League last 16
Apps: 5 **Goals conceded:** 6 **Cards:** 0 0

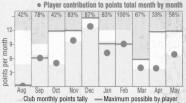

● Player contribution to points total month by month

| 42% | 78% | 42% | 83% | 87% | 83% | 100% | 67% | 33% | 58% |

Club monthly points tally — Maximum possible by player

Aug Sep Oct Nov Dec Jan Feb Mar Apr May

12 Paolo Maldini

▲ Age: 37 • *4th best defender in Italian League* • **Overall World Ranking: 38**

At 37, Paolo Maldini defies his age and his critics, continuing to play football at the very highest level. He has stayed loyal to AC Milan since making his debut for them at 16, but that hasn't prevented him seeing (and winning) it all – including an Italian record 126 caps. He began as a dashing full back but can also play centre half. He scored the opener in this summer's Champions League final before defeat to Liverpool.

Season 2004-05 record

National Team: Italy
Apps: 0 **Goals conceded:** 0 **Cards:** 0 0

Club: AC Milan
Apps: 34 **Goals conceded:** 22 **Cards:** 4 0
Concede rate: Goal every 137 mins
Mins played: 3003 **Ave mins:** 79

Europe: Champions League final
Apps: 12 **Goals conceded:** 7 **Cards:** 0 0

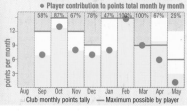

● Player contribution to points total month by month

| 58% | 87% | 67% | 78% | 47% | 100% | 100% | 67% | 25% |

Club monthly points tally — Maximum possible by player

Aug Sep Oct Nov Dec Jan Feb Mar Apr May

13 Jonathan Zebina

▲ Age: 26 • *5th best defender in Italian League* • **Overall World Ranking: 42**

The French international side has only just discovered it can call on one of Serie A's most successful and versatile defenders. Jonathan Zebina was the most effective defender in Italy in 2003-04, playing for Roma, whose miserly defence was the main reason they finished second. Juvé pounced as Zebina came out of contract and he has again topped the Serie A defence charts, conceding a goal every 173 minutes on average.

Season 2004-05 record

National Team: France
Apps: 5 **Goals conceded:** 1 **Cards:** 0 0

Club: Juventus
Apps: 24 **Goals conceded:** 12 **Cards:** 6 0
Concede rate: Goal every 173 mins
Mins played: 2070 **Ave mins:** 54

Europe: Champions League quarter-finals
Apps: 6 **Goals conceded:** 4 **Cards:** 1 0

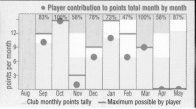

● Player contribution to points total month by month

| 83% | 100% | 58% | 78% | 73% | 47% | 100% | 58% | 87% |

Club monthly points tally — Maximum possible by player

Aug Sep Oct Nov Dec Jan Feb Mar Apr May

14 Carlos Puyol

▲ **Age: 27** • *Best defender in Spanish League* • **Overall World Ranking: 44**

Talismanic captain Carlos Puyol is one of the main reasons Barcelona have transformed from Primeira Liga also-rans to one of the top two sides in Europe. The club won the Spanish league, went out of the Champions League in a classic match against Chelsea and has the best defensive record in Spain. Comfortable at fullback or centre back for Spain or Barça, Puyol seems to have been around for ages but is still only 27.

Season 2004-05 record

National Team: Spain
Apps: 8 **Goals conceded:** 3 **Cards:** 1 ⬜

Club: Barcelona
Apps: 36 **Goals conceded:** 26 **Cards:** 6 ⬜
Concede rate: Goal every 122 mins
Mins played: 3176 **Ave mins:** 84

Europe: Champions League last 16
Apps: 8 **Goals conceded:** 11 **Cards:** 1 ⬜

● Player contribution to points total month by month

	100%	83%	83%	75%	83%	75%	58%	83%	58%	60%

☐ Club monthly points tally — Maximum possible by player

---

15 Mikael Silvestre

▲ **Age: 27** • *5th best defender in Premiership* • **Overall World Ranking: 49**

Silvestre's pace is what keeps him at the top. The undemonstrative Frenchman chose Manchester United over Liverpool in 1999 and became a regular in the side at left back before switching to his preferred position of centre back. He made his French debut in 2001. Now a fixture as Rio Ferdinand's partner, Sylvestre is always a threat at corners and he usually picks up a couple of headed goals each season.

Season 2004-05 record

National Team: France
Apps: 2 **Goals conceded:** 0 **Cards:** 0 ⬜

Club: Man Utd
Apps: 35 **Goals conceded:** 23 **Cards:** 2 🟥
Concede rate: Goal every 128 mins
Mins played: 2949 **Ave mins:** 78

Europe: Champions League last 16
Apps: 8 **Goals conceded:** 7 **Cards:** 1 ⬜

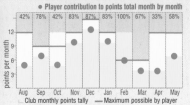

● Player contribution to points total month by month

	42%	78%	42%	83%	87%	83%	100%	67%	33%	58%

☐ Club monthly points tally — Maximum possible by player

16 Eric Abidal

▲ **Age: 25** • *3rd best defender in French League* • **Overall World Ranking: 50**

Cristiano Ronaldo knows all about Eric Abidal. The Lyonnais defender did a pretty good job of marking United's tricky winger in their two Champions League meetings. "As a defender, my aim is to infuriate the opponent," says Abidal. "I want him to be so sick of the sight of me." Played at fullback by Lyon but preferring centre back, Abidal has also broken into the French side in the last two seasons.

Season 2004-05 record

National Team: France
Apps: 7 **Goals conceded:** 2 **Cards:** 0 ⬜

Club: Lyon
Apps: 28 **Goals conceded:** 13 **Cards:** 2 ⬜
Concede rate: Goal every 188 mins
Mins played: 2442 **Ave mins:** 64

Europe: Champions League quarter-finals
Apps: 7 **Goals conceded:** 9 **Cards:** 1 ⬜

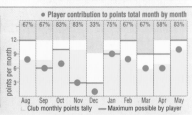

● Player contribution to points total month by month

	67%	67%	83%	83%	33%	75%	67%	67%	58%	83%

☐ Club monthly points tally — Maximum possible by player

---

17 Rafael Marquez

▲ **Age: 26** • *2nd best defender in Spanish League* • **Overall World Ranking: 54**

Mexico has long been rated by FIFA as one of the top ten footballing nations but, unlike their South American rivals Brazil and Argentina, few of their stars play in Europe. Rafael Marquez is an exception. Starting his career with Atlas de Guadalajara, he first played for the Mexican national side in 1999 and was brought to Europe by Monaco. Now at Barcelona he can play centre back or defensive midfield.

Season 2004-05 record

National Team: Mexico
Apps: 7 **Goals conceded:** 6 **Cards:** 0 ⬜

Club: Barcelona
Apps: 35 **Goals conceded:** 22 **Cards:** 7 🟥
Concede rate: Goal every 130 mins
Mins played: 2855 **Ave mins:** 75

Europe: Champions League last 16
Apps: 5 **Goals conceded:** 4 **Cards:** 2 ⬜

● Player contribution to points total month by month

	100%	83%	83%	75%	83%	75%	58%	83%	58%	60%

☐ Club monthly points tally — Maximum possible by player

18 Alex

Age: 23 • *3rd best defender in Dutch League* • **Overall World Ranking: 60**

Alex, full name Alex Rodrigo Dias de Costa, was capped by Brazil at a number of levels but although he has broken into the international team, he has yet to establish himself effectively. The PSV defender can play at fullback or in the centre and has the skill to be both useful in possession and join the attack. Alex had never seen snow until he arrived in Eindhoven in 2004 for talks on his transfer.

Season 2004-05 record

National Team: Brazil
Apps: 0 **Goals conceded:** 0 **Cards:** 0 0

Club: PSV Eindhoven
Apps: 27 **Goals conceded:** 14 **Cards:** 3 1
Concede rate: Goal every 157 mins
Mins played: 2199 **Ave mins:** 65

Europe: Champions League semi-finals
Apps: 12 **Goals conceded:** 10 **Cards:** 1 0

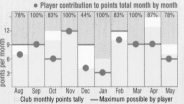

• Player contribution to points total month by month
78% 100% 83% 100% 44% 100% 83% 100% 87% 78%
Aug Sep Oct Nov Dec Jan Feb Mar Apr May
□ Club monthly points tally — Maximum possible by player

19 Roberto Carlos

Age: 32 • *3rd best defender in Spanish League* • **Overall World Ranking: 63**

Small in size, awesome in stature in the game, Roberto Carlos has been a Brazilian legend since his incredible free kick bent around a wall of French defenders and bulged the net of a baffled Fabien Barthez in 1997. He first played for Brazil as an 18-year-old in 1992, establishing his place in 1995 and has been their left back ever since. He has won everything in the game at Real Madrid and was their best defender last season.

Season 2004-05 record

National Team: Brazil
Apps: 9 **Goals conceded:** 6 **Cards:** 0 0

Club: Real Madrid
Apps: 34 **Goals conceded:** 26 **Cards:** 6 0
Concede rate: Goal every 115 mins
Mins played: 3001 **Ave mins:** 79

Europe: Champions League last 16
Apps: 10 **Goals conceded:** 11 **Cards:** 1 0

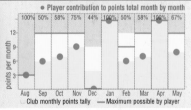

• Player contribution to points total month by month
100% 50% 58% 75% 44% 100% 50% 58% 100% 67%
Aug Sep Oct Nov Dec Jan Feb Mar Apr May
□ Club monthly points tally — Maximum possible by player

20 Juliano Belletti

Age: 29 • *4th best defender in Spanish League* • **Overall World Ranking: 64**

A Brazilian defender who has already seen action for the international side with the 2002 World Cup squad and is favourite to take over from Cafu when he retires. Belletti began his career with Cruzeiro and was brought to Spain by Villarreal before moving to Barcelona in 2004. He played 27 league games in their title win last season and was their most effective defender in terms of keeping goals out.

Season 2004-05 record

National Team: Brazil
Apps: 4 **Goals conceded:** 3 **Cards:** 1 0

Club: Barcelona
Apps: 31 **Goals conceded:** 19 **Cards:** 10 0
Concede rate: Goal every 133 mins
Mins played: 2535 **Ave mins:** 67

Europe: Champions League last 16
Apps: 8 **Goals conceded:** 11 **Cards:** 0 0

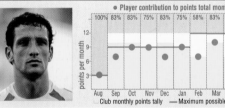
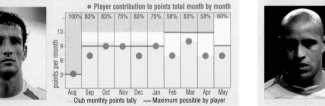

• Player contribution to points total month by month
100% 83% 83% 75% 83% 75% 58% 83% 58% 60%
Aug Sep Oct Nov Dec Jan Feb Mar Apr May
□ Club monthly points tally — Maximum possible by player

21 Gabriel Ivan Heinze

Age: 27 • *6th best defender in Premiership* • **Overall World Ranking: 65**

Arriving at Manchester United around the same time as Wayne Rooney isn't a good way to grab the headlines, so Gabriel Heinze just got on with his job. Strong in the air and never likely to duck a tackle, he tightened United's defence last season. With a German dad and an Italian mum, he was brought-up in Argentinian Patagonia where he learnt Welsh – probably not much help in communicating with Ryan Giggs though!

Season 2004-05 record

National Team: Argentina
Apps: 8 **Goals conceded:** 7 **Cards:** 3 0

Club: Man Utd
Apps: 26 **Goals conceded:** 16 **Cards:** 4 0
Concede rate: Goal every 143 mins
Mins played: 2286 **Ave mins:** 60

Europe: Champions League last 16
Apps: 7 **Goals conceded:** 8 **Cards:** 2 0

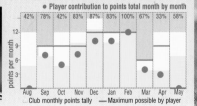

• Player contribution to points total month by month
42% 78% 42% 83% 87% 83% 100% 67% 33% 58%
Aug Sep Oct Nov Dec Jan Feb Mar Apr May
□ Club monthly points tally — Maximum possible by player

22 ▲ Cristiano Zenoni

Age: 28 • *6th best defender in Italian League* • **Overall World Ranking: 67**

Cristiano Zenoni is the mainstay of the Sampdoria defence which achieved fifth place in the Italian Serie A last season. The right back who can also play in midfield began his career with Atalanta in 1995 and moved to Juventus in 2001, coinciding with his one cap for Italy. Tall but rarely getting on the scoresheet, Zenoni has a twin brother Damiano who plays for Atalanta and also has one Italian cap.

Season 2004-05 record

National Team: Italy
Apps: 0 Goals conceded: 0 Cards: 0 0

Club: Sampdoria
Apps: 35 Goals conceded: 27 Cards: 8 1
Concede rate: Goal every 114 mins
Mins played: 3087 Ave mins: 81

Europe: Did not play
Apps: 0 Goals conceded: 0 Cards: 0 0

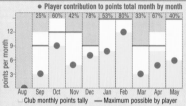
● Player contribution to points total month by month
25% 60% 42% 78% 53% 80% 33% 67% 40%
☐ Club monthly points tally —— Maximum possible by player

---

23 ▲ Cafu

Age: 35 • *7th best defender in Italian League* • **Overall World Ranking: 68**

At 35 Cafu is still performing at the highest level and astonishing football fans with his stamina and energy as he makes the right flank his own territory from corner flag to corner flag. He is the Brazilian captain in their World Cup qualifying campaign and has already played in three World Cup finals. AC Milan have one of the oldest back fours in top-flight football but it is in the top six most effective in Europe.

Season 2004-05 record

National Team: Brazil
Apps: 6 Goals conceded: 4 Cards: 1 0

Club: AC Milan
Apps: 33 Goals conceded: 22 Cards: 6 0
Concede rate: Goal every 129 mins
Mins played: 2828 Ave mins: 74

Europe: Champions League final
Apps: 11 Goals conceded: 9 Cards: 1 0

● Player contribution to points total month by month
58% 87% 67% 78% 47% 100% 100% 67% 25%
☐ Club monthly points tally —— Maximum possible by player

---

24 ▲ Andy Todd

Age: 30 • *7th best defender in Premiership* • **Overall World Ranking: 69**

No-one will be more astonished than Andy Todd to find himself in such exalted company. Blackburn have had a tough year since Graeme Souness left but their defence has proved one of the strongest in the Premier. Todd is a combative son of England star Colin, and in his 26 league games last season Blackburn only conceded 16 goals. He has formed a tight partnership at centre back with Ryan Nelsen.

Season 2004-05 record

National Team: England
Apps: 0 Goals conceded: 0 Cards: 0 0

Club: Blackburn
Apps: 26 Goals conceded: 16 Cards: 4 0
Concede rate: Goal every 143mins
Mins played: 2294 Ave mins: 60

Europe: Did not play
Apps: 0 Goals conceded: 0 Cards: 0 0

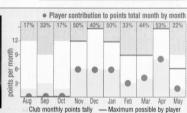
● Player contribution to points total month by month
17% 33% 17% 50% 40% 50% 33% 44% 53% 22%
☐ Club monthly points tally —— Maximum possible by player

---

25 ▲ Ricardo Carvalho

Age: 27 • *8th best defender in Premiership* • **Overall World Ranking: 79**

The fourth member of the almost impenetrable Chelsea back-line is Ricardo Carvalho. Like colleague Paulo Ferreira, Carvalho followed José Mourinho from Champions League-winning Porto to London but with John Terry and William Gallas in the side, he has found it harder to secure a starting spot. For Portugal he was one of the stars of Euro 2004, reaching the final where they were surprisingly beaten by Greece.

Season 2004-05 record

National Team: Portugal
Apps: 6 Goals conceded: 4 Cards: 0 0

Club: Chelsea
Apps: 25 Goals conceded: 13 Cards: 2 0
Concede rate: Goal every 152 mins
Mins played: 1970 Ave mins: 52

Europe: Champions League semi-finals
Apps: 10 Goals conceded: 13 Cards: 2 0

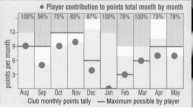
● Player contribution to points total month by month
100% 56% 75% 83% 87% 100% 78% 100% 73% 78%
☐ Club monthly points tally —— Maximum possible by player

#	Player	National Team	Caps	Conceded	Cards	Club	Games	Conceded	Cards	Concede rate	Mins played	Ave mins	Europe	Games	Conceded	Cards
26 ▲	**Presas Oleguer** — Age: 25 • 5th defender in Spain • Overall World Ranking: 87	Spain	0	0	0	Barcelona	35	25	3	Goal every 114 mins	2857	75	Champions League last 16	7	7	0
27 ▲	**Guilio Falcone** — Age: 31 • 8th best defender in Italy • Overall World Ranking: 89	Italy	0	0	0	Sampdoria	28	16	3	Goal every 146 mins	2333	61	Did not play	-	0	0
28 ▲	**Sylvain Distin** — Age: 27 • 9th best defender in Premiership • Overall World Ranking: 96	France	0	0	0	Man City	38	39	3	Goal every 87 mins	3402	90	Did not play	-	0	0
29 ▲	**Habib Kolo Toure** — Age: 24 • 10th best defender in Premiership • Overall World Ranking: 97	Ivory Coast	3	0	0	Arsenal	35	31	1	Goal every 101 mins	3134	82	Champions League last 16	8	9	1
30 ▲	**Ivan Helguera** — Age: 30 • 6th best defender in Spain • Overall World Ranking: 101	Spain	2	3	0	Real Madrid	34	27	7	Goal every 106 mins	2867	75	Champions League last 16	10	11	1
31 ▲	**Etame Mayer Lauren** — Age: 28 • 11th best defender in Premiership • Overall World Ranking: 103	Cameroon	0	0	0	Arsenal	33	29	4	Goal every 101 mins	2939	77	Champions League last 16	7	8	3
32 ▲	**Valerio Bertotto** — Age: 32 • 9th defender in Italy • Overall World Ranking: 117	Italy	0	0	0	Udinese	35	33	2	Goal every 94 mins	3096	81	Did not play	-	3	0
33 ▲	**Richard Dunne** — Age: 25 • 12th best defender in Premiership • Overall World Ranking: 126	Rep of Ireland	4	0	0	Man City	35	36	7	Goal every 87 mins	3123	82	Did not play	-	0	0
34 ▲	**Andre Ooijer** — Age: 30 • 4th best defender in Holland • Overall World Ranking: 127	Holland	3	0	0	PSV Eindhoven	24	14	3	Goal every 141 mins	1972	58	Champions League semi-finals	9	9	3
35 ▲	**Tony Hibbert** — Age: 24 • 13th best defender in Premiership • Overall World Ranking: 129	England	0	0	0	Everton	36	41	9	Goal every 78 mins	3184	84	Did not play	-	0	0
36 ▲	**Alan Stubbs** — Age: 33 • 14th best defender in Premiership • Overall World Ranking: 134	England	0	0	0	Everton	31	24	0	Goal every 102 mins	2439	64	Did not play	-	0	0
37 ▲	**Ledley King** — Age: 24 • 15th best defender in Premiership • Overall World Ranking: 136	England	7	3	0	Tottenham	28	41	2	Goal every 83 mins	3420	90	Did not play	-	0	0
38 ▲	**Pablo Ibanez** — Age: 23 • 7th defender in Spain • Overall World Ranking: 138	Spain	7	0	0	Atl Madrid	35	30	11	Goal every 105 mins	3150	83	Did not play	-	0	0
39 ▲	**Marco Pisano** — Age: 23 • 10th best defender in Italy • Overall World Ranking: 142	Italy	0	0	0	Sampdoria	29	21	3	Goal every 114 mins	2397	63	Did not play	-	0	0
40 ▲	**Ashley Cole** — Age: 24 • 16th best defender in Premiership • Overall World Ranking: 147	England	11	6	3	Arsenal	35	35	7	Goal every 90 mins	3150	83	Champions League last 16	8	6	0
41 ▲	**Efstathios Tavlaridis** — Age: 25 • 4th best defender in France • Overall World Ranking: 156	Greece	0	0	0	Lille	30	23	11	Goal every 115 mins	2643	70	UEFA Cup last 16	8	5	2
42 ▲	**Josip Simunic** — Age: 27 • Best defender in Germany • Overall World Ranking: 166	Croatia	8	5	2	Hertha Berlin	30	27	9	Goal every 97 mins	2616	77	Did not play	-	0	0
43 ▲	**Gareth Southgate** — Age: 34 • 17th best defender in Premiership • Overall World Ranking: 167	England	0	0	0	Middlesbrough	36	39	4	Goal every 83 mins	3240	85	UEFA Cup last 16	10	8	2
44 ▲	**Robert Kovac** — Age: 31 • 2nd best defender in Germany • Overall World Ranking: 172	Croatia	8	5	3	Bayern Munich	23	15	4	Goal every 134 mins	2010	59	Champions League quarter-finals	8	12	3
45 ▲	**Rafael Schmitz** — Age: 24 • 5th defender in France • Overall World Ranking: 176	Brazil	0	0	0	Lille	27	19	7	Goal every 121 mins	2308	61	UEFA Cup last 16	5	2	3
46 ▲	**David Weir** — Age: 35 • 18th best defender in Premiership • Overall World Ranking: 177	Scotland	2	2	0	Everton	34	39	3	Goal every 78 mins	3033	80	Did not play	-	0	0
47 ▲	**Dick Van Burik** — Age: 31 • 3rd best defender in Germany • Overall World Ranking: 178	Holland	0	0	0	Hertha Berlin	26	19	2	Goal every 114 mins	2173	64	Did not play	-	0	0
48 ▲	**Gonzalo Rodriguez** — Age: 21 • 8th best defender in Spain • Overall World Ranking: 185	Argentina	4	2	0	Villarreal	34	34	12	Goal every 90 mins	3060	81	UEFA Cup quarter-finals	9	5	2
49 ▲	**John O'Shea** — Age: 24 • 19th best defender in Premiership • Overall World Ranking: 194	Rep of Ireland	9	4	1	Man Utd	23	9	1	Goal every 166 mins	1490	39	Champions League last 16	5	6	0
50 ▲	**Alberto Lopo** — Age: 26 • 9th best defender in Spain • Overall World Ranking: 195	Spain	0	0	0	Espanyol	36	44	12	Goal every 73 mins	3194	84	Did not play	-	0	0

Do you know your football?

THINK YOU'RE A FOOTY KNOW-IT-ALL? TEST YOUR KNOWLEDGE ON THE FOUR QUIZ PAGES IN THIS ANNUAL. FILL IN YOUR ANSWERS ON PAGE 94 AND SEE HOW MANY YOU SCORED OUT OF 200!

NAME THE MANAGER

Can you name these managers and the former club they are pictured playing for?

1

2

3

4

5

GOAL SCORERS WORD SEARCH

The 20 goalscorers hidden in the grid below all finished in the Top 3 of Match Of The Day's Goal Of The Month competition last season. Can you spot them?

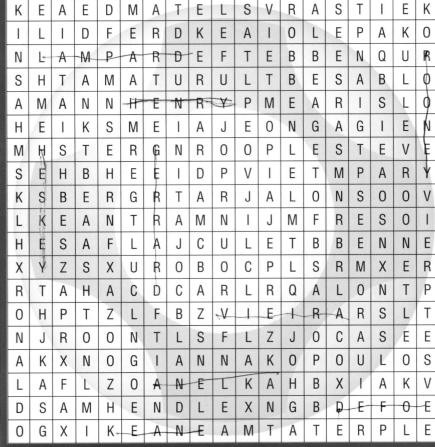

K	E	A	E	D	M	A	T	E	L	S	V	R	A	S	T	I	E	K
I	L	I	D	F	E	R	D	K	E	A	I	O	L	E	P	A	K	O
N	L	A	M	P	A	R	D	E	F	T	E	B	B	E	N	Q	U	R
S	H	T	A	M	A	T	U	R	U	L	T	B	E	S	A	B	L	O
A	M	A	N	N	H	E	N	R	Y	P	M	E	A	R	I	S	L	O
H	E	I	K	S	M	E	I	A	J	E	O	N	G	A	G	I	E	N
M	H	S	T	E	R	G	N	R	O	O	P	L	E	S	T	E	V	E
S	E	H	B	H	E	E	I	D	P	V	I	E	T	M	P	A	R	Y
K	S	B	E	R	G	R	T	A	R	J	A	L	O	N	S	O	O	V
L	K	E	A	N	T	R	A	M	N	I	J	M	F	R	E	S	O	I
H	E	S	A	F	L	A	J	C	U	L	E	T	B	B	E	N	N	E
X	Y	Z	S	X	U	R	O	B	O	C	P	L	S	R	M	X	E	R
R	T	A	H	A	C	D	C	A	R	L	R	Q	A	L	O	N	T	P
O	H	P	T	Z	L	F	B	Z	V	I	E	I	R	A	R	S	L	T
N	J	R	O	O	N	T	L	S	F	L	Z	J	O	C	A	S	E	E
A	K	X	N	O	G	I	A	N	N	A	K	O	P	O	U	L	O	S
L	A	F	L	Z	O	A	N	E	L	K	A	H	B	X	I	A	K	V
D	S	A	M	H	E	N	D	L	E	X	N	G	B	D	E	F	O	E
O	G	X	I	K	E	A	N	E	A	M	T	A	T	E	R	P	L	E

LAST SEASON'S MATCH OF THE DAY GOAL OF THE SEASON

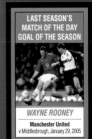

WAYNE ROONEY
Manchester United
v Middlesbrough, January 29, 2005

ALONSO	COLE	HENDRIE	ROBBEN
AMBROSE	DEFOE	HENRY	RONALDO
ANELKA	EDMAN	HESKEY	ROONEY
ASHTON	GERRARD	KEANE	SMITH
BERGER	GIANNAKOPOULOS	LAMPARD	VIEIRA

HOW MUCH CAN YOU REMEMBER ABOUT THE

2004-05 SEASON?

1. Who was Manchester United's top scorer last season in all competitions?

2. Which Premiership team had the most penalties awarded against them last season?

3. Who scored the goals that knocked Manchester United out of last season's Champions League?

4. Who scored two goals on his England debut against USA in the summer?

5. Name the player who made the most international appearances for Holland last season?

6. Who did Chelsea sign Didier Drogba from?

7. Who was Liverpool's most expensive signing last season?

8. Which keeper conceded the most goals in last season's Premiership?

9. Name the player who scored the most goals in last season's Scottish Premier League?

10. Name the city that staged the final of the 2005 Champions League?

11. What club did Robbie Savage begin last season playing for?

12. Who were Spanish champions in 2005?

GUESS THE PUNDIT

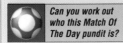
Can you work out who this Match Of The Day pundit is?

GOLDEN BOOTS

Can you match the strikers with the season they were last top scorer in the Premiership?

1. THIERRY HENRY, 25 GOALS	A. 1999-00
2. ALAN SHEARER, 25 GOALS	B. 2002-03
3. KEVIN PHILLIPS, 30 GOALS	C. 2001-02
4. JIMMY FLOYD HASSELBAINK, 23 GOALS	D. 2004-05
5. RUUD VAN NISTELROOY, 25 GOALS	E. 2000-01

6 OF THE BEST

MICHAEL OWEN

1 What year did Michael make his debut for Liverpool?

2 Who did Michael score his first European goal against?

3 Who did Michael make his international debut against?

4 In what year did Michael win BBC Sports Personality Of The Year?

5 Michael scored his first England goal as a sub. Who did he replace?

6 How much did Newcastle United pay to sign Michael?

55

LIVERPOOL SPECTACULARLY REASSERTED their position as British football's most dominant European force in 2005, fighting back from three goals down to lift their fifth European Cup against AC Milan in Istanbul. Gerrard, Smicer, Alonso, Dudek and their team-mates wrote themselves into perhaps the most thrilling chapter of the history of British clubs in Europe's top competition. Despite the FA's initial scepticism towards the tournament when it first started in 1956, and a six-year ban following the 1985 Heysel tragedy, it has been an illustrious history, with these islands producing the European champs an incredible 11 times.

Celtic were the first British side to lift club football's most coveted trophy when they saw off Inter Milan in 1967 with a side born and raised in Glasgow. Between then and multi-national Liverpool's 2005 triumph,

Manchester United, Nottingham Forest and Aston Villa have also ruled the continental roost.

The list of managers who have taken their sides to Euro glory is testament to what it takes to achieve such a feat – Jock Stein, Matt Busby, Bob Paisley and Brian Clough may all be gone now, but their achievements granted them immortality and their legacy can still be seen in the British game to this day. And there can be no doubt about the legacy Sir Alex Ferguson will leave at Old Trafford when he finally decides he's had enough, while we wait with baited breath to see just how far Rafael Benitez can take his current champs.

Here, MOTD Annual relives every European Cup final that has produced a British champion – including an unprecedented run of seven British wins in eight years between 1977 and 1984.

LIVERPOOL 3 AC MILAN 3
(Liverpool won 3-2 on penalties)

2005

WHEN: May 25, 2005
WHERE: Atatürk Stadium, Istanbul
WHO SCORED: Gerrard, Smicer, Alonso
KNOCKED OUT: Grazer AK, Olympiakos & Deportivo, (group), Bayer Leverkusen, Juventus, Chelsea
BEST MOMENT: Vladimir Smicer's strike from outside the box that brought Liverpool back to 3-2 and infused everyone with the belief that the improbable was possible.

In an unprecedented comeback at this level, Liverpool became champions of Europe for a fifth time with three goals in six incredible second-half minutes. Outclassed, the Reds found themselves 3-0 down at half-time. But goals from Gerrard, Smicer and Alonso (following up his own saved penalty) took the game into extra-time and penalties, where the English side triumphed thanks in no small part to some exceptional goalkeeping from Dudek.

CAPTAIN: Steven Gerrard
MANAGER: Rafael Benitez
TEAM: Dudek; Finnan (Hamann); Hyypia, Carragher, Traore; Kewell (Smicer), Alonso, Gerrard, Riise; Luis Garcia, Baros (Cisse)

WHAT THE MOTD PUNDITS SAID...

ALAN HANSEN: *"It was not just the best comeback in a European Cup Final, it was not just the best comeback I have seen in football, it was the best comeback I have seen in sport anywhere in the world. Liverpool were saved by the tactical acumen of Rafael Benitez, the sheer grit and will to fight that had seen them through to the final in Istanbul, and the brilliance of Steven Gerrard. As a performance from a captain of Liverpool it is hard to see how Gerrard's second half could have been bettered. He dragged Liverpool back into the match with the same self-belief shown when they scored three times after the interval to overcome Olympiacos. This was perhaps Liverpool's greatest-ever performance."*

MARK LAWRENSON: *"The first truly momentous victory of Rafael Benitez's reign and the start of what I'm sure everybody hopes will be a trophy-laden era. By overcoming AC Milan in the extraordinary way they did, Benitez sent shockwaves through European football and re-energised the whole club.*
"What a night and what a game. I was working on the European Cup Final for Five Live and it was an absolute privilege to be at the match. From the lowest low to the highest high inside one game is some achievement, but Liverpool did it... The first 15 minutes of the second half, including the six minutes where they got the goals, were just mesmerising. Milan looked shellshocked and had no answer until Liverpool drew breath. Then, when Dudek made his double save from Shevchenko, you knew it was Liverpool's night."

1967

CELTIC 2 INTER MILAN 1

The first Brits to reach a European Cup final, Celtic were a goal down before they had even settled, Mazzolo converting from the spot for Inter. But the Bhoys were not to be denied, with Tommy Gemmell equalising just after the hour and Steve Chalmers diverting Murdoch's shot into the net with five minutes to go. With that goal, the European Cup came to Britain for the first time.

WHEN:	May 25, 1967
WHERE:	Estadio Nacional, Lisbon
WHO SCORED:	Gemmill, Chalmers
KNOCKED OUT:	FC Zurich, FC Nantes, FK Vojvodina, Dukla Prague
BEST MOMENT:	Gemmell's 20-yard screamer that gave Celtic their parity their play deserved in the 62nd minute.
CAPTAIN:	Billy McNeil
MANAGER:	Jock Stein
TEAM:	Simpson, Craig, McNeill, Gemmell, Murdoch, Clark, Wallace, Johnstone, Chalmers, Auld, Lennox

1968

MANCHESTER UNITED 4 BENFICA 1

Ten years after the Munich air disaster, United became the first English winners of the European Cup. The game came alive in the second half, with Bobby Charlton scoring before Graca equalised for the Portuguese side. United took over in extra-time with Best beating two defenders to put them back in the lead before Kidd and Charlton again sealed the win.

WHEN:	May 29, 1968
WHERE:	Wembley Stadium, London
WHO SCORED:	Charlton (2), Best, Kidd
KNOCKED OUT:	Hibernians (Malta), FK Sarajevo, Gornik Zarbze, Real Madrid
BEST MOMENT:	George Best dancing through the Benfica defence to restore United's lead in extra-time.
CAPTAIN:	Bobby Charlton
MANAGER:	Matt Busby
TEAM:	Stepney, Brennan, Stiles, Foulkes, Dunne, Crerand, Charlton, Sadler, Best, Kidd, Aston

1977

LIVERPOOL 3 B.MÖNCHENGLADBACH 1

Liverpool won their first European title with a terrific display. Terry McDermott met Steve Heighway's cross to put the Brits ahead, but the Germans snatched an equaliser after the break. The Reds continued to press and, after Smith had headed home another Heighway cross, Vogts hauled down Keegan to give Phil Neal the chance to seal victory from the spot.

WHEN:	May 25, 1977
WHERE:	Olympic Stadium, Rome
WHO SCORED:	McDermott, Smith, Neal
KNOCKED OUT:	Crusaders, FC Zurich, Trabzonspor, Saint-Etienne
BEST MOMENT:	When McDermott's opener fizzed home – it was to be the start of a special relationship between Liverpool and the European Cup.
CAPTAIN:	Emlyn Hughes
MANAGER:	Bob Paisley
TEAM:	Clemence, Neal, Jones, Smith, Hughes; Case, Kennedy, Callaghan, McDermott, Keegan, Heighway

1978

LIVERPOOL 1 CLUB BRUGGE 0

Brugge knew they had their work cut out facing the reigning European champs in their own country, but their defensive approach made this final much less of a spectacle than the previous year's affair in Rome. Liverpool stuck to their task though, and got their reward not long after the hour when Kenny Dalglish struck the goal that ensured the Cup would remain in the Anfield trophy cabinet.

WHEN:	May 10, 1978
WHERE:	Wembley Stadium, London
WHO SCORED:	Dalglish
KNOCKED OUT:	Dynamo Dresden, Benfica, Borussia Mönchengladbach
BEST MOMENT:	Dalglish latched on to a lovely ball from Souness to dink home over the advancing Jensen.
CAPTAIN:	Emlyn Hughes
MANAGER:	Bob Paisley
TEAM:	Clemence, Neal, Thompson, Hansen, Hughes, McDermott, Kennedy, Souness, Case (Heighway), Fairclough, Dalglish

EUROPEAN CUP: COUNTRY BY COUNTRY

ENGLAND	10 wins
ITALY	10 wins
SPAIN	10 wins
GERMANY	6 wins
HOLLAND	6 wins
PORTUGAL	4 wins
FRANCE	1 win
ROMANIA	1 win
SCOTLAND	1 win
SERBIA & MONTENEGRO	1 win

1979

NOTTINGHAM FOREST 1 MALMÖ 0

Trevor Francis justified his £1 million price tag scoring the only goal of the game to earn Forest their first European title against a weakened Swedish outfit. Francis's goal came seconds before half-time from a John Robertson cross, the midfielder heading home at the far post. Malmö struggled to create a chance of any note barring a Ljungberg free-kick.

WHEN:	May 30, 1979
WHERE:	Olympic Stadium, Munich
WHO SCORED:	Francis
KNOCKED OUT:	Liverpool, AEK Athens, Grasshoppers Zurich, Cologne
BEST MOMENT:	Francis's winner proved that Ol' Big 'Ead knew what he was doing when he made him the first million pound player.
CAPTAIN:	John McGovern
MANAGER:	Brian Clough
TEAM:	Shilton, Anderson, Lloyd, Burns, Clark, Francis, McGovern, Bowyer, Robertson, Woodcock, Birtles

1980

NOTTINGHAM FOREST 1 HAMBURG 0

Kevin Keegan returned to the European Cup final, lining up for German side Hamburg, but he was upstaged by John Robertson, whose goal earned Forest their second European title. Forest played cannily on the counter-attack throughout the match, and hit the winner in the 19th minute when Robertson played a neat one-two with Birtles before firing home from the edge of the box.

WHEN:	May 28, 1980
WHERE:	Bernabéu Stadium, Madrid
WHO SCORED:	Robertson
KNOCKED OUT:	Osters IF Vaxjo, Arges Pitesti, Dynamo Berlin, Ajax
BEST MOMENT:	The neat interplay, leading to the goal was Clough's Forest at their most effective.
CAPTAIN:	John McGovern
MANAGER:	Brian Clough
TEAM:	Shilton, Anderson, Gray (Gunn), Lloyd, Burns, Clark, O'Neill, McGovern, Bowyer, Mills (O'Hare), Robertson, Birtles

1981

LIVERPOOL 1 REAL MADRID 0

A tight game that saw each side's premier playmaker (Dalglish for Liverpool, Stielike for Real) well marshalled was settled by a single goal. Liverpool only came to life after the break, responding to increasing Madrid pressure, and their efforts culminated in Alan Kennedy beating Cortes before scoring from an acute angle to give Liverpool and manager Bob Paisley a third European Cup.

WHEN:	May 27, 1981
WHERE:	Parc Des Princes, Paris
WHO SCORED:	A Kennedy
KNOCKED OUT:	OPS Oulu, Aberdeen, CSKA Sofia, Bayern Munich
BEST MOMENT:	It may not have been a great final, but Kennedy's goal was a worthy winner.
CAPTAIN:	Phil Thompson
MANAGER:	Bob Paisley
TEAM:	Clemence, Neal, Thompson, Hansen, A Kennedy; Lee, McDermott, Souness, R Kennedy, Dalglish (Case), Johnson

1982

ASTON VILLA 1 BAYERN MUNICH 0

Against a mighty Bayern team including Hoeness and Rummenigge, Villa suffered an early setback when keeper Jimmy Rimmer had to be replaced by inexperienced sub Nigel Spink. The 23-year-old was up to the task, however, making a series of great saves. As a result of his clean sheet, when Peter Withe turned home Tony Morley's cross in the 67th minute the goal was enough to win the trophy.

WHEN: May 26, 1982	
WHERE: De Kuip, Rotterdam	
WHO SCORED: Withe	
KNOCKED OUT: Valur, Dynamo Berlin, Dinamo Kiev, Anderlecht	
BEST MOMENT: Nigel Spink's two world class saves in 60 seconds, first from Durnberger and then Rummenigge, spurred his team on.	
CAPTAIN: Dennis Mortimer	
MANAGER: Tony Barton	
TEAM: Rimmer (Spink), Swain, Evans, McNaught, Williams, Bremner, Cowans, Mortimer, Shaw, Withe, Morley	

1984

LIVERPOOL 1 ROMA 1 *(Liverpool won 4-2 on penalties)*

European Cup finals don't come much more daunting than playing the Italian champions in their own stadium. Nevertheless Liverpool took the game to Roma, Phil Neal scoring in the 14th minute after Tancredi spilled Craig Johnstone's cross. A Roman onslaught followed, but they managed just one goal and the game went into extra-time and pens, Alan Kennedy scoring the decisive spot kick.

WHEN: May 30, 1984	
WHERE: Olympic Stadium, Rome	
WHO SCORED: Neal	
KNOCKED OUT: OB Odense, Athletic Bilbao, Benfica, Dinamo Bucharest	
BEST MOMENT: Bruce Grobbelaar's famous 'spaghetti legs' routine that won Liverpool the penalty shoot-out.	
CAPTAIN: Graeme Souness	
MANAGER: Joe Fagan	
TEAM: Grobbelaar, Neal, Lawrenson, Hansen, A Kennedy, Johnston (Nicol), Lee, Souness, Whelan, Dalglish (Robinson), Rush	

1999

MAN. UNITED 2 BAYERN MUNICH 1

United finally sealed a second European Cup with football's all-time greatest sucker punch. Bayern seemed destined to lift the trophy, leading 1-0 in stoppage time, before two Beckham corners turned the match on its head. First he found Giggs, whose effort was turned in by Sheringham, and then a second corner was flicked on by Sheringham for Solskjaer to win the cup.

WHEN: May 26, 1999	
WHERE: Nou Camp, Barcelona	
WHO SCORED: Sheringham, Solskjaer	
KNOCKED OUT: LKS Lodz, Barcelona & Brondby (group), Inter Milan, Juventus	
BEST MOMENT: Solskjaer's winner, stabbed home as United fans were still celebrating their team's late equaliser.	
CAPTAIN: Peter Schmeichel	
MANAGER: Alex Ferguson	
Team: Schmeichel, G Neville, Johnsen, Stam, Irwin, Beckham, Butt, Giggs, Blomqvist (Sheringham), Yorke, Cole (Solskjaer)	

THE WORLD'S TOP 25

GOAL

Who are the best keepers in world football? The MOTD computer picks the Top 25.

OVER THE LAST 12 MONTHS WE'VE FOLLOWED 5,000 OF THE BEST PLAYERS IN world football to check on their form. Are they playing for teams that win? Do they make a difference to how goals are scored or conceded? We've turned the info into a chart for world's best strikers, midfielders, defenders and keepers. In doing this, we also show you where the player is ranked positionally in his domestic league (ie. 3rd best goalkeeper in the Premiership) and what their Overall World Ranking is (where they are ranked in the list of the world's best players, regardless of position).

To be a top keeper you need to be good stopper. But good keepers also need to be able to organise the defence in front of them. Are they collecting clean sheets? How often do they concede a goal? Averaging 90 minutes means he's conceding exactly a goal a game – Liverpool's **Jose Reina** managed a goal every 92 minutes at Villarreal last season.

THE WORLD'S TOP 100 PLAYERS: CLUB BY CLUB

While working out the Top 50 players in every position, our MOTD computer also compiled a chart of the Top 100 Players in the world, regardless of position – which has given every player an Overall World Ranking in addition to their positional ranking and their ranking within their own domestic league. Barcelona have the most players in the Top 100 with ten, followed by Chelsea with nine.

	Top clubs	no. of players	League pos.
1	BARCELONA	10	1
2	CHELSEA	9	1
=	PSV	9	1
4	JUVENTUS	8	1
5	MAN UTD	7	3
6	AC MILAN	6	2
7	LYON	4	1
=	FEYENOORD	4	4

UNDERSTANDING THE GRAPH

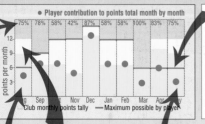

The figure at the top of the column shows what percentage of achievable points were won by the club each month. If the club got 9 points from a possible 12, then it would show 75%.

The red bar indicates the maximum number of points that the player's club could have got if they had won ALL the games that he played in. The May column shows the club could have won up to 6 points when the player was in the team.

The dark yellow bar show how many points the player's club won during the month. The August column here shows that the club won 9 points.

The light yellow bar stops at the maximum points the player's club could have won. The August column here shows the club could have won up to 12 points during the month.

The red spot indicates how many points the club actually won in games when the player was on the pitch. The May column shows that this player's club won three points when he played.

• Player contribution to points total month by month

75% 78% 58% 42% 87% 58% 58% 100% 83% 75%

points per month

Aug Sep Oct Nov Dec Jan Feb Mar Apr May

Club monthly points tally — Maximum possible by player

KEEPERS

Age: 23 • *Best keeper in Premiership* • **Overall World Ranking: 1**

In his first year in the Premiership Petr Cech has won the title, set records which may never be broken, and established himself as the best goalkeeper in world football. Chelsea conceded the fewest goals ever in a Premier season and in 35 games, Cech kept 24 clean sheets, saving an astonishing ten shots for each goal conceded. A Czech international, he was already winning praise at Rennes – now he's winning trophies.

Season 2004-05 record

National Team: Czech Republic
Apps: 8 **Goals conceded:** 6 **Cards:** 0 0

Club: Chelsea
Apps: 35 **Goals conceded:** 13 **Cards:** 0 0
Concede rate: Goal every 242 mins
Mins played: 3150 **Ave mins:** 83

Europe: Champions League semi-finals
Apps: 11 **Goals conceded:** 13 **Cards:** 0 0

● **Player contribution to points total month by month**

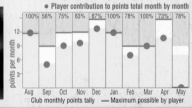

	Aug	Sep	Oct	Nov	Dec	Jan	Feb	Mar	Apr	May
	100%	56%	75%	83%	87%	100%	78%	100%	73%	78%

points per month

□ Club monthly points tally ── Maximum possible by player

2 Heurelho Gomes

Age: 24 • *Best keeper in Dutch League* • **Overall World Ranking: 8**

Heurelho Gomes is waiting in the wings should Brazil's goalkeeper Dida slip up. The talented 24-year-old admires his rival, who he rates as the best Brazilian keeper ever. Gomes conceded only one more league goal than Chelsea's Petr Cech last season and kept 21 clean sheets, missing only one game as PSV's ultra tight defence helped the club secure the Dutch title by a clear ten points.

Season 2004-05 record

National Team: Brazil
Apps: 0 **Goals conceded:** 0 **Cards:** 0 0

Club: PSV Eindhoven
Apps: 30 **Goals conceded:** 14 **Cards:** 0 0
Concede rate: Goal every 189 mins
Mins played: 2650 **Ave mins:** 78

Europe: Champions League semi-finals
Apps: 11 **Goals conceded:** 14 **Cards:** 2 0

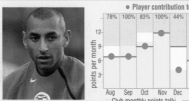
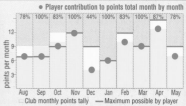

• Player contribution to points total month by month

78% 100% 83% 100% 44% 100% 83% 100% 87% 78%

Aug Sep Oct Nov Dec Jan Feb Mar Apr May
☐ Club monthly points tally — Maximum possible by player

3 Gianluigi Buffon

Age: 27 • *Best keeper in Italian League* • **Overall World Ranking: 11**

4 Nelson Dida

Age: 31 • *2nd best keeper in Italian League* • **Overall World Ranking: 20**

Hard on Gianluigi Buffon's heels in Serie A is Nelson Dida. Not so long ago Brazilian goalkeepers were derided, now they have two in our top five. Another tall man at 1.95m, Dida played for two of Brazil's most famous clubs (Cruzeira and Corinthians) before joining Swiss side FC Lugano and then moving to AC Milan. Last season he hit the headlines after being struck by a flare thrown by the Inter Milan crowd.

Season 2004-05 record

National Team: Brazil
Apps: 5 **Goals conceded:** 4 **Cards:** 0 0

Club: AC Milan
Apps: 36 **Goals conceded:** 23 **Cards:** 0 1
Concede rate: Goal every 137 mins
Mins played: 3157 **Ave mins:** 83

Europe: Champions League final
Apps: 12 **Goals conceded:** 9 **Cards:** 0 0

• Player contribution to points total month by month

58% 87% 67% 78% 47% 100% 100% 67% 25%

Aug Sep Oct Nov Dec Jan Feb Mar Apr May
☐ Club monthly points tally — Maximum possible by player

5 Francesco Antonioli

Age: 35 • *3rd best keeper in Italian League* • **Overall World Ranking: 21**

Francesco Antonioli kept goal behind the third best defence in Italy. The 36-year-old is in his second season at Sampdoria but he has transferred ten times in 20 years of Italian football since his debut for Monza in the 1986-87 season. It includes two spells at AC Milan and he had four years at Roma, where he shared the shirt with Ivan Pellizzoli. He played 37 games for Sampdoria last season, conceding just 26 goals.

Season 2004-05 record

National Team: Italy
Apps: 0 **Goals conceded:** 0 **Cards:** 0 0

Club: Sampdoria
Apps: 37 **Goals conceded:** 26 **Cards:** 0 1
Concede rate: Goal every 126 mins
Mins played: 3267 **Ave mins:** 86

Europe: Did not play
Apps: 0 **Goals conceded:** 0 **Cards:** 0 0

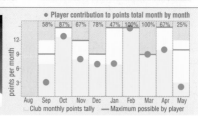

Buffon made his Serie A debut in 1995, making several stunning saves for Parma against a powerful AC Milan side. Anyone watching would have noted the 17-year-old as one to keep an eye on. 'Gigi' was called up to the Italian squad in 1997 and joined Juventus for £32 million in 2001. He is Italy's national keeper but also the best in a cosmopolitan Serie A, conceding only 23 goals in 37 games last season.

Season 2004-05 record

National Team: Italy
Apps: 8 **Goals conceded:** 7 **Cards:** 0 0

Club: Juventus
Apps: 37 **Goals conceded:** 23 **Cards:** 0 0
Concede rate: Goal every 143 mins
Mins played: 3285 **Ave mins:** 86

Europe: Champions League quarter-finals
Apps: 11 **Goals conceded:** 6 **Cards:** 0 0

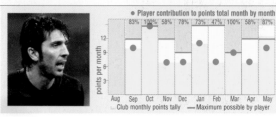

• Player contribution to points total month by month

83% 100% 58% 78% 73% 47% 100% 58% 87%

Aug Sep Oct Nov Dec Jan Feb Mar Apr May
☐ Club monthly points tally — Maximum possible by player

• Player contribution to points total month by month

25% 60% 42% 78% 53% 80% 33% 67% 40%

Aug Sep Oct Nov Dec Jan Feb Mar Apr May
☐ Club monthly points tally — Maximum possible by player

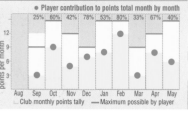

6 Victor Valdes

Age: 23 • *Best keeper in Spanish League* • **Overall World Ranking:** 25

Valdes is a product of the Barcelona youth policy, having joined them as a youngster in 1992. He finally broke into the first team in 2002 and last year he beat off a challenge for the Barça jersey from experienced Turkish international keeper Rustu. Now he has kept goal behind a title-winning defence but he still faces a battle at international level to challenge Real Madrid's highly-rated Iker Casillas – just one year older.

Season 2004-05 record

National Team: Spain
Apps: 0 **Goals conceded:** 0 **Cards:** 0 0

Club: Barcelona
Apps: 35 **Goals conceded:** 25 **Cards:** 2 1
Concede rate: Goal every 125 mins
Mins played: 3133 **Ave mins:** 82

Europe: Champions League last 16
Apps: 8 **Goals conceded:** 11 **Cards:** 0 0

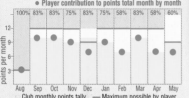

● Player contribution to points total month by month

	Aug	Sep	Oct	Nov	Dec	Jan	Feb	Mar	Apr	May
	100%	83%	83%	75%	83%	75%	58%	83%	58%	60%

□ Club monthly points tally — Maximum possible by player

7 Roy Carroll

Age: 27 • *2nd best keeper in Premiership* • **Overall World Ranking:** 28

8 Nigel Martyn

Age: 38 • *3rd best keeper in Premiership* • **Overall World Ranking:** 35

Nigel Martyn's career seemed on the downward spiral as he lost his place in the England squad and his place in the Leeds side to Paul Robinson. Instead, his move to Everton has brought out the best in Martyn. He only conceded 26 league goals in 32 appearances, a record of one goal conceded every 109 minutes – they let in a goal every 29 minutes when Martyn didn't play! He also saved eight shots for every goal conceded.

Season 2004-05 record

National Team: England
Apps: 0 **Goals conceded:** 0 **Cards:** 0 0

Club: Everton
Apps: 32 **Goals conceded:** 26 **Cards:** 0 0
Concede rate: Goal every 109 mins
Mins played: 2834 **Ave mins:** 75

Europe: Did not play
Apps: 0 **Goals conceded:** 0 **Cards:** 0 0

● Player contribution to points total month by month

	Aug	Sep	Oct	Nov	Dec	Jan	Feb	Mar	Apr	May
	58%	100%	58%	58%	67%	33%	58%	0%	47%	33%

□ Club monthly points tally — Maximum possible by player

The bizarre "goal that wasn't" from Tottenham's Mendes which Roy Carroll dropped over his line could have blighted his year, as could on-going contract talks which ultimately ended with him leaving Manchester United for West Ham. Brought in as cover for Fabien Barthez, Carroll forced his way into United's team and last season only conceded a goal every 146 minutes, the fourth best record in Europe.

Season 2004-05 record

National Team: Northern Ireland
Apps: 8 **Goals conceded:** 3 **Cards:** 0 0

Club: Man Utd
Apps: 26 **Goals conceded:** 16 **Cards:** 0 0
Concede rate: Goal every 146 mins
Mins played: 2340 **Ave mins:** 62

Europe: Champions League last 16
Apps: 5 **Goals conceded:** 5 **Cards:** 0 0

● Player contribution to points total month by month

	Aug	Sep	Oct	Nov	Dec	Jan	Feb	Mar	Apr	May
	42%	78%	42%	83%	87%	83%	100%	67%	33%	58%

□ Club monthly points tally — Maximum possible by player

9 Tony Mario Sylva

Age: 30 • *Best keeper in French League* • **Overall World Ranking:** 39

Tony Mario Sylva shone for Senegal in the 2002 World Cup, but by that time he had already been playing in France for seven years. He moved to Monaco in 1995 aged 20 but spent his time as cover and didn't get to make his first team debut until late 1999. He joined Lille in 2004 and made Monaco pay for not promoting him – Lille's defensive record was the key to beating their rivals into third place in the French league.

Season 2004-05 record

National Team: Senegal
Apps: 5 **Goals conceded:** 5 **Cards:** 0 0

Club: Lille
Apps: 38 **Goals conceded:** 29 **Cards:** 1 0
Concede rate: Goal every 116 mins
Mins played: 3375 **Ave mins:** 89

Europe: UEFA Cup last 16
Apps: 10 **Goals conceded:** 6 **Cards:** 0 0

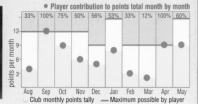

● Player contribution to points total month by month

	Aug	Sep	Oct	Nov	Dec	Jan	Feb	Mar	Apr	May
	33%	100%	75%	50%	56%	53%	33%	12%	100%	60%

□ Club monthly points tally — Maximum possible by player

10 Iker Casillas

Age: 24 • *2nd best keeper in Spanish League* • **Overall World Ranking: 41**

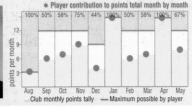

"Iker is the most galactic of galacticos," said rival keeper Jose Reina. A poll carried out among journalists from 20 countries agreed, naming Casillas as the world's best keeper ahead of Petr Cech and Gianluigi Buffon. Only 24 years old, Casillas is already a veteran of seven years at the Bernabéu. Strong, brave and a natural shot-stopper, he is thought to have a weakness on crosses but is still Spain's No.1.

Season 2004-05 record

National Team: Spain
Apps: 9 Goals conceded: 1 Cards: 0 0

Club: Real Madrid
Apps: 38 Goals conceded: 32 Cards: 2 0
Concede rate: Goal every 106 mins
Mins played: 3383 Ave mins: 89

Europe: Champions League last 16
Apps: 10 Goals conceded: 11 Cards: 0 0

● Player contribution to points total month by month

100% 50% 58% 75% 44% 100% 50% 58% 100% 67%

points per month

Aug Sep Oct Nov Dec Jan Feb Mar Apr May
Club monthly points tally — Maximum possible by player

---

11 Gregory Coupet

Age: 32 • *2nd best keeper in French League* • **Overall World Ranking: 46**

Fabien Barthez is still France's last line of defence but many think Lyon's Gregory Coupet should now be given the goalkeeping jersey. Coupet made his professional debut for Saint-Etienne before moving to Lyon, where he has now played for nine seasons. There, he has won four French Ligue 1 titles in the last four seasons but has not made the French keeping position his own despite winning his first cap in 2001.

Season 2004-05 record

National Team: France
Apps: 9 Goals conceded: 2 Cards: 0 0

Club: Lyon
Apps: 31 Goals conceded: 18 Cards: 0 0
Concede rate: Goal every 155 mins
Mins played: 2790 Ave mins: 73

Europe: Champions League quarter-finals
Apps: 8 Goals conceded: 9 Cards: 0 0

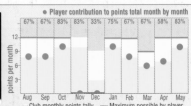

● Player contribution to points total month by month

67% 67% 83% 83% 33% 75% 67% 67% 58% 83%

points per month

Aug Sep Oct Nov Dec Jan Feb Mar Apr May
Club monthly points tally — Maximum possible by player

---

12 David James

Age: 34 • *4th best keeper in Premiership* • **Overall World Ranking: 59**

David James was already England keeper when Manchester City paid £2 million for him as replacement for David Seaman. Error-strewn appearances for England against the likes of Austria and Denmark have seen him replaced in England's side by Paul Robinson, but good displays behind a much-improved City defence have made him a favourite at the City Of Manchester Stadium. He played every league game last term.

Season 2004-05 record

National Team: England
Apps: 6 Goals conceded: 4 Cards: 0 0

Club: Man City
Apps: 38 Goals conceded: 39 Cards: 0 0
Concede rate: Goal every 88 mins
Mins played: 3420 Ave mins: 90

Europe: Did not play
Apps: 0 Goals conceded: 0 Cards: 0 0

● Player contribution to points total month by month

33% 33% 44% 60% 27% 58% 42% 0% 60% 78%

points per month

Aug Sep Oct Nov Dec Jan Feb Mar Apr May
Club monthly points tally — Maximum possible by player

---

13 Christian Fiedler

Age: 30 • *Best keeper in German League* • **Overall World Ranking: 62**

Only Bayern Munich's great Oliver Khan had a better defensive record in the Bundesliga than Christian Fiedler last season. The Hertha Berlin keeper conceded just 31 goals despite playing every league game. Germany has many fine keepers, with Jens Lehmann and Khan battling for the international spot, while Rangers' Stefan Klos and Fiedler wait in the wings – but Fiedler is the youngest and may yet have his day.

Season 2004-05 record

National Team: Germany
Apps: 0 Goals conceded: 0 Cards: 0 0

Club: Hertha Berlin
Apps: 34 Goals conceded: 31 Cards: 1 0
Concede rate: Goal every 99 mins
Mins played: 3060 Ave mins: 90

Europe: Did not play
Apps: 0 Goals conceded: 0 Cards: 0 0

● Player contribution to points total month by month

33% 22% 60% 67% 100% 33% 75% 56% 60% 56%

points per month

Aug Sep Oct Nov Dec Jan Feb Mar Apr May
Club monthly points tally — Maximum possible by player

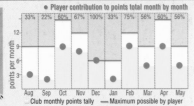

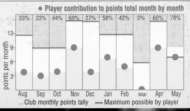

14 Jose Reina

Age: 22 • *3rd best keeper in Spanish League* • **Overall World Ranking: 73**

"The best goalkeeper in Spain," said Rafael Benitez as he signed Jose Reina to Liverpool. Reina played every game bar one for Villarreal in a demanding last season, in which the 'Yellow Submarines' finished third in La Liga and reached the latter stages of the UEFA Cup. He also saved seven penalties out of nine faced. Son of the former Atletico Madrid keeper, Miguel, Reina was born in Madrid but first played for Barcelona.

Season 2004-05 record

National Team: Spain
Apps: 1 **Goals conceded:** 0 **Cards:** 0 0

Club: Villarreal
Apps: 38 **Goals conceded:** 37 **Cards:** 1 0
Concede rate: Goal every 92 mins
Mins played: 3420 **Ave mins:** 90

Europe: UEFA Cup quarter-finals
Apps: 11 **Goals conceded:** 6 **Cards:** 0 0

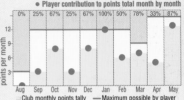

● Player contribution to points total month by month

| 0% | 25% | 67% | 25% | 67% | 100% | 50% | 78% | 33% | 87% |

Aug Sep Oct Nov Dec Jan Feb Mar Apr May
— Club monthly points tally — Maximum possible by player

15 Leonardo Franco

Age: 28 • *4th best keeper in Spanish League* • **Overall World Ranking: 86**

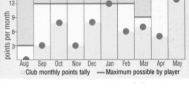

Leonardo Franco began his career with Independiente in Argentina before moving to Spanish lower league side Merida in 1997, then to Mallorca. Tall and agile, he was Mallorca's main keeper for five years before moving to Atletico Madrid in 2004 – the same year he won his first Argentinian cap. The 'other' Madrid finished only 11th last season, but in 37 games Franco had the third best defensive record in La Liga.

Season 2004-05 record

National Team: Argentina
Apps: 6 **Goals conceded:** 1 **Cards:** 0 0

Club: Atl Madrid
Apps: 37 **Goals conceded:** 32 **Cards:** 1 0
Concede rate: Goal every 104 mins
Mins played: 3330 **Ave mins:** 88

Europe: Did not play
Apps: 0 **Goals conceded:** 0 **Cards:** 0 0

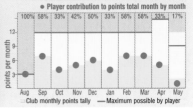

● Player contribution to points total month by month

| 100% | 58% | 33% | 42% | 50% | 33% | 58% | 58% | 33% | 17% |

Aug Sep Oct Nov Dec Jan Feb Mar Apr May
— Club monthly points tally — Maximum possible by player

16 Carlos Kameni

Age: 21 • *5th best keeper in Spanish League* • **Overall World Ranking: 108**

Idriss Carlos Kameni has emerged as one of the most sought-after keepers in Spain. The Cameroonian was the youngest-ever footballer to win an Olympic medal in 2000, aged just 16. He won gold in Sydney with a sensational performance in the final penalty shoot-out. He moved from Le Havre in the French lower divisions to play every game for Espanyol last season, helping them to fifth spot in La Liga.

Season 2004-05 record

National Team: Cameroon
Apps: 5 **Goals conceded:** 7 **Cards:** 0 0

Club: Espanyol
Apps: 38 **Goals conceded:** 47 **Cards:** 3 0
Concede rate: Goal every 72 mins
Mins played: 3398 **Ave mins:** 89

Europe: Did not play
Apps: 0 **Goals conceded:** 0 **Cards:** 0 0

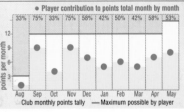

● Player contribution to points total month by month

| 33% | 75% | 33% | 75% | 58% | 42% | 50% | 42% | 58% | 53% |

Aug Sep Oct Nov Dec Jan Feb Mar Apr May
— Club monthly points tally — Maximum possible by player

17 Morgan De Sanctis

Age: 28 • *4th best keeper in Italian League* • **Overall World Ranking: 122**

Suddenly, after ten years, Morgan De Sanctis has become an overnight success. After three seasons with Serie B side Pescara, he moved to Juventus but barely got a game. He made little impression on moving to Udinese in 1999, yet in the last two seasons he's played almost every game and taken his team to fourth in Serie A. He's been linked with several clubs, including Arsenal, and was called into the Italian squad in 2005.

Season 2004-05 record

National Team: Italy
Apps: 2 **Goals conceded:** 0 **Cards:** 0 0

Club: Udinese
Apps: 36 **Goals conceded:** 38 **Cards:** 2 0
Concede rate: Goal every 84 mins
Mins played: 3177 **Ave mins:** 84

Europe: Did not play
Apps: 0 **Goals conceded:** 3 **Cards:** 0 0

● Player contribution to points total month by month

| 42% | 47% | 83% | 100% | 20% | 53% | 67% | 42% | 60% |

Aug Sep Oct Nov Dec Jan Feb Mar Apr May
— Club monthly points tally — Maximum possible by player

18 Brad Friedel

Age: 34 • *5th best keeper in Premiership* • **Overall World Ranking:** 123

Since Blackburn returned to the Premiership, Brad Friedel has barely missed a game, earning a reputation as one of the most consistent keepers around. He won a Worthington Cup medal in 2002 before taking his place in the USA World Cup team which reached the quarter-finals. Last season his 45 appearances in all competitions included 17 clean sheets, but for USA Kasey Keller has beaten him to the No.1 jersey.

Season 2004-05 record

National Team: United States
Apps: 0 **Goals conceded:** 0 **Cards:** o o

Club: Blackburn
Apps: 38 **Goals conceded:** 43 **Cards:** o o
Concede rate: Goal every 80 mins
Mins played: 3420 **Ave mins:** 90

Europe: Did not play
Apps: 0 **Goals conceded:** 0 **Cards:** o o

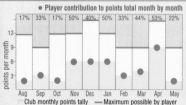

• Player contribution to points total month by month

	17%	33%	17%	50%	40%	50%	33%	44%	53%	22%
	Aug	Sep	Oct	Nov	Dec	Jan	Feb	Mar	Apr	May

☐ Club monthly points tally — Maximum possible by player

19 Oliver Kahn

Age: 36 • *2nd best keeper in German League* • **Overall World Ranking:** 125

A veteran of three World Cups and six Bundesliga titles, Oliver Kahn is one of Germany's sporting legends. He captained Germany to the finals of the 2002 World Cup where FIFA voted him best goalkeeper and the tournament's MVP – most valuable player. Still winning titles in his 11th season at Bayern, he was recently stripped of the German captaincy and challenged to see off Jens Lehmann for the goalkeeping slot.

Season 2004-05 record

National Team: Germany
Apps: 8 **Goals conceded:** 5 **Cards:** o o

Club: Bayern Munich
Apps: 32 **Goals conceded:** 28 **Cards:** o o
Concede rate: Goal every 100 mins
Mins played: 2790 **Ave mins:** 82

Europe: Champions League quarter-finals
Apps: 10 **Goals conceded:** 13 **Cards:** o o

• Player contribution to points total month by month

	44%	78%	60%	100%	33%	67%	75%	67%	100%	100%
	Aug	Sep	Oct	Nov	Dec	Jan	Feb	Mar	Apr	May

☐ Club monthly points tally — Maximum possible by player

20 Paul Robinson

Age: 25 • *6th best keeper in Premiership* • **Overall World Ranking:** 128

By the end of the 2003-04 season, Paul Robinson needed an escape route. He had just endured a torrid season, propping up a Leeds team in freefall, conceding 85 goals and letting in one in four shots on target. He moved to Spurs and picked up four clean sheets in his first six games. By the end of the season, he had made the England goalkeeping spot his own and helped Spurs push close to Europe.

Season 2004-05 record

National Team: England
Apps: 9 **Goals conceded:** 2 **Cards:** o o

Club: Tottenham
Apps: 36 **Goals conceded:** 40 **Cards:** o o
Concede rate: Goal every 80 mins
Mins played: 3214 **Ave mins:** 85

Europe: Did not play
Apps: 0 **Goals conceded:** 0 **Cards:** o o

• Player contribution to points total month by month

	67%	22%	25%	25%	87%	33%	67%	33%	40%	44%
	Aug	Sep	Oct	Nov	Dec	Jan	Feb	Mar	Apr	May

☐ Club monthly points tally — Maximum possible by player

21 ▲ Francesco Toldo

Age: 33 • *5th best keeper in Italian League* • **Overall World Ranking: 131**

Francesco Toldo started his career at AC Milan but he has spent the last four seasons as the goalkeeper at rivals Inter. He didn't get a look in at AC Milan and switched clubs until he arrived at Fiorentina and helped them into Serie A. The following year he won his first cap for Italy. Standing 1.96m tall, Toldo conceded just 28 goals in 30 appearances last season as Inter claimed third place.

Season 2004-05 record

National Team: Italy
Apps: 0 **Goals conceded:** 0 **Cards:** 0 0

Club: Inter Milan
Apps: 30 **Goals conceded:** 28 **Cards:** 2 1
Concede rate: Goal every 95 mins
Mins played: 2659 **Ave mins:** 70

Europe: Champions League quarter-finals
Apps: 8 **Goals conceded:** 8 **Cards:** 0 0

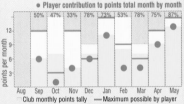

● Player contribution to points total month by month

| | 50% | 47% | 33% | 78% | 73% | 53% | 78% | 75% | 87% |

points per month — Club monthly points tally — Maximum possible by player
Aug Sep Oct Nov Dec Jan Feb Mar Apr May

22 ▲ Jussi Jaaskelainen

Age: 30 • *7th best keeper in Premiership* • **Overall World Ranking: 137**

Bolton picked up Jussi Jaaskelainen for just £100,000 from VPS Vaasa in 1997. It turned out to be a bargain as the Lancashire side established themselves in the Premiership under Sam Allardyce, embarrassing more fashionable teams. Last season the Finnish international was picking up rave reviews and being linked with the top sides in the Premiership. He stayed to help Bolton secure their first ever European qualification.

Season 2004-05 record

National Team: Finland
Apps: 0 **Conceded:** 0 **Cards:** 0 0

Club: Bolton
Apps: 36 **Conceded:** 40 **Cards:** 1 1
Concede rate: Goal every 81 mins
Mins played: 3236 **Ave mins:** 85

Europe: Did not play
Apps: 0 **Conceded:** 0 **Cards:** 0 0

● Player contribution to points total month by month

| | 75% | 33% | 75% | 17% | 0% | 83% | 58% | 100% | 53% | 44% |

points per month — Club monthly points tally — Maximum possible by player
Aug Sep Oct Nov Dec Jan Feb Mar Apr May

23 ▲ Stephane Porato

Age: 31 • *3rd best keeper in French League* • **Overall World Ranking: 146**

The small French club of AC Ajaccio is punching above its weight in defensive terms. The club finished 14th in the league last season but had the sixth best defensive rating in the tightest league in Europe. Keeper Stephane Porato is part of the reason. Understudy to Fabien Barthez during five years at Monaco, he helped Marseille to second spot in France in 1999. Last season, he conceded barely a goal a game.

Season 2004-05 record

National Team: France
Apps: 0 **Goals conceded:** 0 **Cards:** 0 0

Club: AC Ajaccio
Apps: 35 **Goals conceded:** 35 **Cards:** 1 0
Concede rate: Goal every 90 mins
Mins played: 3150 **Ave mins:** 83

Europe: Did not play
Apps: 0 **Goals conceded:** 0 **Cards:** 0 0

● Player contribution to points total month by month

| | 8% | 42% | 25% | 42% | 22% | 50% | 33% | 33% | 83% | 50% |

points per month — Club monthly points tally — Maximum possible by player
Aug Sep Oct Nov Dec Jan Feb Mar Apr May

24 ▲ Ulrich Rame

Age: 32 • *4th best keeper in French League* • **Overall World Ranking: 179**

Ulrich Rame was France's substitute goalkeeper when Les Bleus won the European Championships in 2000. He was also part of the French squad which crashed out of the World Cup in 2002. He won his only Ligue 1 title with Bordeaux in 1999 and has stayed loyal to the club as they have slipped to mid-table. But his performances earned 16 clean sheets last season and kept him in the French squad.

Season 2004-05 record

National Team: France
Apps: 0 **Goals conceded:** 0 **Cards:** 0 0

Club: Bordeaux
Apps: 37 **Goals conceded:** 38 **Cards:** 2 0
Concede rate: Goal every 88 mins
Mins played: 3330 **Ave mins:** 88

Europe: Did not play
Apps: 0 **Goals conceded:** 0 **Cards:** 0 0

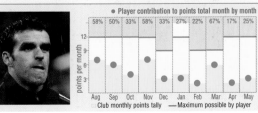

● Player contribution to points total month by month

| | 58% | 50% | 33% | 58% | 33% | 27% | 22% | 67% | 17% | 25% |

points per month — Club monthly points tally — Maximum possible by player
Aug Sep Oct Nov Dec Jan Feb Mar Apr May

25 ▲ Charles-Hubert Itandje

Age: 22 • *5th best keeper in French League* • **Overall World Ranking: 197**

One of the up-and-coming keepers in France's Ligue 1 is 22-year-old Charles-Hubert Itandje. He took over the number one spot at Lens at the start of 2004 and was watched by both Spurs and Liverpool, where former Reds boss Gerard Houllier invited him for a trial. Itandje stayed at Lens where he was ever-present last season as they flirted with Europe before finishing seventh. Strongly tipped as the future French keeper.

Season 2004-05 record

National Team: France
Apps: 0 **Goals conceded:** 0 **Cards:** 0 0

Club: Lens
Apps: 38 **Goals conceded:** 39 **Cards:** 1 0
Concede rate: Goal every 88 mins
Mins played: 3420 **Ave mins:** 90

Europe: Did not play
Apps: 0 **Goals conceded:** 0 **Cards:** 0 0

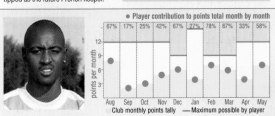

● Player contribution to points total month by month

| | 67% | 17% | 25% | 42% | 67% | 27% | 78% | 67% | 33% | 58% |

points per month — Club monthly points tally — Maximum possible by player
Aug Sep Oct Nov Dec Jan Feb Mar Apr May

FOOTBALL CHALLENGE QUIZ 4

Do you know your football?

THINK YOU'RE A FOOTY KNOW-IT-ALL? TEST YOUR KNOWLEDGE ON THE FOUR QUIZ PAGES IN THIS ANNUAL. FILL IN YOUR ANSWERS ON PAGE 94 AND SEE HOW MANY YOU SCORED OUT OF 200!

FOREIGN LEGION

Can you name the nationalities of these Chelsea stars

1 PETR CECH

2 EIDUR GUDJOHNSEN

3 ARJEN ROBBEN

4 HERMAN CRESPO

5 RICARDO CARVALHO

THE ROAD TO WEMBLEY

With the all-new Wembley set to open its doors next year, what better time to test your knowledge of the new national stadium and its history.

1. What match will see the opening of the new Wembley Stadium?
2. Who will the new Wembley footbridge be named after?
3. Who were England's opponents in the final game at the old Wembley Stadium?
4. What was the original name of Wembley Stadium?
5. What was the first football game to be played at Wembley when it opened in 1923?
6. Did England always use the North or South dressing room at the old stadium?
7. Who scored the last goal of the 1966 World Cup Final at Wembley?
8. What year were the Twin Towers of Wembley knocked down?
9. What rock band will be the first entertainers to play at the new Wembley Stadium?
10. How high in metres is the arch over the new Wembley stadium?

HOW MUCH CAN YOU REMEMBER ABOUT THE 2004-05 SEASON?

1. Shaun Wright Phillips was joint top goalscorer for Manchester City last season. Who did he tie with?
2. Which foreign country had the most players represented in the Premiership last season?
3. Who was Celtic's manager last season?
4. Who did Liverpool beat in the League Cup semi-final?
5. How many England goals did Wayne Rooney manage to score last season?
6. What was the score when Norwich played Manchester United at Carrow Road?
7. Who was Birmingham City's leading goalscorer?
8. How many league goals did Michael Owen score for Real Madrid in his first season?
9. What foreign country had the most players appear in the Spanish Liga?
10. What team finished bottom of the Scottish Premier League?
11. Who were Italian champions?
12. Last season who knocked Newcastle out of the UEFA Cup?

GUESS THE PUNDIT

Can you work out who this Match Of The Day pundit is?

I'M FREE

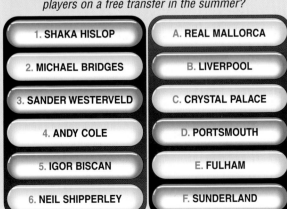

Can you name the football clubs who released these players on a free transfer in the summer?

1. SHAKA HISLOP
2. MICHAEL BRIDGES
3. SANDER WESTERVELD
4. ANDY COLE
5. IGOR BISCAN
6. NEIL SHIPPERLEY

A. REAL MALLORCA
B. LIVERPOOL
C. CRYSTAL PALACE
D. PORTSMOUTH
E. FULHAM
F. SUNDERLAND

6 OF THE BEST

ALAN SHEARER

1. How many goals did Alan score on his league debut for Southampton?
2. Which country did Alan win his first England cap against?
3. Alan has won the Premiership title just once. Who was he playing for?
4. Alan's 100th premier goal came in December 1995. Who was it against?
5. Signing Alan cost Newcastle a British record fee. How much did they pay?
6. Against what team did Alan played his last England game at Euro 2000?

It's taken big money to make Chelsea the best club in England!

WHEN WEALTHY RUSSIAN OIL TYCOON ROMAN Abramovich paid £140 million to buy Chelsea Football Club on July 2, 2003 he sent shockwaves through the English game. Chelsea had firmly established themselves as a top five Premiership side and their Stamford Bridge ground had been impressively redeveloped. However, the club was buckling under a reported debt of £80m and chairman Ken Bates was desperate to find a buyer who'd stabilise the Blues' finances and, hopefully, take them to the next level on the pitch, too. In the last two years, Abramovich has done all that and more.

The 39-year-old billionaire has splashed out nearly £240 million on new players, persuaded Manchester United chief executive Peter Kenyon to quit the club for Stamford Bridge, and snapped up Champions League-winning manager José Mourinho from Porto.

The effect of all this spending has been instant and far reaching. Chelsea were crowned league champions for the first time in 50 years last season and also lifted the Carling Cup. Abramovich's financial muscle means Chelsea are able to bid for any player that takes their fancy and that Mourinho has at least two world-class players for every position in his first team.

For the first time since the Premiership began it's Man United and Arsenal that are scrabbling to play catch up as the Blues seek to dominate English football for the forseeable future. It's all a far cry from the Chelsea of ten years ago, who played in a stadium with only three sides, had never paid more than a couple of million pounds for a player, and hadn't won a trophy worth the name in more than 20 years.

SEA

ABRAMOVICH'S BIG MONEY SPENDING

* * * * * * * * * * * *

PLAYER	FROM	FEE
Glen Johnson	West Ham	£6m
Geremi	Real Madrid	£7m
Damien Duff	Blackburn	£17m
Wayne Bridge	Southampton	£7m
Juan Veron	Man Utd	£15m
Joe Cole	West Ham	£6.6m
Adrian Mutu	Parma	£15.8m
Alexei Smertin	Bordeaux	£3.45m
Hernan Crespo	Inter	£16.8m
Claude Makelele	Real Madrid	£16.6m
Scott Parker	Charlton	£10m
Petr Cech	Rennes	£7m
Arjen Robben	PSV Eindhoven	£12m
Paulo Ferreira	Porto	£13.2m
Mateja Kezman	PSV Eindhoven	£5m
Didier Drogba	Marseille	£24m
Tiago Mendes	Benfica	£8m
Ricardo Carvalho	Porto	£19.85m
Asier Del Horno	Ath. Bilbao	£8m
Shaun Wright-Phillips	Man City	£21m
Lassana Diarra	Le Havre	£2.8m
Michael Essien	Lyon	£24.4m

PLAYERS TOTAL
£266.15m

- - - - - - - - - - - - - - - - -

Cost of buying club	£140m
Wages 2003-04	£73m
Wages 2004-05	£115m

PURCHASE & WAGES TOTAL
£569.75m

- - - - - - - - - - - - - - - - -

* * * * * * * * * * * *

OVERALL TOTAL
£835.9m

* * * * * * * * * * * *

OF WINNING

CHELSEA: NOW & THEN!

An awful lot can happen to a club in ten years, as our comparison between Chelsea of today and their poorer, less successful counterparts from 1995-96 proves...

THE MANAGER

THEN Glenn Hoddle had taken over the manager's hot seat at the Bridge in the summer of 1993. The ex-England international had enjoyed a glittering career as a player with Tottenham and Monaco, and kicked off life as a manager impressively by winning promotion to the Premier League with Swindon. This alerted Chelsea supremo Ken Bates and Hoddle was soon warming the dug-out at Stamford Bridge. During his tenure in west London Hoddle took the Blues to the final of the FA Cup and the semi-final of the European Cup Winners' Cup, before quitting to manage England in 1996.

NOW José Mourinho joined the Blues after winning the Champions League with Porto in 2004. The charismatic boss had already turned the unfashionable side into Portugal's most successful club, leading them to the UEFA Cup in 2003, two league titles and a domestic cup. Not bad for a man who started his career in football as translator to Bobby Robson at Sporting Lisbon and had never made it as a player. In his first season in charge at the Bridge, Mourinho led Chelsea to a league and Carling Cup double success.

THE BADGE

THEN IN 1986, keen to distance his reign as Chelsea owner from the previous regime, Ken Bates ditched the 33-year-old 'lion rampant' club badge in favour of something supposedly more modern. Unfortunately, the new badge was never popular with fans who felt it looked far too much like that of reviled London rivals Millwall.

NOW To celebrate Chelsea's centenary year, the club has decided to bring back the 'lion rampant' design that had been the official club badge between 1953 and 1986. Inspired by the civic coat of arms of the Metropolitan Borough of Chelsea, the lion was derived from the Arms of Earl Cadogan, who was president of the club and also held the title Viscount Chelsea. (Chelsea's original badge from 1905 had featured the face of a Chelsea pensioner but was replaced in 1952 under manager Ted Drake who was seeking a brand new image for the club.)

THE RECORD SIGNING

THEN In June 1995, When Glenn Hoddle signed Dan Petrescu from Sheffield Wednesday, for £2.3 million, the Romanian wing-back became Chelsea's joint record signing, equal to the amount the club had coughed up in May 1994 for striker Paul Furlong from Oxford United. The record remained until July 1996, when Ruud Gullit paid £4.9m to Lazio for midfielder Roberto di Matteo.

NOW Despite winning a league title and Carling Cup double in his first season in charge, Blues boss José Mourinho was keen to strengthen his squad with another top class midfielder to play alongside Frank Lampard and Claude Makelele. The club was initially expected to wrap up a new British record £32 million deal for Liverpool's Steven Gerrard, but when the England star decided to stay on Merseyside, Mourinho moved for Lyon's 24-year-old Ghana international Michael Essien. After weeks of negotiations Chelsea finally got their man for £24.4 million – some £400,000 more expensive than previous record signing Didier Drogba, the striker who had joined the club from Marseille the previous season. The deal for Essien is the third biggest in British transfer history behind Manchester United's signings of Rio Ferdinand (£29 million) and Juan Sebastian Veron (£28.1 million).

THE OWNER

THEN Ken Bates bought Chelsea FC and its debts for just £1 in April 1982 and over the next 22 years would transform both the stadium and the team, turning a ramshackled old ground into one of the best in the Premiership, and funding extensive spending on players that saw Chelsea rise from the depths of the old Second Division to seriously challenge for the title on several occasions. He wasn't always popular with the football authorities or even his own club's fans (especially after sacking beloved manager Gianluca Vialli), but no one doubts that he left Chelsea FC in far better condition than that in which he had inherited it.

NOW Russian billionaire Roman Abramovich bought Chelsea FC and its debts for £140m in July 2004 and made it clear from the start that his ambition was to make 'The Blues' the biggest team in the world. The oil magnate is certainly off to a good start, his seemingly unlimited reservoirs of cash allowing José Mourinho to build a squad packed with world-class players. The new Blues won their first league title for 50 years in Abramovich's second season in charge and are now focused on conquering the heights of the Champions League.

THE GROUND

THEN After emerging victorious in a long and bitter battle to wrest control of Stamford Bridge from its then owners (the ground had been sold off in the '70s to property developers), Ken Bates began to redevelop the stadium. By the mid-90s the process had begun but the work needed to demolish and rebuild three sides of the ground left it looking like a building site. No wonder Ruud Gullit wasn't impressed when he first set foot in the place, commenting: "I thought that coming to Chelsea was the best idea I'd ever had. That is until I saw Stamford Bridge. It was a terrible mess and a real shock. I thought to myself, 'Jesus Christ, what did I do?'"

NOW The impressive redevelopment is one of the few improvements of the last ten years Roman Abramovich can't take any credit for. Three sides of the ground have been demolished and rebuilt (only the East Stand, erected in 1973, survived the process) and Bates even found room to include a leisure and entertainment complex on the site, which houses two four-star hotels, five restaurants, shops, conference and banqueting facilities, a nightclub, an underground car park, a health club and a business centre. The ground's capacity stands at 42,522.

PREMIERSHIP CLUB GUIDE

Everything you needed to know about the Premiership, club by club!

SATURDAY NIGHT IN FRONT OF THE TELLY watching *Match Of The Day* will be so much easier now you have the *Match Of The Day Annual 2006* to keep you informed. You'll be able to keep it with you while you watch the show and look up the players to see what kind of form they've been in for club and country throughout the last season.

For every club in the Premiership we list this year's squads, with each player's record from *last* season. So even if a player was turning out for another club somewhere else in the world, you can see how well he was performing. Michael Owen might have been at Real Madrid last year, but you'll find his full record on the Newcastle club page.

For each striker and midfielder we show their attacking strengths, and for each defender and goalkeeper we highlight how many goals their team has conceded while the player was on the pitch. This way you get a clear picture of just how much each player contributed to his team's performance.

Through the last year we've studied the contributions made by every major player to his team's performance, and it has helped us to come up with a series of rankings for every player in the Premiership, regardless of where they played last year. You can see where they are ranked within their respective leagues, you can see where they are ranked in the world by position, and you can see where they are ranked in the world regardless of position. That's how we know that Petr Cech is currently the best player in the world!

Added to all that, we show you who each club's star players were last season. And we also give you all of last season's results, so you can see how each team is doing compared to last year. Sounds like stat heaven!

>>>>> >>>> > NOW TURN OVER >>>> >>>>>

Premiership 04-05 **2nd**
FA Cup **Winners**
Coca-Cola Cup **Quarter final**
Champions League **Last 16**

ARSENAL FACTS

MANAGER	CAPTAIN
ARSENE WENGER	THIERRY HENRY

ADDITIONS TO SQUAD 2005-06

▼ PLAYERS IN	▼ FROM	▼ COST
Alexander Hleb	VfB Stuttgart	£10m
Alex Song	Bastia	Loan

CLUB

Stadium: Arsenal Stadium
Capacity: 38,500
Pitch Size: 110 yds by 73 yds
Website: www.arsenal.com

RECORDS

Record Home Attendance: 73,707 v RC Lens (European Cup; at Wembley) Nov.25, 1998
Record Victory: 12-0 v Loughborough Town (league) Mar.12, 1900; v Ashford United (FA Cup) Oct.14, 1893
Record Defeat: 0-6 v Derby County (FA Cup) Jan.28, 1899
Most League Goals: Cliff Bastin (150)
Most League Apps: David O'Leary (558)
Most Capped Player: Kenny Samson, 77 (England)

HONOURS

Premiership: 1998, 2002, 2004
Division One: 1931, 1933, 1934, 1935, 1938, 1948, 1953, 1971, 1989, 1991
FA Cup: 1930, 1936, 1950, 1971, 1979, 1993, 1998, 2002, 2003, 2005
League Cup: 1987, 1993
UEFA Cup: 1970 (as Fairs Cup)
European Cup Winners Cup: 1994

CURRENT SQUAD RECORD 2004-05

	CLUB				INTERNATIONAL			POSITIONAL RANKING		OVERALL RANKING
	Games	Goals	Mins per goal	% played	Country	Games	Goals	Domestic	World	All positions
GOALKEEPERS			CONCEDED				CONCEDED			
JENS LEHMANN	28	27	93	73	Germany	7	3	8	26	206
MANUEL ALMUNIA	10	9	100	26	Spain	0	0	19	102	1206
DEFENDERS			CONCEDED				CONCEDED			
HABIB KOLO TOURE	35	31	101	91	Ivory Coast	3	0	10	29	97
ETAME MAYER LAUREN	33	29	101	85	Cameroon	0	0	11	31	104
ASHLEY COLE	35	35	90	92	England	11	6	16	40	151
PHILIPPE SENDEROS	13	6	181	31	Switzerland	2	0	27	100	394
GAEL CLICHY	15	4	195	22	France	0	0	41	178	627
SOL CAMPBELL	16	14	101	41	England	4	0	59	264	895
PASCAL CYGAN	15	22	58	37	France	0	0	94	489	1569
MIDFIELDERS			SCORED				SCORED			
CESC FABREGAS	33	1	2118	61	Spain	0	0	7	35	122
ROBERT PIRES	33	14	165	67	France	5	0	8	36	125
ALEXANDER HLEB * Stuttgart	34	2	1507	98	Belarus	3	0	15	84	244
FREDRIK LJUNGBERG	27	10	208	60	Sweden	8	7	27	106	292
GILBERTO SILVA	13	1	1124	32	Brazil	5	0	39	216	579
MATHIEU FLAMINI	21	1	960	28	France	0	0	66	354	883
FORWARDS			SCORED				SCORED			
THIERRY HENRY	32	25	113	82	France	8	1	1	2	5
JOSE ANTONIO REYES	30	9	223	58	Spain	6	0	6	42	110
DENNIS BERGKAMP	29	8	240	56	Holland	0	0	8	56	158
ROBIN VAN PERSIE	25	4	226	26	Holland	2	0	50	259	1201

KEY: Club stats are all for the 2004-05 season. Games = appearances in the league for club; Goals conceded = goals let in when the player is on the pitch; Goals scored = scored by the player; Mins per goal = number of minutes on average between each goal conceded or scored; % played = the percentage of the league season player played; Domestic = player ranking by position in domestic league; World = player ranking by position in World; Overall Position = player ranking in world across all positions. * = player record from previous club

THE STARS OF LAST SEASON

TEAM OF THE SEASON

G Lehman

D Lauren D Senderos D Toure D Cole

M Ljungberg M Fabregas M Vieira M Pires

F Reyes F Henry

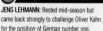

G STAR GOALKEEPER

JENS LEHMANN: Rested mid-season but came back strongly to challenge Oliver Kahn for the position of German number one.

Average goals per game conceded by club	0.95
Goals per game conceded when player on pitch	0.96
Points per game conceded club won when player on pitch	2.25
Minutes played	2520	Clean sheets	11

D STAR DEFENDER

HABIB KOLO TOURE: A superb athlete who took over from the injured Sol Campbell as Wenger's most reliable defender.

Goals per game conceded when player on pitch	0.89
Points per game club won when player on pitch	2.2
Goals scored by player	0
Minutes played	3134	Clean sheets	15

M STAR MIDFIELDER

PATRICK VIEIRA: An accomplished and competitive midfield player who has left a huge gap with his departure to Juventus.

Goals per game conceded when player on pitch	0.90
Goals per game club scored when player on pitch	1.91
Goals scored by player	6
Minutes played	2794	Assists	6

F STAR FORWARD

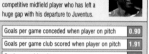

THIERRY HENRY: One of the top strikers in the world and the most complete with pace, control and a deadly finish.

Average goals per game scored by club	2.29
Goals per game scored when player on pitch	2.43
% of club goals scored by player	28.7
Minutes played	2826	Assists	16

2004-05 SEASON REVIEW OF THE LEAGUE

■ Games won ■ Games lost ■ Games drawn   League position game by game

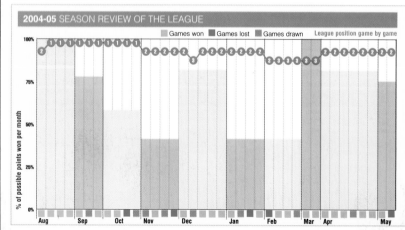

Aug Sep Oct Nov Dec Jan Feb Mar Apr May

2004-05 RESULTS ROUND-UP

□ Premiership □ League Cup □ FA Cup □ UEFA Cup □ Champions League

Everton	A	4-1	Man Utd	A	0-1	Bolton	A	1-0
Middlesbrough	H	5-3	**Birmingham**	H	3-0	Blackburn	A	1-0
Blackburn	H	3-0	**Rosenborg BK**	H	5-1	Norwich	H	4-1
Norwich	A	4-1	Chelsea	H	2-2	Middlesbrough	H	1-0
Fulham	A	3-0	Portsmouth	H	1-0	**Blackburn**	N	3-0
PSV Eindhoven	H	1-0	**Fulham**	H	2-0	Chelsea	A	0-0
Bolton	H	2-2	Newcastle	A	1-0	**Tottenham**	H	1-0
Man City	A	1-0	Charlton	A	3-1	West Brom	A	2-0
Rosenborg BK	A	1-1	**Man City**	H	1-1	**Liverpool**	A	2-1
Charlton	H	4-0	Stoke	H	2-1	Everton	H	7-0
Aston Villa	H	3-1	Bolton	A	0-1	Birmingham	A	1-2
Panathinaikos	A	2-2	Newcastle	H	1-0	Man Utd	H	0-0*
Man Utd	A	0-2	**Wolverhampton**	H	2-0			
Man City	A	2-1	Man Utd	H	2-4	*Won on penalties		
Southampton	H	2-2	Aston Villa	A	3-1			
Panathinaikos	H	1-1	**Crystal Palace**	H	5-1			
Crystal Palace	A	1-1	Sheff Utd	H	1-1			
Everton	H	3-1	Bayern Munich	A	1-3			
Tottenham	H	5-4	Southampton	A	3-1			
West Brom	H	1-1	Sheff Utd	A	0-0*			
PSV Eindhoven	H	1-1	Portsmouth	A	1-0			
Liverpool	A	1-2	**Bayern Munich**	H	1-0			

STAR SIGNING

ALEXANDER HLEB

The powerhouse in Stuttgart's midfield last season, Hleb played every league game and helped the club through the group stages of the UEFA Cup before being knocked out by Parma. He has won 18 caps for Belarus and in the world's top midfielders chart, Hleb is rated 84th.

ASTON VILLA

ASTON VILLA FACTS

MANAGER	CAPTAIN
DAVID O'LEARY	OLOF MELLBERG

ADDITIONS TO SQUAD 2005-06

▼ PLAYERS IN	▼ FROM	▼ COST
Milan Baros	Liverpool	£6.5m
Wilfred Bouma	PSV Eindhoven	£3.5m
Aaron Hughes	Newcastle	£1.5m
Kevin Phillips	Southampton	£1m
Stuart Taylor	Arsenal	£1m
Patrik Berger	Portsmouth	FREE

CLUB

Stadium: Villa Park
Capacity: 42,584
Pitch Size: 115 yds by 72 yds
Website: www.avfc.co.uk

RECORDS

Record Home Attendance: 76,588 v Derby County, Mar.2, 1946 (FA Cup)

Record Victory: 13-0 v Wednesday Old Athletic (FA Cup) Oct.30 1886

Record Defeat: 1-8 v Blackburn (FA Cup) Feb.16, 1889

Most League Goals: Harry Hampton (215)

Most League Apps: Charlie Aitken (561)

Most Capped Player: Steve Staunton, 64 (Republic Of Ireland)

HONOURS

Division One: 1894, 1896, 1897, 1899, 1900, 1910, 1981

Division Two: 1938, 1960

Division Three: 1972

FA Cup: 1887, 1895, 1897, 1905, 1913, 1920, 1957

League Cup: 1961, 1975, 1977, 1994, 1996

European Cup: 1982

CURRENT SQUAD RECORD 2004-05	CLUB				INTERNATIONAL			POSITIONAL RANKING		OVERALL RANKING
	Games	Goals	Mins per goal	% played	Country	Games	Goals	Domestic	World	All positions
GOALKEEPERS			CONCEDED				CONCEDED			
THOMAS SORENSEN	36	43	74	93	Denmark	6	7	**11**	**46**	339
DEFENDERS			CONCEDED				CONCEDED			
JLLOYD SAMUEL	35	46	65	87	England	0	0	**42**	**199**	684
OLOF MELLBERG	30	37	71	77	Sweden	9	5	**48**	**215**	726
ULISES DE LA CRUZ	34	42	67	82	Ecuador	7	7	**53**	**231**	781
MARK DELANEY	31	39	65	74	Wales	7	11	**62**	**269**	905
AARON HUGHES *Newcastle	22	29	57	49	N Ireland	8	14	**90**	**472**	1511
LIAM RIDGEWELL	15	20	56	33	England	0	0	**109**	**565**	1790
MARTIN LAURSEN	12	19	54	30	Denmark	2	0	**113**	**574**	1837
MIDFIELDERS			SCORED				SCORED			
PATRIK BERGER *Portsmouth	32	3	832	72	Czech Rep.	0	0	**40**	**219**	588
GARETH BARRY	34	7	405	82	England	0	0	**55**	**305**	785
LEE HENDRIE	29	5	404	59	England	0	0	**60**	**335**	841
GAVIN MCCANN	20	1	1763	51	England	0	0	**83**	**431**	1092
STEVEN DAVIS	28	1	1899	55	N. Ireland	5	0	**114**	**578**	1456
PETER WHITTINGHAM	13	1	573	16	England	0	0	**141**	**737**	1888
MATHIEU BERSON	11	0	-	18	France	0	0	**146**	**765**	1953
ERIC DJEMBA-DJEMBA	6	0	-	10	Cameroon	4	0	**163**	**849**	2141
FORWARDS			SCORED				SCORED			
KEVIN PHILLIPS *Southampton	30	10	209	61	England	0	0	**26**	**151**	618
MILAN BAROS *Liverpool	26	9	205	54	Czech Rep.	8	3	**21**	**111**	418
JUAN PABLO ANGEL	35	7	388	79	Colombia	5	1	**28**	**157**	651
LUKE MOORE	25	1	849	24	England	0	0	**74**	**440**	1899

*KEY: Club stats are all for the 2004-05 season. Games = appearances in the league for club; Goals conceded = goals let in when the player is on the pitch; Goals scored = scored by the player; Mins per goal = number of minutes on average between each goal conceded or scored; % played = the percentage of the league season the player played; Domestic = player ranking by position in domestic league; World = player ranking by position in World; Overall Position = player ranking in world across all positions. * = player record from previous club*

THE STARS OF LAST SEASON

TEAM OF THE SEASON

G Sorensen
D De La Cruz | D Mellberg | D Delaney | D Samuel
M Solano | M Hendrie | M Hitzlsperger | M Barry
F Angel | F Cole

G STAR GOALKEEPER

THOMAS SORENSEN: A consistent stopper for both Denmark and Villa with the instant reactions of a brilliant line keeper.

Average goals per game conceded by club	1.37
Goals per game conceded when player on pitch	1.19
Points per game club won when player on pitch	1.34
Minutes played	3195	Clean sheets	11

D STAR DEFENDER

JLLOYD SAMUEL: Played the most league games in a tight-knit defence and got onto the verges of the England squad.

Goals per game conceded when player on pitch	1.31
Points per game club won when player on pitch	1.44
Goals scored by player	0
Minutes played	3009	Clean sheets	11

M STAR MIDFIELDER

NOLBERTO SOLANO: Arguably O'Leary's best buy and not surprising that Newcastle re-signed one of the Premier's top wingers.

Goals per game conceded when player on pitch	1.34
Goals per game club scored when player on pitch	1.18
Goals scored by player	8
Minutes played	2794	Assists	6

F STAR FORWARD

JUAN PABLO ANGEL: A revelation with 23 goals in 2003-04, but couldn't find that form last season in a misfiring forward line.

Average goals per game scored by club	1.18
Goals per game scored when player on pitch	1.20
% of club goals scored by player	15.5
Minutes played	2717	Assists	4

2004-05 SEASON REVIEW OF THE LEAGUE

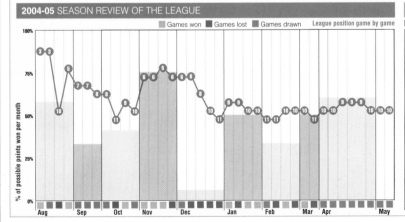

■ Games won ■ Games lost ■ Games drawn   — League position game by game

Aug Sep Oct Nov Dec Jan Feb Mar Apr May

2004-05 RESULTS ROUND-UP

☐ Premiership ☐ League Cup ☐ FA Cup ☐ UEFA Cup ☐ Champions League

Southampton	H	2-0	**Blackburn**	H	1-0	Birmingham	A	0-2
West Brom	A	1-1	Crystal Palace	A	0-2	Newcastle	A	3-0
Charlton	A	0-3	Sheff Utd	A	1-3	**West Brom**	H	1-1
Newcastle	H	4-2	**Norwich**	H	3-0	Southampton	A	3-2
Chelsea	H	0-0	Man Utd	A	1-3	**Charlton**	H	0-0
Norwich	A	0-0	Fulham	A	1-1	**Bolton**	H	1-1
QPR	H	3-1	**Arsenal**	H	1-3	Tottenham	A	1-5
Crystal Palace	H	1-1	Portsmouth	A	2-1	**Man City**	H	1-2
Blackburn	A	2-2	**Everton**	H	1-3	Liverpool	A	1-2
Arsenal	A	1-3	Middlesbrough	H	2-0			
Fulham	H	2-0						
Burnley	A	1-3						
Everton	A	1-1						
Portsmouth	H	3-0						
Bolton	A	2-1						
Tottenham	H	1-0						
Man City	H	0-2						
Liverpool	H	1-1						
Birmingham	H	1-2						
Middlesbrough	A	0-3						
Chelsea	A	0-1						
Man Utd	H	0-1						

STAR SIGNING

KEVIN PHILLIPS

A consistently prolific striker for Sunderland before two seasons with Southampton, he had a respectable strike rate of a goal every 209 minutes last season. Phillips has won eight caps for England.

BIRMINGHAM CITY

Premiership 04-05 **12th**
FA Cup **Round 4**
Coca-Cola Cup **Round 3**

BIRMINGHAM FACTS

MANAGER	CAPTAIN
STEVE BRUCE	KENNY CUNNINGHAM

ADDITIONS TO SQUAD 2005-06

▼ PLAYERS IN	▼ FROM	▼ COST
Mikael Forssell	Chelsea	£3m
Walter Pandiani	Deportivo	£3m
Mehdi Nafti	Racing Santander	*
Nicky Butt	Newcastle	Loan
Jiri Jarosik	Chelsea	Loan

Fee Undisclosed

CLUB

Stadium: St Andrew's

Capacity: 30,009

Pitch Size: 110yds x 74yds

Website: www.bcfc.com

RECORDS

Record Home Attendance: 66,844 v Everton (FA Cup) Mar.11, 1939

Record Victory: 9-2 v Burton (FA Cup) Oct.31, 1885

Record Defeat: 1-9 Sheffield Wednesday (league) Dec.13, 1930; v Blackburn (league) Jan.5, 1895

Most League Goals: Joe Bradford (249)

Most League Apps: Frank Womack (491)

Most Capped Player: Malcolm Page, 28 (Wales)

HONOURS

Division Two: 1893, 1921, 1948, 1955, 1995

League Cup: 1963

CURRENT SQUAD RECORD 2004-05

	CLUB				INTERNATIONAL			POSITIONAL RANKING		OVERALL RANKING
	Games	Goals	Mins per goal	% played	Country	Games	Goals	Domestic	World	All positions
GOALKEEPERS			CONCEDED				CONCEDED			
MAIK TAYLOR	38	46	74	100	N Ireland	9	15	9	31	219
DEFENDERS			CONCEDED				CONCEDED			
MATTHEW UPSON	36	42	77	94	England	2	0	25	79	309
KENNY CUNNINGHAM	36	44	71	92	Rep of Ire.	10	5	30	106	411
MARIO MELCHIOT	34	38	74	83	Holland	5	0	37	160	560
JAMIE CLAPHAM	27	24	69	49	England	0	0	72	357	1140
OLIVIER TEBILY	15	11	69	22	Ivory Coast	0	0	102	530	1681
MARTIN TAYLOR	7	7	51	10	England	0	0	134	692	2251
MIDFIELDERS			SCORED				SCORED			
DAMIEN JOHNSON	36	0	-	90	N. Ireland	7	0	34	169	460
STAN LAZARIDIS	20	0	-	39	Australia	1	0	89	462	1179
ROBBIE SAVAGE	18	4	402	47	Wales	4	0	95	491	1239
DAVID DUNN	11	2	358	20	England	0	0	106	551	1396
JULIAN GRAY	31	2	945	55	England	0	0	111	570	1437
NICKY BUTT *Newcastle*	18	1	1423	41	England	0	0	116	582	1462
STEPHEN CLEMENCE	22	0	-	37	England	0	0	121	593	1483
JIRI JAROSIK *Chelsea*	14	0	-	13	Czech Rep.	5	0	78	419	1061
JERMAINE PENNANT	11	0	-	29	England	0	0	127	636	1618
MUSTAFA IZZET	8	1	817	23	Turkey	0	0	136	718	1822
MEHDI NAFTI	10	0	-	17	Tunisia	4	1	147	770	1961
FORWARDS			SCORED				SCORED			
EMILE HESKEY	32	10	290	84	England	2	0	18	90	320
WALTER PANDIANI	14	4	258	30	Uruguay	0	0	42	195	881

KEY: Club stats are all for the 2004-05 season. Games = appearances in the league for club; Goals conceded = goals let in when the player is on the pitch; Goals scored = scored by the player; Mins per goal = number of minutes on average between each goal conceded or scored; % played = the percentage of the league season the player played; Domestic = player ranking by position in domestic league; World = player ranking by position in World; Overall Position = player ranking in world across all positions. * = player record from previous club

THE STARS OF LAST SEASON

TEAM OF THE SEASON

G Taylor

D Melchiot — D Cunningham — D Upson — D Clapham

M Johnson — M Savage — M Dunn — M Lazaridis

F Pandiani — F Heskey

G STAR GOALKEEPER

MAIK TAYLOR: Played every minute of the season and has impressed everyone since his days understudying van der Sar at Fulham.

Average goals per game conceded by club	1.21
Goals per game conceded when player on pitch	1.21
Points per game club won when player on pitch	1.18
Minutes played	3420	Clean sheets	9

D STAR DEFENDER

MATTHEW UPSON: A powerful pillar in the Blues' defence, whose performances earned two caps for England last season.

Goals per game conceded when player on pitch	1.17
Points per game club won when player on pitch	1.25
Goals scored by player	2
Minutes played	3240	Clean sheets	9

M STAR MIDFIELDER

DAMIEN JOHNSON: City's key midfielder as other players went in and out around him. His 11 cards show his competitive nature.

Goals per game conceded when player on pitch	1.15
Goals per game club scored when player on pitch	1.05
Goals scored by player	0
Minutes played	3104	Assists	1

F STAR FORWARD

EMILE HESKEY: The robust former Liverpool and England forward has many Premiership admirers and is usually a handful.

Average goals per game scored by club	1.05
Goals per game scored when player on pitch	1.03
% of club goals scored by player	25
Minutes played	2903	Assists	5

2004-05 SEASON REVIEW OF THE LEAGUE

■ Games won ■ Games lost ■ Games drawn — League position game by game

(Graph of % of possible points won per month and league position game by game, Aug through May)

2004-05 RESULTS ROUND-UP

□ Premiership □ League Cup □ FA Cup □ UEFA Cup □ Champions League

Portsmouth	A	1-1		Newcastle	A	1-2		West Brom	A	0-2
Chelsea	H	0-1		Bolton	H	1-2		**Aston Villa**	H	2-0
Man City	H	1-0		Leeds	H	3-0		Tottenham	H	1-1
Tottenham	A	0-1		Charlton	A	1-3		Chelsea	A	1-1
Middlesbrough	A	1-2		**Fulham**	H	1-2		Portsmouth	H	0-0
Charlton	H	1-1		Chelsea	A	0-2		Man City	A	0-3
Lincoln	H	3-1		**Southampton**	H	2-1		Everton	A	1-1
Bolton	H	1-1		Man Utd	A	0-2		**Blackburn**	H	0-1
Newcastle	H	2-2		Liverpool	H	2-0		Norwich	A	0-1
Man Utd	H	0-0		Crystal Palace	A	0-2		**Arsenal**	H	2-1
Southampton	A	0-0								
Fulham	H	0-1								
Crystal Palace	H	0-1								
Liverpool	A	1-1								
Everton	H	0-1								
Blackburn	A	3-3								
Norwich	H	1-1								
Arsenal	A	0-3								
Aston Villa	H	0-0								
West Brom	H	4-0								
Middlesbrough	H	2-0								
Fulham	A	3-2								

STAR SIGNING

MIKAEL FORSSELL

Led the line brilliantly for the Blues in the 2003-04 season when on loan from Chelsea. He scored 42 per cent of the club's goals at a strike rate of one every 155 minutes. Spent most of last season injured at Chelsea but has now transferred permanently.

BLACKBURN ROVERS

BLACKBURN FACTS

MANAGER	CAPTAIN
MARK HUGHES	ANDY TODD

ADDITIONS TO SQUAD 2005-06

▼ PLAYERS IN	▼ FROM	▼ COST
Craig Bellamy	Newcastle	£5m
Shefki Kuqi	Ipswich	Free
Zurab Khizanifhvili	Rangers	Free

CLUB

Stadium: Ewood Park
Capacity: 31,367
Pitch Size: 115 yds by 72 yds
Website: www.rovers.co.uk

RECORDS

Record Home Attendance: 62,522 v Bolton, Mar.2, 1929 (FA Cup)
Record Victory: 11-0 v Rossendale (FA Cup) Oct.13, 1884
Record Defeat: 0-8 v Arsenal (league) Feb.25, 1933
Most League Goals: Simon Garner (168)
Most League Apps: Derek Fazackerley (596)
Most Capped Player: Hennning Berg, 52 (Norway)

HONOURS

Premiership: 1995
Division One: 1912, 1914
Division Two: 1939
Division Three: 1975
FA Cup: 1884, 1885, 1886, 1890, 1891, 1928
League Cup: 2002

CURRENT SQUAD RECORD 2004-05

	CLUB				INTERNATIONAL			POSITIONAL RANKING		OVERALL RANKING
	Games	Goals	Mins per goal	% played	Country	Games	Goals	Domestic	World	All positions
GOALKEEPERS		CONCEDED					CONCEDED			
BRAD FRIEDEL	38	43	79	100	USA	0	0	5	18	124
DEFENDERS		CONCEDED					CONCEDED			
ANDY TODD	26	16	143	67	England	0	0	7	24	69
LUCAS NEILL	36	41	76	92	Australia	0	0	24	78	308
RYAN NELSEN	15	9	150	39	N. Zealand	1	0	29	102	403
DOMINIC MATTEO	28	29	77	65	Scotland	0	0	51	227	776
JAMES McEVELEY	5	7	64	13	England	0	0	122	625	2019
LORENZO AMORUSO	6	7	64	13	Italy	0	0	124	643	2071
MICHAEL GRAY	9	20	40	23	England	0	0	126	649	2103
MIDFIELDERS		SCORED					SCORED			
BRETT EMERTON	37	4	771	90	Australia	2	2	38	214	577
STEVEN REID	28	2	980	57	Rep of Ire.	2	0	70	380	969
MORTEN GAMST PEDERSEN	19	4	384	45	Norway	0	0	80	423	1066
KERIMOGLU TUGAY	21	0	-	36	Turkey	0	0	97	498	1255
AARON MOKOENA	16	0	-	37	S. Africa	6	0	99	506	1286
GARRY FLITCROFT	19	0	-	42	England	0	0	107	553	1398
DAVID THOMPSON	24	0	-	34	England	0	0	118	590	1477
ROBBIE SAVAGE	9	0	-	21	Wales	4	0	142	742	1905
FORWARDS		SCORED					SCORED			
CRAIG BELLAMY *Newcastle	21	7	254	52	Wales	8	3	12	71	224
PAUL DICKOV	29	5	261	68	England	0	0	20	107	392
PAUL GALLAGHER	16	2	265	15	England	0	0	64	367	1650
MATTHEW JANSEN	7	2	150	8	England	0	0	73	435	1890
JAY BOTHROYD	11	1	488	14	England	0	0	81	477	2093
SHEFKI KUQI *Ipswich	43	19	178	82	Finland	-	-	-	-	-

KEY: Club stats are all for the 2004-05 season. Games = appearances in the league for club; Goals conceded = goals let in when the player is on the pitch; Goals scored = scored by the player; Mins per goal = number of minutes on average between each goal conceded or scored; % played = the percentage of the league season the player played; Domestic = player ranking by position in domestic league; World = player ranking by position in World; Overall Position = player ranking in world across all positions. * = player record from previous club

THE STARS OF LAST SEASON

TEAM OF THE SEASON

- G: Friedel
- D: Neill, Nelsen, Todd, Matteo
- M: Emerton, Ferguson, Reid, Pedersen
- F: Stead, Dickov

G STAR GOALKEEPER

BRAD FRIEDEL: A World Cup keeper with the USA whose experience, instinct and bravery put him in our World's Top 25 Keepers list.

Average goals per game conceded by club	1.13
Goals per game conceded when player on pitch	1.13
Points per game club won when player on pitch	1.11
Minutes played	3420	Clean sheets	15

D STAR DEFENDER

ANDY TODD: A strong and consistent centre-back in a team battling relegation, he was a surprise entry into our Top 25 Defenders list.

Goals per game conceded when player on pitch	0.61
Points per game club won when player on pitch	1.4
Goals scored by player	1
Minutes played	2294	Clean sheets	14

M STAR MIDFIELDER

BARRY FERGUSON: Highly rated by Graeme Souness who signed him, he didn't fit Mark Hughes' plans and rejoined Rangers.

Goals per game conceded when player on pitch	1.43
Goals per game club scored when player on pitch	0.95
Goals scored by player	2
Minutes played	1890	Assists	1

F STAR FORWARD

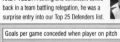

PAUL DICKOV: Nicknamed 'the Pest' for his ability to irritate the hell out of defenders and then pounce on their mistakes.

Average goals per game scored by club	0.84
Goals per game scored when player on pitch	1.03
% of club goals scored by player	28.1
Minutes played	2354	Assists	2

2004-05 SEASON REVIEW OF THE LEAGUE

■ Games won ■ Games lost ■ Games drawn — League position game by game

2004-05 RESULTS ROUND-UP

☐ Premiership ☐ League Cup ☐ FA Cup ☐ UEFA Cup ☐ Champions League

West Brom	H	1-1	**Charlton**	H	1-0	Liverpool	A	0-0
Southampton	A	2-3	Cardiff	A	1-1	**Arsenal**	H	0-1
Arsenal	A	0-3	Portsmouth	A	1-0	Man Utd	A	0-0
Man Utd	H	1-1	**Cardiff**	H	3-2	**Southampton**	H	3-0
Newcastle	A	0-3	Bolton	H	0-1	Arsenal	A	0-3
Portsmouth	H	1-0	Colchester	H	3-0	**Crystal Palace**	H	1-0
Bournemouth	H	3-3*	Chelsea	A	0-1	**Man City**	H	0-0
Charlton	A	0-1	Middlesbrough	A	0-1	West Brom	A	1-1
Aston Villa	H	2-2	**Norwich**	H	3-0	Birmingham	A	1-2
Middlesbrough	H	0-4	Burnley	A	0-0	Fulham	A	1-3
Chelsea	A	0-4	**Burnley**	H	2-1	Tottenham	A	0-0
Liverpool	H	2-2	Everton	A	1-0	*Lost on penalties
Norwich	A	1-1	**Leicester**	H	1-0	
Man City	H	1-1				
Birmingham	H	3-3				
Fulham	A	2-0				
Tottenham	H	0-1				
Crystal Palace	A	0-0				
Everton	H	0-0				
Newcastle	H	2-2				
Bolton	A	0-0				
Aston Villa	A	0-1				

STAR SIGNING

CRAIG BELLAMY

Blackburn were the lowest scorers in the Premiership last season. Bellamy and Ipswich striker Shefki Kuqi are Mark Hughes' response to that. The controversial Bellamy scored freely for both Newcastle and Celtic in a season disrupted by arguments.

BOLTON WANDERERS

BOLTON FACTS

MANAGER

SAM ALLARDYCE

CAPTAIN
JAY-JAY OKOCHA

ADDITIONS TO SQUAD 2005-06

▼ PLAYERS IN	▼ FROM	▼ COST
Jared Borgetti	Pachuca	£1m
El Hadji Diouf	Liverpool	*
Abdoulaye Faye	Lens	Loan
Ian Walker	Leicester	Free
Hidetoshi Nakata	Fiorentina	Loan

Fee Undisclosed

CLUB

Stadium: Reebok Stadium
Capacity: 28,723
Pitch Size: 114 yds by 74 yds
Website: www.bwfc.co.uk

RECORDS

Record Home Attendance: 69,912 v Man. City (FA Cup) Feb.18, 1933
Record Victory: 13-0 v Sheffield United (FA Cup) Feb.1, 1890
Record Defeat: 1-9 v Preston (FA Cup) Dec.10, 1887
Most League Goals: Nat Lofthouse (255)
Most League Apps: Eddie Hopkinson (519)
Most Capped Player: Mark Fish, 34 (South Africa)

HONOURS

Division One: *1997
Division Two: 1909, 1978
Division Three: 1909,
FA Cup: 1923, 1926, 1929, 1958

CURRENT SQUAD RECORD 2004-05

	CLUB				INTERNATIONAL			POSITIONAL RANKING		OVERALL RANKING
	Games	Goals	Mins per goal	% played	Country	Games	Goals	Domestic	World	All positions
GOALKEEPERS		CONCEDED				CONCEDED				
JUSSI JAASKELAINEN	36	40	80	94	Finland	2	8	**7**	**22**	140
DEFENDERS		CONCEDED				CONCEDED				
RICARDO GARDNER	33	29	92	78	Jamaica	6	6	**20**	**55**	229
BRUNO N'GOTTY	37	41	79	95	France	0	0	**21**	**56**	230
NICKY HUNT	29	31	77	70	England	0	0	**36**	**157**	549
TAL BEN HAIM	21	19	92	51	Israel	6	6	**49**	**217**	733
RADHI JAIDI	27	28	65	53	Tunisia	5	4	**74**	**361**	1152
MIDFIELDERS		SCORED				SCORED				
GARY SPEED	38	1	3337	97	Wales	5	1	**18**	**71**	205
KEVIN NOLAN	36	4	624	73	England	0	0	**30**	**147**	398
STELIOS GIANNAKOPOULOS	34	7	336	68	Greece	8	2	**31**	**158**	426
JAY-JAY OKOCHA	31	6	402	70	Nigeria	5	1	**33**	**167**	450
IVAN CAMPO	27	0	-	50	Spain	0	0	**64**	**346**	866
HIDETOSHI NAKATA *Fiorentina*	20	0	-	34	Japan	3	0	**101**	**535**	1356
ABDOULAYE FAYE *Lens*	26	0	-	60	Senegal	5	1	**117**	**764**	1951
FORWARDS		SCORED				SCORED				
EL HADJI DIOUF	27	9	227	59	Senegal	3	2	**17**	**89**	318
KEVIN DAVIES	35	8	354	82	England	0	0	**19**	**101**	366
HENRIK PEDERSEN	27	6	226	39	Denmark	3	0	**43**	**204**	922

KEY: Club stats are all for the 2004-05 season. Games = appearances in the league for club; Goals conceded = goals let in when the player is on the pitch; Goals scored = scored by the player; Mins per goal = number of minutes on average between each goal conceded or scored; % played = the percentage of the league season the player played; Domestic = player ranking by position in domestic league; World = player ranking by position in World; Overall Position = player ranking in world across all positions. * = player record from previous club

THE STARS OF LAST SEASON

TEAM OF THE SEASON

G
Jaaskelainen

D Hunt | D Ben Haim | D N'Gotty | D Gardner

M Nolan | M Okocha | M Speed | M Stelios

F Diouf | F Davies

G STAR GOALKEEPER

JUSSI JAASKELAINEN: Won rave reviews for his consistent and occasionally inspired style and was linked with Arsenal and Man United.

Average goals per game conceded by club	1.16
Goals per game conceded when player on pitch	1.11
Points per game club won when player on pitch	1.58
Minutes played	3236	Clean sheets	8

D STAR DEFENDER

RICARDO GARDNER: Bolton's top defender, the Jamaican adds speed on the left, both in defence and supporting the attack.

Goals per game conceded when player on pitch	0.88
Points per game club won when player on pitch	1.72
Goals scored by player	0
Minutes played	2678	Clean sheets	8

M STAR MIDFIELDER

GARY SPEED: A model pro leading Sam Allardyce to claim he'd win the Champions League if he had ten more like him.

Goals per game conceded when player on pitch	1.15
Goals per game club scored when player on pitch	1.23
Goals scored by player	1
Minutes played	3337	Assists	6

F STAR FORWARD

EL HADJI DIOUF: Hasn't won many friends because of his fiery temper but he has won respect and the Bolton top scorer's crown.

Average goals per game scored by club	1.29
Goals per game scored when player on pitch	1.29
% of club goals scored by player	18.4
Minutes played	2043	Assists	4

2004-05 SEASON REVIEW OF THE LEAGUE

■ Games won ■ Games lost ■ Games drawn — League position game by game

% of possible points won per month

Aug Sep Oct Nov Dec Jan Feb Mar Apr May

2004-05 RESULTS ROUND-UP

□ Premiership □ League Cup □ FA Cup □ UEFA Cup □ Champions League

Charlton	H	4-1	West Brom	H	1-1	Man City	A	1-0
Fulham	A	0-2	Birmingham	A	2-1	Arsenal	H	0-1
Southampton	A	2-1	Ipswich	A	3-1	Norwich	A	1-0
Liverpool	H	1-0	**Arsenal**	H	1-0	Liverpool	A	0-1
Man Utd	H	2-2	Blackburn	A	1-0	Fulham	H	1-0
Arsenal	A	2-2	Oldham	A	1-0	Charlton	A	2-1
Yeovil	H	3-0	**Tottenham**	H	3-1	Southampton	A	1-1
Birmingham	H	1-1	Crystal Palace	A	1-0	Aston Villa	A	1-1
West Brom	A	1-2	**Middlesbrough**	H	0-0	**Chelsea**	H	0-2
Crystal Palace	H	3-2	Fulham	H	1-0	Portsmouth	A	1-1
Tottenham	A	2-1	Newcastle	A	1-2	**Everton**	H	3-2
Tottenham	H	3-4						
Newcastle	A	2-1						
Middlesbrough	H	1-1						
Aston Villa	H	1-2						
Chelsea	A	2-2						
Portsmouth	H	0-1						
Everton	A	2-3						
Norwich	A	2-3						
Man City	H	0-1						
Man Utd	H	0-1						
Blackburn	H	0-1						

STAR SIGNING

HIDETOSHI NAKATA

The Japanese international made 20 appearances for Fiorentina in a subdued season in Italy's Serie A. He is a national hero back in Japan but his career has slipped in Italy. Sam Allardyce is hoping to rediscover the 28-year-old's best form this season.

CHARLTON ATHLETIC

CHARLTON FACTS

MANAGER

ALAN CURBISHLEY

CAPTAIN

MATT HOLLAND

ADDITIONS TO SQUAD 2005-06

▼ PLAYERS IN	▼ FROM	▼ COST
Darren Bent	Ipswich	£2.5m
Darren Ambrose	Newcastle	£700,000
Alexei Smertin	Chelsea	Loan
Jonathon Spector	Man. United	Loan
Gonzalo Sorondo	Inter Milan	Loan
Chris Powell	West Ham	Free
Thomas Myhre	Sunderland	Free

CLUB

Stadium: The Valley

Capacity: 27,116

Pitch Size: 111 yds by 73 yds

Website: www.cafc.co.uk

RECORDS

Record Home Attendance: 75,031 v Aston Villa (FA Cup) Feb.12, 1938

Record Victory: 8-1 v Middlesbrough (league) Sept.12, 1953

Record Defeat: 1-11 v Aston Villa (league) Nov.14, 1959

Most League Goals: Stuart Leary (153)

Most League Apps: Sam Bartram (583)

Most Capped Player: John Robinson, 30 (Wales)

HONOURS

Division One: 2000

Division Three (South): 1929, 1935

FA Cup: 1947

CURRENT SQUAD RECORD 2004-05

	CLUB				INTERNATIONAL			POSITIONAL RANKING		OVERALL RANKING
	Games	Goals	Mins per goal	% played	Country	Games	Goals	Domestic	World	All positions
GOALKEEPERS				CONCEDED			CONCEDED			
DEAN KIELY	36	53	61	94	Rep of Ire.	0	0	12	66	567
STEPHAN ANDERSEN	2	3	60	5	Denmark	1	2	-	-	-
DEFENDERS				CONCEDED			CONCEDED			
HERMANN HREIDARSSON	34	46	64	86	Iceland	5	14	43	203	700
LUKE YOUNG	36	56	57	94	England	0	0	52	228	777
TALAL EL KARKOURI	32	36	69	73	Morocco	5	4	56	244	824
JONATHAN FORTUNE	31	43	60	75	England	0	0	70	317	1018
CHRIS PERRY	19	23	65	43	England	0	0	86	452	1441
CHRIS POWELL *West Ham	36	0	-	76	England	0	0	-	-	-
MIDFIELDERS				SCORED			SCORED			
DANNY MURPHY	38	3	1080	94	England	0	0	41	228	602
ALEXEI SMERTIN *Chelsea	16	0	-	22	Russia	6	0	44	238	638
MATT HOLLAND	32	3	896	78	England	0	0	54	304	783
RADOSTIN KISHISHEV	31	0	-	64	Bulgaria	4	0	71	384	979
JEROME THOMAS	24	3	567	49	England	0	0	73	401	1020
DENNIS ROMMEDAHL	26	2	828	48	Denmark	7	1	109	558	1408
BRYAN HUGHES	17	1	964	28	Wales	0	0	134	690	1761
DARREN AMBROSE *Newcastle	12	3	247	21	England	0	0	144	749	1915
FORWARDS				SCORED			SCORED			
SHAUN BARTLETT	25	6	340	59	S. Africa	3	1	35	182	813
JONATAN JOHANSSON	26	4	363	42	Finland	7	1	56	324	1489
JASON EUELL	26	2	475	27	England	0	0	70	419	1830
KEVIN LISBIE	17	1	1134	33	Jamaica	0	0	75	443	1924
DARREN BENT *Ipswich	45	20	197	82	England	1	0	13	-	-

*Stephan Andersen did not play enough games to receive a ranking. KEY: Club stats are all for the 2004-05 season. Games = appearances in the league for club; Goals conceded = goals let in when the player is on the pitch; Goals scored = scored by the player; Mins per goal = number of minutes on average between each goal conceded or scored; % played = the percentage of the league season the player played; Domestic = player ranking by position in domestic league; World = player ranking by position in World; Overall Position = player ranking in world across all positions. * = player record from previous club*

THE STARS OF LAST SEASON

TEAM OF THE SEASON

G Kiely

D Fortune / D El Karkouri / D Fortune / D Hreidarsson

M Thomas / M Murphy / M Holland / M Kishishev

F Bartlett / F Johansson

G STAR GOALKEEPER

DEAN KIELY: When Kiely has 'one of his days' it doesn't matter what the opposition throw at him – he'll keep them out.

Average goals per game conceded by club	1.53
Goals per game conceded when player on pitch	1.47
Points per game club won when player on pitch	1.28
Minutes played 3240	Clean sheets 12

D STAR DEFENDER

HERMANN HREIDARSSON: The big Icelandic fullback is powerful on the flanks and a danger when he gets into the opposition box.

Goals per game conceded when player on pitch	1.35
Points per game club won when player on pitch	1.36
Goals scored by player	1
Minutes played 2959	Clean sheets 12

M STAR MIDFIELDER

DANNY MURPHY: Taken over Matt Holland's crown as Charlton's 'Mr Reliable'. Always likely to score or to set up a colleague.

Goals per game conceded when player on pitch	1.45
Goals per game club scored when player on pitch	1.02
Goals scored by player	3
Minutes played 3241	Assists 6

F STAR FORWARD

SHAUN BARTLETT: Charlton's leading scorer despite netting only six goals last season but the South African leads the line selflessly.

Average goals per game scored by club	1.11
Goals per game scored when player on pitch	1.25
% of club goals scored by player	14.3
Minutes played 2041	Assists 3

2004-05 SEASON REVIEW OF THE LEAGUE

■ Games won ■ Games lost ■ Games drawn — League position game by game

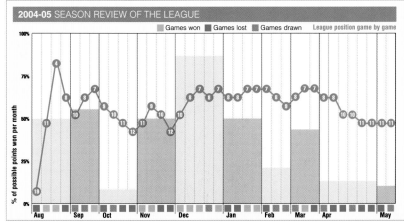

% of possible points won per month

100% / 75% / 50% / 25% / 0%

Aug Sep Oct Nov Dec Jan Feb Mar Apr May

2004-05 RESULTS ROUND-UP

□ Premiership □ League Cup □ FA Cup □ UEFA Cup □ Champions League

Bolton	A	1-4	Arsenal	H	1-3	Tottenham	H	2-0
Portsmouth	H	2-1	Blackburn	A	0-1	**West Brom**	H	1-4
Aston Villa	H	3-0	Rochdale	A	4-1	**Man City**	H	2-2
Man City	A	0-4	**Birmingham**	H	3-1	Portsmouth	A	2-4
Southampton	H	0-0	Everton	A	1-0	**Bolton**	H	1-2
Birmingham	A	1-1	**Yeovil**	H	3-2	Aston Villa	A	0-0
Grimsby	A	2-0	**Liverpool**	H	1-2	Norwich	A	0-1
Blackburn	H	1-0	Newcastle	A	1-1	**Man Utd**	H	0-4
Arsenal	H	0-4	**Leicester**	H	1-2	Chelsea	A	0-1
Newcastle	H	1-1	Middlesbrough	A	2-2	**Crystal Palace**	H	2-2
Liverpool	A	0-2	Fulham	A	0-0			
Crystal Palace	H	1-2						
Middlesbrough	H	1-2						
Tottenham	A	3-2						
Norwich	H	4-0						
Man Utd	A	0-2						
Chelsea	H	0-1						
Crystal Palace	A	1-0						
West Brom	H	1-0						
Fulham	H	2-1						
Southampton	A	2-0						
Everton	H	2-0						

STAR SIGNING

DARREN BENT

Not to be confused with Everton's Marcus Bent who also played at Ipswich, Darren Bent has made an impressive start at Charlton, scoring twice on his debut. He hit 20 goals in 45 appearances, taking Ipswich into the play-offs last season.

CHELSEA FACTS

MANAGER	CAPTAIN
JOSÉ MOURINHO	JOHN TERRY

ADDITIONS TO SQUAD 2005-06

▼ PLAYERS IN	▼ FROM	▼ COST
Michael Essien	Lyon	£24.4m
Shaun Wright-Phillips	Man City	£21m
Asier del Horno	Athletic Bilbao	£8m
Lassana Diarra	Le Havre	*
Scott Sinclair	Bristol Rovers	*

* Fee Undisclosed

CLUB

Stadium: Stamford Bridge
Capacity: 42,522
Pitch Size: 113 yds by 74 yds
Website: www.chelseafc.com

RECORDS

Record Home Attendance: 82,905, v Arsenal (league) Oct.12, 1935
Record Victory: 13-0 v Jeunesse Hautcharage (ECWC) Sept. 29, 1971
Record Defeat: 1-8 v Wolves (league) Sept.26
Most League Goals: Bobby Tambling (164)
Most League Apps: Ron Harris (655)
Most Capped Player: Marcel Desailly, 48 (France)

HONOURS

League Champions: 1955, 2005
FA Cup: 1970, 1997, 2000
League Cup: 1965, 1998, 2005
European Cup Winners Cup: 1971, 1998

CURRENT SQUAD RECORD 2004-05

	CLUB				INTERNATIONAL			POSITIONAL RANKING		OVERALL RANKING
	Games	Goals	Mins per goal	% played	Country	Games	Goals	Domestic	World	All positions
GOALKEEPERS			CONCEDED				CONCEDED			
PETR CECH	35	13	242	92	Czech Rep.	8	6	1	1	1
CARLO CUDICINI	3	2	130	7	Italy	0	0	25	124	1756
DEFENDERS			CONCEDED				CONCEDED			
JOHN TERRY	36	13	249	94	England	8	4	1	1	2
PAULO FERREIRA	29	10	261	76	Portugal	8	6	2	2	3
WILLIAM GALLAS	28	10	244	71	France	10	4	3	3	4
RICARDO CARVALHO	25	13	151	57	Portugal	6	4	8	25	79
GLEN JOHNSON	17	8	144	33	England	1	0	34	136	481
WAYNE BRIDGE	15	1	1149	33	England	3	4	38	164	582
ASIER DEL HORNO *Bilbao	29	31	69	62	Spain	6	0	59	304	991
ROBERT HUTH	10	5	108	15	Germany	6	2	95	492	1574
MIDFIELDERS			SCORED				SCORED			
FRANK LAMPARD	38	13	262	99	England	9	3	1	1	6
CLAUDE MAKELELE	36	1	3238	94	France	1	0	2	2	10
DAMIEN DUFF	30	6	399	70	Rep of Ire.	10	0	3	9	40
ARJEN ROBBEN	18	7	179	36	Holland	3	2	9	39	134
MICHAEL ESSIEN *Lyon	37	4	799	93	Ghana	0	0	1	33	120
JOE COLE	28	8	203	47	England	8	1	10	40	135
S. WRIGHT-PHILLIPS *Man.City	34	10	299	87	England	7	1	13	48	159
GEREMI NITJAP	13	0	-	17	Cameroon	0	0	82	430	1090
FORWARDS			SCORED				SCORED			
EIDUR GUDJOHNSEN	22	12	207	72	Iceland	6	5	3	21	56
DIDIER DROGBA	12	10	162	47	Ivory Coast	2	3	10	62	174
HERMAN CRESPO	33	10	201	59	Argentina	2	3	16	62	230

KEY: Club stats are all for the 2004-05 season. Games = appearances in the league for club; Goals conceded = goals let in when the player is on the pitch; Goals scored = scored by the player; Mins per goal = number of minutes on average between each goal conceded or scored; % played = the percentage of the league season the player played; Domestic = player ranking by position in domestic league; World = player ranking by position in World; Overall Position = player ranking in world across all positions. * = player record from previous club

THE STARS OF LAST SEASON

TEAM OF THE SEASON

- G Cech
- D Ferreira
- D Terry
- D Carvalho
- D Gallas
- M Robben
- M Lampard
- M Makelele
- M Duff
- F Drogba
- F Gudjohnsen

G STAR GOALKEEPER

PETR CECH: The best player in world football, Cech saved an astonishing 9.9 shots-on-target for every goal he conceded last season.

Average goals per game conceded by club	0.39
Goals per game conceded when player on pitch	0.37
Points per game club won when player on pitch	2.51
Minutes played	3150	Clean sheets	24

D STAR DEFENDER

JOHN TERRY: A clenched fist of determination in the middle of Chelsea's formidable defence and now England's first choice too.

Goals per game conceded when player on pitch	0.36
Points per game club won when player on pitch	2.53
Goals scored by player	3
Minutes played	3240	Clean sheets	25

M STAR MIDFIELDER

FRANK LAMPARD: A record of 19 goals from midfield and 18 assists helped make Lampard the best midfielder anywhere last season.

Goals per game conceded when player on pitch	0.40
Goals per game club scored when player on pitch	1.91
Goals scored by player	13
Minutes played	3412	Assists	18

F STAR FORWARD

EIDUR GUDJOHNSEN: An intelligent and imaginative striker but 12 goals was a poor return for a table-topping side.

Average goals per game scored by club	1.89
Goals per game scored when player on pitch	1.91
% of club goals scored by player	16.7
Minutes played	2494	Assists	8

2004-05 SEASON REVIEW OF THE LEAGUE

■ Games won ■ Games lost ■ Games drawn ● League position game by game

y-axis: % of possible points won per month (0% – 100%)
x-axis: Aug Sep Oct Nov Dec Jan Feb Mar Apr May

2004-05 RESULTS ROUND-UP

☐ Premiership ☐ League Cup ☐ FA Cup ☐ UEFA Cup ☐ Champions League

Man Utd	H	1-0	Fulham	A	2-1	**Barcelona**	H	4-2
Birmingham	A	1-0	Newcastle	H	4-0	**West Brom**	H	1-0
Crystal Palace	A	2-0	Porto	A	1-2	**Crystal Palace**	H	4-1
Southampton	H	2-1	Arsenal	A	2-2	Southampton	A	3-1
Aston Villa	A	0-0	**Norwich**	H	4-0	**Bayern Munich**	H	4-2
Paris SG	A	3-0	**Aston Villa**	H	1-0	**Birmingham**	H	1-1
Tottenham	H	0-0	Portsmouth	A	2-0	Bayern Munich	A	2-3
Middlesbrough	A	1-0	Liverpool	H	1-0	**Arsenal**	H	0-0
Porto	H	3-1	Middlesbrough	H	2-0	Fulham	H	3-1
Liverpool	H	1-0	**Scunthorpe**	H	3-1	**Liverpool**	H	0-0
Man City	A	0-1	**Man Utd**	H	0-0	Bolton	A	2-0
CSKA Moscow	H	2-0	Tottenham	A	2-0	Liverpool	A	0-1
Blackburn	H	4-0	Portsmouth	H	3-0	**Charlton**	H	1-0
West Ham	H	1-0	Man Utd	A	2-1	Man Utd	A	3-1
West Brom	A	4-1	**Birmingham**	H	2-0	Newcastle	A	1-1
CSKA Moscow	A	1-0	Blackburn	A	1-0			
Everton	H	1-0	**Man City**	H	0-0			
Newcastle	A	2-0	Everton	A	1-0			
Fulham	A	4-1	Newcastle	A	0-1			
Bolton	H	2-2	**Barcelona**	H	1-2			
Paris SG	H	0-0	Liverpool	A	3-2			
Charlton	A	4-0	Norwich	A	3-1			

STAR SIGNING

MICHAEL ESSIEN

The on-off saga surrounding Michael Essien's transfer from Lyon used up a lot of newsprint in the summer. The Ghanaian midfield player is viewed as 'the new Vieira' in France. At £24.4 million he is Chelsea's record signing.

EVERTON

EVERTON FACTS

MANAGER	CAPTAIN
DAVID MOYES	DAVID WEIR

ADDITIONS TO SQUAD 2005-06

▼ PLAYERS IN	▼ FROM	▼ COST
Per Koldrup	Udinese	£5m
Simon Davies	Tottenham	£4m
Phil Neville	Man. United	£3.5m
Mikel Arteta	Real Sociedad	£2m
Andy van der Meyde	Inter Milan	£1.8
Nuno Valente	Porto	£1.5m
John Ruddy	Cambridge	£250,000

CLUB

Stadium: Goodison Park

Capacity: 40,170

Pitch Size: 110 yds by 70 yds

Website: www.evertonfc.com

RECORDS

Record Home Attendance: 78,299 v Liverpool (league) Sept.18, 1948

Record Victory: 11-2 v Derby County (FA Cup) Jan.18, 1890

Record Defeat: 4-10 v Tottenham (League) Oct.11, 1958

Most League Goals: William 'Dixie' Dean (349)

Most League Apps: Neville Southall (578)

Most Capped Player: Neville Southall, 92 (Wales)

HONOURS

Division One: 1891, 1915, 1928, 1932, 1939, 1963, 1970, 1985, 1987

Division Two: 1931

FA Cup: 1906, 1933, 1966, 1984, 1995

European Cup Winners Cup: 1985

TEAM OF THE SEASON

G Martyn

D Hibbert | D Stubbs | D Weir | D Pistone

M Carsley | M Cahill | M Gravesen | M Kilbane

F Bent | F Ferguson

(G) STAR GOALKEEPER

NIGEL MARTYN: Gets better with age and no keeper did more to paper over the cracks of his back four than Martyn did.

Average goals per game conceded by club	1.21
Goals per game conceded when player on pitch	0.81
Points per game club won when player on pitch	1.84

Minutes played	2834	Clean sheets	13

(D) STAR DEFENDER

TONY HIBBERT: One of the quiet heroes in this hard-working Everton team who puts in every ounce of effort.

Goals per game conceded when player on pitch	1.14
Points per game club won when player on pitch	1.74
Goals scored by player	0

Minutes played	3184	Clean sheets	13

(M) STAR MIDFIELDER

KEVIN KILBANE: Nicknamed 'Zinedine Kilbane', the Irish left-midfielder has been a huge hit with the Goodison crowd.

Goals per game conceded when player on pitch	1.23
Goals per game club scored when player on pitch	1.1
Goals scored by player	1

Minutes played	3215	Assists	3

(F) STAR FORWARD

MARCUS BENT: A mobile forward with pace and the ability to strike a wonder goal from nowhere as he did against Saints.

Average goals per game scored by club	1.18
Goals per game scored when player on pitch	1.3
% of club goals scored by player	13.3

Minutes played	2659	Assists	3

CURRENT SQUAD RECORD 2004-05

	CLUB				INTERNATIONAL			POSITIONAL RANKING		OVERALL RANKING
	Games	Goals	Mins per goal	% played	Country	Games	Goals	Domestic	World	All positions
GOALKEEPERS			CONCEDED				CONCEDED			
NIGEL MARTYN	31	26	109	82	England	0	0	3	8	35
RICHARD WRIGHT	7	20	29	17	England	0	0	30	159	2194
DEFENDERS			CONCEDED				CONCEDED			
TONY HIBBERT	36	41	77	93	England	0	0	13	35	130
DAVID WEIR	34	39	77	88	Scotland	2	2	18	46	182
ALESSANDRO PISTONE	33	39	70	80	Italy	0	0	26	99	388
PER KROLDRUP *Udinese	26	24	86	60	Denmark	6	0	32	187	649
JOSEPH YOBO	27	35	50	51	Nigeria	4	2	81	409	1294
GARY NAYSMITH	11	8	58	13	Scotland	5	7	123	626	2020
MIDFIELDERS			SCORED				SCORED			
KEVIN KILBANE	38	1	3215	94	Rep of Ire.	10	0	16	60	188
LEE CARSLEY	36	4	757	88	Rep of Ire.	0	0	17	63	192
TIM CAHILL	33	11	245	78	Australia	2	4	21	89	254
LEON OSMAN	29	6	359	63	England	0	0	36	179	497
SIMON DAVIES *Tottenham	16	0	-	47	Wales	5	0	74	406	1031
PHIL NEVILLE *Man.Utd	19	0	-	31	England	3	0	92	478	1212
MIKEL ARTETA	12	1	808	23	Spain	0	0	128	642	1632
FORWARDS			SCORED				SCORED			
MARCUS BENT	37	6	443	77	England	0	0	15	86	312
DUNCAN FERGUSON	35	5	244	35	Scotland	0	0	32	172	729
JAMES BEATTIE	11	1	567	16	England	0	0	68	409	1800
JAMES MCFADDEN	23	1	768	22	Scotland	5	2	72	434	1884

KEY: Club stats are all for the 2004-05 season. Games = appearances in the league for club; Goals conceded = goals let in when the player is on the pitch; Goals scored = scored by the player; Mins per goal = number of minutes on average between each goal conceded or scored; % played = the percentage of the league season the player played; Domestic = player ranking by position in domestic league; World = player ranking by position in World; Overall Position = player ranking in world across all positions. * = player record from previous club

2004-05 SEASON REVIEW OF THE LEAGUE

- Games won ■ Games lost ■ Games drawn — League position game by game

% of possible points won per month

Aug Sep Oct Nov Dec Jan Feb Mar Apr May

2004-05 RESULTS ROUND-UP

□ Premiership □ League Cup □ FA Cup □ UEFA Cup □ Champions League

Arsenal	H	1-4	Charlton	A	0-2	**Blackburn**	H	0-1
Crystal Palace	A	3-1	Tottenham	A	2-5	Liverpool	A	1-2
West Brom	H	2-1	**Portsmouth**	H	2-1	West Brom	A	0-1
Man Utd	H	0-0	Plymouth	A	3-1	**Crystal Palace**	H	4-0
Man City	A	1-0	Middlesbrough	A	1-1	**Man Utd**	H	1-0
Middlesbrough	H	1-0	**Charlton**	H	0-1	Birmingham	A	1-1
Bristol City	A	2-2*	**Sunderland**	H	3-0	Fulham	H	0-2
Portsmouth	A	1-0	Norwich	H	1-0	**Newcastle**	H	2-0
Tottenham	H	0-1	Southampton	A	2-2	Arsenal	A	0-7
Southampton	H	1-0	**Chelsea**	H	0-1	Bolton	A	2-3
Norwich	A	3-2	Man Utd	H	0-2	
Preston	H	2-0	Aston Villa	A	3-1	*Won on penalties
Aston Villa	H	1-0	
Chelsea	A	0-1	
Arsenal	A	1-3	
Birmingham	A	1-0	
Fulham	H	1-0	
Newcastle	A	1-1	
Bolton	H	3-2	
Liverpool	H	1-0	
Blackburn	A	0-0	
Man City	H	2-1	

STAR SIGNING

PER KROLDRUP

With the reliable Alan Stubbs leaving the club, David Moyes needed to find a class act at centre-half. He turned to Danish international Per Kroldrup, who took Italian side Udinese to fourth spot and a Champions League place last season.

FULHAM

FULHAM FACTS

MANAGER	CAPTAIN
CHRIS COLEMAN	LUIS BOA MORTE

ADDITIONS TO SQUAD 2005-06

▼ PLAYERS IN	▼ FROM	▼ COST
Heider Helguson	Watford	£1.3m
Jaroslav Drobny	Panionios	*
Niclas Jensen	Borussia Dortmund	*
Ahmed Erlich	Busan Icons	*
Tony Warner	Cardiff	Loan

* Fee Undisclosed

CLUB

Stadium: Craven Cottage
Capacity: 22,000
Pitch Size: 110 yds by 75 yds
Website: www.fulhamfc.com

RECORDS

Record Home Attendance: 49,335 v Millwall (league) Oct.8, 1938
Record Victory: 10-1 v Ipswich (league) Dec.26, 1963
Record Defeat: 0-10 v Liverpool (League Cup) Sept.23, 1986
Most League Goals: Gordon Davies (159)
Most League Apps: Johnny Haynes (594)
Most Capped Player: Johnny Haynes, 56 (England)

HONOURS

Division One: 2001
Division Two: 1949, 1999
Division Three South: 1932

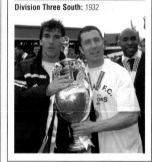

CURRENT SQUAD RECORD 2004-05

	CLUB				INTERNATIONAL			POSITIONAL RANKING		OVERALL RANKING
	Games	Goals	Mins per goal	% played	Country	Games	Goals	Domestic	World	All positions
GOALKEEPERS		CONCEDED					CONCEDED			
MARK CROSSLEY	6	9	53	13	Wales	5	0	28	152	2091
TONY WARNER *Cardiff	26	31	73	55	England	0	0	-	-	-
DEFENDERS		CONCEDED					CONCEDED			
ZATYIAH KNIGHT	35	56	56	91	England	0	0	57	253	858
MORITZ VOLZ	31	48	57	81	Germany	1	0	61	267	900
CARLOS BOCANEGRA	28	44	54	69	USA	10	5	78	380	1213
ZESHAN REHMAN	17	25	58	42	England	0	0	89	465	1495
ALAIN GOMA	16	23	61	41	France	0	0	92	484	1544
LIAM ROSENIOR	17	26	55	41	England	0	0	98	503	1600
IAN PEARCE	11	12	65	22	England	0	0	119	589	1887
ADAM GREEN	4	7	51	10	England	0	0	133	688	2233
MIDFIELDERS		SCORED					SCORED			
LUIS BOA MORTE	31	8	325	76	Portugal	7	0	35	176	482
PAPA BOUBA DIOP	29	6	418	73	Senegal	4	1	45	245	648
MARK PEMBRIDGE	28	0	-	68	Wales	5	0	59	332	835
STEED MALBRANQUE	19	6	314	55	France	0	0	61	336	845
NICLAS JENSEN *Dortmund	16	1	1238	36	Denmark	8	0	86	585	1465
SYLVAIN LEGWINSKI	15	1	1127	32	France	0	0	132	676	1722
CLAUS JENSEN	12	0	-	22	Denmark	4	1	148	771	1968
FORWARDS		SCORED					SCORED			
TOMASZ RADZINSKI	35	6	368	64	Canada	4	0	29	158	653
BRIAN MCBRIDE	31	6	255	44	USA	10	3	39	190	847
COLLINS JOHN	27	4	296	34	Holland	2	0	55	305	1400

KEY: *Club stats are all for the 2004-05 season. Games = appearances in the league for club; Goals conceded = goals let in when the player is on the pitch; Goals scored = scored by the player; Mins per goal = number of minutes on average between each goal conceded or scored; % played = the percentage of the league season the player played; Domestic = player ranking by position in domestic league; World = player ranking by position in World; Overall Position = player ranking in world across all positions. * = player record from previous club*

2004-05 SEASON REVIEW OF THE LEAGUE

■ Games won ■ Games lost ■ Games drawn — League position game by game

% of possible points won per month

100% / 75% / 50% / 25% / 0%

Aug Sep Oct Nov Dec Jan Feb Mar Apr May

2004-05 RESULTS ROUND-UP

□ Premiership □ League Cup □ FA Cup □ UEFA Cup □ Champions League

Man City	A	1-1	Arsenal	A	0-2	Tottenham	A	0-2
Bolton	H	2-0	Birmingham	H	2-3	**Charlton**	H	0-0
Middlesbrough	H	0-2	**Crystal Palace**	H	3-1	Man Utd	H	0-1
Portsmouth	A	3-4	Southampton	A	3-3	**Portsmouth**	H	3-1
Arsenal	H	0-3	Watford	A	1-1	Bolton	A	1-3
West Brom	A	4-1	**West Brom**	H	1-0	**Man City**	H	1-1
Boston	A	4-1	Watford	H	2-0	Middlesbrough	A	1-3
Southampton	H	1-0	Birmingham	A	2-1	Chelsea	A	1-3
Crystal Palace	A	0-2	Derby	H	1-1	**Everton**	H	1-1
Liverpool	H	2-4	**Aston Villa**	H	1-1	Newcastle	A	1-3
Aston Villa	A	0-2	Liverpool	A	1-3	Blackburn	A	3-1
Birmingham	H	1-0	**Derby**	H	4-2	Norwich	H	6-0
Tottenham	H	2-0	Bolton	A	0-1			
Newcastle	A	4-1						
Nottm Forest	A	4-2						
Chelsea	H	1-4						
Everton	A	0-1						
Blackburn	H	0-2						
Chelsea	H	1-0						
Norwich	A	1-0						
Man Utd	H	1-1						
Charlton	A	1-2						

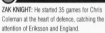

LIVERPOOL

Premiership position 04-05 **5th**
FA Cup **Round 3**
Coca-Cola Cup **Runners Up**
Champions League **Winners**

LIVERPOOL FACTS

MANAGER	CAPTAIN
RAFAEL BENITEZ	STEVEN GERRARD

ADDITIONS TO SQUAD 2005-06

▼ PLAYERS IN	▼ FROM	▼ COST
Peter Crouch	Southampton	£7m
Jose Reina	Villarreal	£6m
Mohamed Sissoko	Valencia	£5m
Boudewijn Zendon	Middlesbrough	Free
Mark Gonzalez	Albacete	*
Antwi Godwin	Real Zaragoza	*
Antonio Barragan	Seville	*

* Fee Undisclosed

CLUB

Stadium: Anfield
Capacity: 45,362
Pitch Size: 111 yds by 74 yds
Website: www.liverpoolfc.tv

RECORDS

Record Home Attendance: 61,905 v Wolves (FA Cup) Feb.2, 1952
Record Victory: 11-0 v Stromgodset (ECWC) Sept.17, 1974
Record Defeat: 1-9 v Birmingham City (league) Dec.11, 1954
Most League Goals: Roger Hunt (245)
Most League Apps: Ian Callaghan (640)
Most Capped Player: Ian Rush, 67 (Wales)

HONOURS

Division One: 1901, 1906, 1922, 1923, 1947, 1964, 1966, 1973, 1976, 1977, 1979, 1980, 1982, 1983, 1984, 1986, 1988, 1990
Division Two: 1894, 1896, 1905, 1962
FA Cup: 1965, 1974, 1986, 1989, 1992, 2001
League Cup: 1981, 1982, 1983, 1984, 1995, 2001, 2003
European Cup: 1977, 1978, 1981, 1984, 2005
UEFA Cup: 1973, 1976, 2001
European Cup Winners Cup: 1977, 2001

CURRENT SQUAD RECORD 2004-05

	CLUB				INTERNATIONAL			POSITIONAL RANKING		OVERALL RANKING
	Games	Goals	Mins per goal	% played	Country	Games	Goals	Domestic	World	All positions
GOALKEEPERS		CONCEDED				CONCEDED				
JOSE REINA *Villarreal	38	37	92	100	Spain	1	0	3	14	73
JERZY DUDEK	24	25	86	63	Poland	0	0	14	68	629
SCOTT CARSON	4	3	120	10	England	0	0	26	133	1855
DEFENDERS		CONCEDED				CONCEDED				
JAMIE CARRAGHER	38	41	83	100	England	7	1	23	65	257
STEVE FINNAN	33	30	84	74	England	0	0	35	144	498
SAMI HYYPIA	32	36	77	81	Finland	7	15	39	165	583
DJIMI TRAORE	18	25	71	51	France	0	0	75	365	1158
STEPHEN WARNOCK	19	8	100	23	England	0	0	93	487	1554
MIGUEL JOSEMI	15	18	62	32	Spain	0	0	105	547	1730
MIDFIELDERS		SCORED				SCORED				
BOUDEWIJN ZENDEN *Mboro	36	5	611	89	Holland	1	0	14	50	164
JOHN ARNE RIISE	37	6	495	86	Norway	6	0	24	96	263
XABI ALONSO	24	2	903	52	Spain	5	0	48	276	732
STEVEN GERRARD	30	7	353	72	England	6	2	52	290	757
DIETMAR HAMANN	30	0	-	59	Germany	0	0	53	294	765
FORWARDS		SCORED				SCORED				
HARRY KEWELL	18	1	1403	41	Australia	0	0	90	464	1182
PETER CROUCH *Southampton	28	12	156	54	England	0	0	14	79	278
JAVIER LUIS GARCIA	29	8	292	68	Spain	0	0	24	128	507
DJIBRIL CISSE	16	4	233	27	France	6	2	47	245	1148
NEIL MELLOR	9	2	238	13	England	0	0	66	382	1699
F. SINAMA-PONGOLLE	15	2	329	19	France	0	0	71	423	1840

KEY: Club stats are all for the 2004-05 season. Games = appearances in the league for club; Goals conceded = goals let in when the player is on the pitch; Goals scored = scored by the player; Mins per goal = number of minutes on average between each goal conceded or scored; % played = the percentage of the league season the player played; Domestic = player ranking by position in domestic league; World = player ranking by position in World; Overall Position = player ranking in world across all positions. * = player record from previous club

THE STARS OF LAST SEASON

TEAM OF THE SEASON

- G: Dudek
- D: Finnan, Carragher, Hyypia, Traore
- M: Alonso, Gerrard, Hamann, Riise
- F: Baros, Luis Garcia

(G) STAR GOALKEEPER

JERZY DUDEK: Fought off Scott Carson and Chris Kirkland and won the Champions League with his penalty shoot-out antics.

Average goals per game conceded by club	1.08
Goals per game conceded when player on pitch	1.04
Points per game club won when player on pitch	1.58
Minutes played	2160	Clean sheets	5

(D) STAR DEFENDER

JAMIE CARRAGHER: Beloved by supporters as a 'scouser' who gives everything, Carragher had a stunning Champions League campaign.

Goals per game conceded when player on pitch	1.08
Points per game club won when player on pitch	1.53
Goals scored by player	0
Minutes played	3420	Clean sheets	7

(M) STAR MIDFIELDER

JOHN ARNE RIISE: In an ever-changing midfield he put in 57 appearances and offered greater consistency than Stevie Gerrard.

Goals per game conceded when player on pitch	1.02
Goals per game club scored when player on pitch	1.43
Goals scored by player	6
Minutes played	2975	Assists	6

(F) STAR FORWARD

MILAN BAROS: Off the back of rave reviews for the Czech Republic in Euro 2004, he still managed 13 goals in a patchy season.

Average goals per game scored by club	1.37
Goals per game scored when player on pitch	1.53
% of club goals scored by player	17.3
Minutes played	1853	Assists	2

2004-05 SEASON REVIEW OF THE LEAGUE

■ Games won ■ Games lost ■ Games drawn League position game by game

% of possible points won per month

Aug Sep Oct Nov Dec Jan Feb Mar Apr May

2004-05 RESULTS ROUND-UP

☐ Premiership ☐ League Cup ☐ FA Cup ☐ UEFA Cup ☐ Champions League

Grazer AK	A 2-0	**Arsenal**	H 2-1	B Leverkusen	A 3-1
Tottenham	A 1-1	Tottenham	H 1-1*	**Blackburn**	H 0-0
Man City	H 2-1	Aston Villa	A 1-1	**Everton**	H 2-1
Grazer AK	H 0-1	**Olympiakos**	H 3-1	**Bolton**	H 1-0
Bolton	A 0-1	Everton	A 2-1	**Juventus**	H 2-1
West Brom	H 3-0	**Portsmouth**	H 1-1	Man City	A 0-1
Monaco	H 2-0	**Newcastle**	H 1-1	Juventus	A 0-0
Man Utd	A 1-2	West Brom	A 5-0	**Tottenham**	H 2-2
Norwich	H 3-0	**Southampton**	H 2-0	Portsmouth	A 2-1
Olympiakos	A 0-1	Chelsea	H 0-1	Crystal Palace	A 0-0
Chelsea	A 0-1	Norwich	A 2-1	Chelsea	A 0-0
Fulham	H 4-2	Watford	H 1-0	**Middlesbrough**	H 1-1
Deportivo	H 0-0	**Man Utd**	H 0-1	**Chelsea**	H 1-0
Charlton	H 2-0	Burnley	A 1-3	Arsenal	A 1-3
Millwall	A 3-0	Southampton	A 0-2	**Aston Villa**	H 2-1
Blackburn	A 2-2	Watford	A 1-0	AC Milan	A 4-2*
Deportivo	A 1-0	Charlton	A 2-1	*Won on penalties*	
Birmingham	H 1-0	**Fulham**	H 3-1		
Middlesbrough	H 2-0	Birmingham	H 0-2		
Crystal Palace	H 3-2	B Leverkusen	H 3-1		
Middlesbrough	A 0-2	**Chelsea**	H 2-3		
Monaco	A 0-1	Newcastle	A 0-1		

STAR SIGNING

JOSE REINA

Rafael Benitez used his knowledge of the Spanish league to prise Jose Reina away from Villarreal. Reina is 14th in our list of the World's top keepers and has also experienced the pressure of playing for top Spanish club Barcelona.

83

MANCHESTER CITY

Premiership position 04-05 **8th**
FA Cup **Round 3**
Coca-Cola Cup **Round 3**

MAN. CITY FACTS

 MANAGER
STUART PEARCE

 CAPTAIN
SYLVAIN DISTIN

ADDITIONS TO SQUAD 2005-06

▼ PLAYERS IN	▼ FROM	▼ COST
Darius Vassell	Aston Villa	£2m
Andy Cole	Fulham	Free
Kiki Musampa	Atletico Madrid	Loan

CLUB

Stadium: City Of Manchester Stadium
Capacity: 48,000
Pitch Size: 116.5 yds by 75 yds
Website: www.mcfc.co.uk

RECORDS

Record Home Attendance: 84,569 v Stoke (FA Cup) Mar.3, 1934
Record Victory: 10-1 v Huddersfield (league) Nov.7, 1987; v Swindon (FA Cup) Jan.29, 1930
Record Defeat: 1-9 v Everton (league) Sept. 3, 1906
Most League Goals: Tommy Johnson (158)
Most League Apps: Alan Oakes (565)
Most Capped Player: Colin Bell, 48 (England)

HONOURS

Division One: 1937, 1968, *2002
Division Two: 1899, 1903, 1910, 1928, 1947, 1966
FA Cup: 1904, 1934, 1956, 1969
League Cup: 1970, 1976
European Cup Winners Cup: 1970

Nationwide
FOOTBALL LEAGUE
DIVISION 1 CHAMPIONS
MANCHESTER CITY F.C.

CURRENT SQUAD RECORD 2004-05

	CLUB				INTERNATIONAL			POSITIONAL RANKING		OVERALL RANKING
	Games	Goals	Mins per goal	% played	Country	Games	Goals	Domestic	World	All positions
GOALKEEPERS		CONCEDED					CONCEDED			
DAVID JAMES	38	39	87	100	England	10	4	**4**	**12**	59
DEFENDERS		CONCEDED					CONCEDED			
SYLVAIN DISTIN	38	39	87	99	France	0	0	**9**	**28**	96
RICHARD DUNNE	35	36	86	91	Rep of Ire.	4	0	**12**	**34**	128
DANNY MILLS	32	33	79	76	England	0	0	**31**	**107**	412
STEPHEN JORDAN	19	18	90	47	England	0	0	**44**	**206**	709
BEN THATCHER	18	17	90	45	Wales	4	7	**50**	**225**	771
NEDUM ONUOHA	17	10	106	31	England	0	0	**55**	**240**	806
SUN JIHAI	6	2	166	9	China PR	0	0	**114**	**577**	1845
MIDFIELDERS		SCORED					SCORED			
JOEY BARTON	31	1	2502	73	England	0	0	**15**	**55**	175
ANTOINE SIBIERSKI	35	4	714	83	France	0	0	**19**	**74**	213
CLAUDIO REYNA	17	2	731	42	USA	4	0	**63**	**338**	849
KIKI MUSAMPA	14	3	414	36	Holland	0	0	**75**	**407**	1033
WILLO FLOOD	9	1	381	11	Rep of Ire.	0	0	**152**	**800**	2035
TREVOR SINCLAIR	4	1	194	5	England	0	0	**156**	**822**	2080
FORWARDS		SCORED					SCORED			
ROBBIE FOWLER	32	10	251	73	England	0	0	**9**	**57**	162
ANDREW COLE *Fulham	31	12	208	73	England	0	0	**16**	**87**	316
DARIUS VASSELL *Villa	21	2	699	40	England	3	0	**59**	**352**	1589

KEY: Club stats are all for the 2004-05 season. Games = appearances in the league for club; Goals conceded = goals let in when the player is on the pitch; Goals scored = scored by the player; Mins per goal = number of minutes on average between each goal conceded or scored; % played = the percentage of the league season the player played; Domestic = player ranking by position in domestic league; World = player ranking by position in World; Overall Position = player ranking in world across all positions. * = player record from previous club

THE STARS OF LAST SEASON

TEAM OF THE SEASON

G
James

D — D — D — D
Mills — Distin — Dunne — Jordan

M — M — M — M
S Wright-Phillips — Barton — Bosvelt — Sibierski

F — F
Anelka — Fowler

G STAR GOALKEEPER

DAVID JAMES: Lost the confidence of England fans but Man City fans suddenly saw their defence performing for the first time in years.

Average goals per game conceded by club	1.03
Goals per game conceded when player on pitch	1.03
Points per game club won when player on pitch	1.37
Minutes played 3420	Clean sheets 11

D STAR DEFENDER

SYLVAIN DISTIN: Played all but 18 minutes of City's season and the main reason why they had the fourth best defence in the Premiership.

Goals per game conceded when player on pitch	1.02
Points per game club won when player on pitch	1.37
Goals scored by player	1
Minutes played 3402	Clean sheets 11

M STAR MIDFIELDER

SHAUN WRIGHT-PHILLIPS: Made Beckham justify his place in the England side and his 11 goals opened Chelsea's cheque-book.

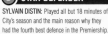

Goals per game conceded when player on pitch	1.02
Goals per game club scored when player on pitch	1.27
Goals scored by player	10
Minutes played 2998	Assists 6

F STAR FORWARD

ROBBIE FOWLER: Under Stuart Pearce he rediscovered his sharpness in front of goal to make up for Nicolas Anelka's departure.

Average goals per game scored by club	1.24
Goals per game scored when player on pitch	1.34
% of club goals scored by player	21.3
Minutes played 2515	Assists 4

2004-05 SEASON REVIEW OF THE LEAGUE

■ Games won ■ Games lost ■ Games drawn   League position game by game

% of possible points won per month

100%
75%
50%
25%
0%

Aug Sep Oct Nov Dec Jan Feb Mar Apr May

2004-05 RESULTS ROUND-UP

□ Premiership □ League Cup □ FA Cup □ UEFA Cup □ Champions League

Fulham	H	1-1	Southampton	H	2-1	Tottenham	A	1-2
Liverpool	A	1-2	Arsenal	A	1-1	Charlton	A	2-2
Birmingham	H	0-1	Oldham	A	0-1	Liverpool	H	1-0
Charlton	H	4-0	Crystal Palace	H	3-1	Fulham	A	1-1
Everton	H	0-1	West Brom	A	0-2	Birmingham	A	3-0
Crystal Palace	A	2-1	Newcastle	H	1-1	Blackburn	A	0-0
Barnsley	H	7-1	Chelsea	A	0-0	Portsmouth	H	2-0
Arsenal	H	0-1	Man Utd	H	0-2	Aston Villa	A	2-1
Southampton	A	0-0	Norwich	A	3-2	Middlesbrough	H	1-1
Chelsea	H	1-0	Bolton	H	0-1			
Newcastle	A	3-4						
Arsenal	H	1-2						
Norwich	H	1-1						
Man Utd	A	0-0						
Blackburn	H	1-1						
Portsmouth	A	3-1						
Aston Villa	H	2-0						
Middlesbrough	A	2-3						
Tottenham	H	0-1						
Bolton	A	1-0						
Everton	A	1-2						
West Brom	H	1-1						

STAR SIGNING

ANDY COLE

"I had to look into his eyes," said Stuart Pearce. He looked and came away convinced that Cole still had something to prove. Pearce will also be hoping that Cole forms a good partnership with another former England striker Darius Vassell.

MAN. UTD FACTS

MANAGER	CAPTAIN
SIR ALEX FERGUSON	ROY KEANE

ADDITIONS TO SQUAD 2005-06

▼ PLAYERS IN	▼ FROM	▼ COST
Ji-Sung Park	PSV	£4m
Edwin van der Sar	Fulham	£2m
Ben Foster	Stoke	£1m

CLUB

Stadium: Old Trafford
Capacity: 68,210
Pitch Size: 116 yds by 76 yds
Website: www.manutd.com

RECORDS

Record Home Attendance: 70,504 v Aston Villa (league) Dec.27, 1920
Record Victory: 10-0 v RSC Anderlecht (EC) Sept.26, 1956
Record Defeat: 0-7 v Blackburn (league) Dec.27, 1930; v Wolves (league) Dec.26, 1931
Most League Goals: Bobby Charlton (199)
Most League Apps: Bobby Charlton (606)
Most Capped Player: Bobby Charlton, 106 (England)

HONOURS

Premier League: 1993, 1994, 1996, 1997, 1999, 2000, 2001, 2003
Division One: 1908, 1911, 1952, 1956, 1957, 1965, 1967
FA Cup: 1909, 1948, 1963, 1977, 1983, 1985, 1990, 1994, 1996, 1999, 2004
League Cup: 1992
European Cup: 1968, 1999
European Cup Winners Cup: 1991

CURRENT SQUAD RECORD 2004-05

	CLUB				INTERNATIONAL			POSITIONAL RANKING		OVERALL RANKING
	Games	Goals	Mins per goal	% played	Country	Games	Goals	Domestic	World	All positions
GOALKEEPERS			CONCEDED				CONCEDED			
EDWIN VAN DER SAR *Fulham*	34	51	57	86	Holland	10	5	16	76	764
TIM HOWARD	12	10	108	31	USA	0	0	18	100	1189
DEFENDERS			CONCEDED				CONCEDED			
RIO FERDINAND	31	20	139	81	England	5	1	4	11	36
MIKAEL SILVESTRE	35	23	128	86	France	2	0	5	15	49
GABRIEL IVAN HEINZE	26	16	142	66	Argentina	8	7	6	21	65
JOHN O'SHEA	23	9	165	43	Rep of Ire.	9	4	19	49	200
WES BROWN	21	12	136	48	England	3	1	22	60	241
GARY NEVILLE	22	18	104	55	England	9	3	40	167	599
MIDFIELDERS			SCORED				SCORED			
JI-SUNG PARK *PSV Eindhoven*	28	7	339	78	South Korea	5	1	2	4	27
ROY KEANE	31	1	2610	76	Rep of Ire.	6	1	5	22	91
RYAN GIGGS	32	6	386	67	Wales	3	0	6	25	99
PAUL SCHOLES	33	9	289	76	England	0	0	11	42	142
CRISTIANO RONALDO	33	5	484	70	Portugal	9	6	26	103	278
DARREN FLETCHER	18	3	456	40	Scotland	5	0	32	160	431
QUINTON FORTUNE	17	0	-	30	S. Africa	0	0	85	444	1125
KEIRON RICHARDSON *WBA*	12	3	295	25	England	0	0	108	555	1402
LIAM MILLER	8	0	-	7	Rep of Ire.	7	0	161	842	2127
FORWARDS			SCORED				SCORED			
WAYNE ROONEY	29	11	198	63	England	6	0	5	33	85
ALAN SMITH	31	7	291	59	England	8	0	25	134	528
RUUD VAN NISTELROOY	17	6	227	39	Holland	5	3	36	184	828
LOUIS SAHA	14	1	672	19	France	3	0	76	446	1933

KEY: Club stats are all for the 2004-05 season. Games = appearances in the league for club; Goals conceded = goals let in when the player is on the pitch; Goals scored = scored by the player; Mins per goal = number of minutes on average between each goal conceded or scored; % played = the percentage of the league season the player played; Domestic = player ranking by position in domestic league; World = player ranking by position in World; Overall Position = player ranking in world across all positions. * = player record from previous club

THE STARS OF LAST SEASON

TEAM OF THE SEASON

G Carroll

D O'Shea **D** Ferdinand **D** Silvestre **D** Heinze

M Ronaldo **M** Keane **M** Scholes **M** Giggs

F Smith **F** Rooney

G STAR GOALKEEPER

ROY CARROLL: Apart from 'the goal that wasn't' against Spurs, Carroll had a great season and earned a Northern Ireland recall.

Average goals per game conceded by club	0.68
Goals per game conceded when player on pitch	0.62
Points per game club won when player on pitch	2.31
Minutes played	2340	Clean sheets	15

D STAR DEFENDER

RIO FERDINAND: Back from his ban and it couldn't have come soon enough for United who were leaking goals without him.

Goals per game conceded when player on pitch	0.64
Points per game club won when player on pitch	2.1
Goals scored by player	0
Minutes played	2790	Clean sheets	17

M STAR MIDFIELDER

ROY KEANE: Still the man that Ferguson must ultimately replace if United are going to challenge for honours into the future.

Goals per game conceded when player on pitch	0.66
Goals per game club scored when player on pitch	1.66
Goals scored by player	1
Minutes played	2610	Assists	2

F STAR FORWARD

WAYNE ROONEY: Began his United career as he left off his Euro 2004 campaign and has become more vital than Ruud.

Average goals per game scored by club	1.53
Goals per game scored when player on pitch	1.91
% of club goals scored by player	19.0
Minutes played	2181	Assists	5

2004-05 SEASON REVIEW OF THE LEAGUE

Games won Games lost Games drawn League position game by game

(graph: % of possible points won per month, Aug–May)

2004-05 RESULTS ROUND-UP

Premiership League Cup FA Cup UEFA Cup Champions League

Dinamo Buch.	A 2-1	Lyon	H 2-1	AC Milan	H 0-1
Chelsea	A 0-1	West Brom	A 3-0	Portsmouth	H 2-1
Norwich	H 2-1	Arsenal	H 1-0	Crystal Palace	A 0-0
Dinamo Buch.	H 3-0	Southampton	H 3-0	AC Milan	A 0-1
Blackburn	A 1-1	Fenerbahce	A 0-3	Southampton	A 4-0
Everton	H 0-0	Fulham	A 1-1	Fulham	H 0-0
Bolton	A 2-2	Crystal Palace	H 5-2	Blackburn	H 0-0
Lyon	A 2-2	Bolton	H 2-0	Norwich	A 0-2
Liverpool	H 2-1	Aston Villa	A 1-0	Newcastle	A 4-1
Tottenham	H 0-0	Middlesbrough	A 0-2	Everton	A 0-1
Fenerbahce	H 6-2	Tottenham	H 0-0	Newcastle	H 2-1
Middlesbrough	H 1-1	Exeter	H 0-0	Charlton	A 4-0
Birmingham	A 0-0	Chelsea	A 0-0	West Brom	H 1-1
Sparta Prague	A 0-0	Liverpool	A 0-1	Chelsea	H 1-3
Arsenal	H 2-0	Exeter	A 2-0	Southampton	A 2-1
Crewe	A 3-0	Aston Villa	H 3-1	Arsenal	N 0-0*
Portsmouth	A 0-2	Chelsea	H 1-2		
Sparta Prague	H 4-1	Middlesbrough	H 2-0	+Lost on penalties
Man City	H 0-0	Arsenal	A 4-2	
Crystal Palace	H 2-0	Birmingham	H 2-0	
Newcastle	A 3-1	Man City	A 2-0	
Charlton	H 2-0	Everton	A 2-0	

STAR SIGNING

PARK JI-SUNG

The Korean winger won rave reviews as an energetic cog in PSV's phenomenal midfield last season. They ran away with the Dutch title and outplayed AC Milan in the semi-finals of the Champions League. United, who failed to make any impression on Milan, took note.

BORO FACTS

MANAGER	CAPTAIN
STEVE McCLAREN	GARETH SOUTHGATE

ADDITIONS TO SQUAD 2005-06

▼ PLAYERS IN	▼ FROM	▼ COST
Ayegbeni Yakubu	Portsmouth	£7.5m
Emanuel Pogatetz	B.Leverkusen	£1.8m
Fabio Rochemback	Barcelona	£1m
Abel Xavier	Unattached	Free

CLUB

Stadium: The Riverside Stadium
Capacity: 35,049
Pitch Size: 115 yds by 75 yds
Website: www.mfc.co.uk

RECORDS

Record Home Attendance: 53,536 v Newcastle (league) Dec.27, 1949
Record Victory: 9-0 v Brighton (league) Aug.23, 1958
Record Defeat: 0-9 v Blackburn (league) Nov.6, 1954
Most League Goals: George Camsell (325)
Most League Apps: Ted Williamson (563)
Most Capped Player: Wilf Mannion, 26 (England)

HONOURS

Division One: 1995
Division Two: 1927, 1929, 1974
League Cup: 2004

CURRENT SQUAD RECORD 2004-05

	CLUB				INTERNATIONAL			POSITIONAL RANKING		OVERALL RANKING
	Games	Goals	Mins per goal	% played	Country	Games	Goals	Domestic	World	All positions
GOALKEEPERS	CONCEDED					CONCEDED				
MARK SCHWARZER	31	39	71	81	Australia	0	0	10	45	338
BRADLEY JONES	5	3	150	13	USA	0	0	23	114	1481
DEFENDERS	CONCEDED					CONCEDED				
GARETH SOUTHGATE	36	39	83	94	England	0	0	17	43	171
FRANCK QUEUDRUE	31	36	76	80	France	0	0	33	126	459
STUART PARNABY	19	13	101	38	England	0	0	63	278	931
CHRIS RIGGOTT	21	24	74	51	England	0	0	64	280	935
UGO EHIOGU	10	6	117	20	England	0	0	79	399	1266
ANTHONY MCMAHON	13	15	71	31	England	0	0	83	427	1354
COLIN COOPER	15	19	54	30	England	0	0	110	566	1796
MIDFIELDERS	SCORED					SCORED				
STEWART DOWNING	35	5	540	78	England	1	0	20	88	253
GEORGE BOATENG	25	3	749	65	Holland	0	0	23	94	261
RAY PARLOUR	33	0	-	81	England	0	0	29	112	301
DORIVA	26	0	-	43	Brazil	0	0	110	569	1436
GAIZKA MENDIETA	7	0	-	15	Spain	0	0	130	671	1711
JAMES MORRISON	14	0	-	15	England	0	0	139	731	1871
FORWARDS	SCORED					SCORED				
JIMMY-FLOYD HASSELBAINK	36	13	248	94	Holland	0	0	4	29	77
AYEGBENI YAKUBU *Portsmth	30	13	189	71	Nigeria	5	2	11	69	220
SZILARD NEMETH	31	4	424	49	Slovakia	8	3	38	189	844
MARK VIDUKA	16	5	219	32	Australia	0	0	40	192	862

KEY: Club stats are all for the 2004-05 season. Games = appearances in the league for club; Goals conceded = goals let in when the player is on the pitch; Goals scored = scored by the player; Mins per goal = number of minutes on average between each goal conceded or scored; % played = the percentage of the league season the player played; Domestic = player ranking by position in domestic league; World = player ranking by position in World; Overall Position = player ranking in world across all positions. * = player record from previous club

THE STARS OF LAST SEASON

TEAM OF THE SEASON

G Schwarzer

D Parnaby | Riggott | Southgate | Queudrue

M Zenden | Parlour | Boateng | Downing

F Hasselbaink | Nemeth

G STAR GOALKEEPER

MARK SCHWARZER: The tall Aussie is a calm presence with a better shot-stopping record than most of his Premiership rivals.

Average goals per game conceded by club	1.21
Goals per game conceded when player on pitch	1.26
Points per game club won when player on pitch	1.55
Minutes played	2790	Clean sheets	9

D STAR DEFENDER

GARETH SOUTHGATE: His England days may be over but he is still one of the most consistent and tidy defenders in the game.

Goals per game conceded when player on pitch	1.08
Points per game club won when player on pitch	1.5
Goals scored by player	0
Minutes played	3240	Clean sheets	11

M STAR MIDFIELDER

BOUDEWIJN ZENDEN: Converted from winger to central midfied by Steve McClaren, his creative spark attracted Liverpool's attention.

Goals per game conceded when player on pitch	1.3
Goals per game club scored when player on pitch	1.48
Goals scored by player	5
Minutes played	3055	Assists	1

F STAR FORWARD

JIMMY FLOYD-HASSELBAINK: Not his best season but that fierce shot and hunger for goals still make him one of the world's top strikers.

Average goals per game scored by club	1.39
Goals per game scored when player on pitch	1.43
% of club goals scored by player	24.5
Minutes played	3234	Assists	7

2004-05 SEASON REVIEW OF THE LEAGUE

■ Games won ■ Games lost ■ Games drawn   League position game by game

2004-05 RESULTS ROUND-UP

□ Premiership □ League Cup □ FA Cup □ UEFA Cup □ Champions League

Newcastle	H	2-2	**Man City**	H	3-2	Crystal Palace	A	1-0
Arsenal	A	3-5	Southampton	A	2-2	**Arsenal**	H	0-1
Fulham	H	2-0	**Partizan**	H	3-0	Fulham	A	1-1
Crystal Palace	H	2-1	Aston Villa	H	3-0	**West Brom**	H	4-0
Birmingham	H	2-1	Birmingham	A	0-2	Newcastle	A	0-0
Banik Ostrava	H	3-0	**Norwich**	H	2-0	Liverpool	A	1-1
Everton	A	0-1	**Man Utd**	H	2-0	**Tottenham**	H	1-0
Chelsea	H	0-1	Chelsea	A	0-0	Man City	A	1-1
Banik Ostrava	A	1-1	Notts County	A	2-1			
Man Utd	A	1-1	**Everton**	H	1-1			
Blackburn	A	4-0	Norwich	A	4-4			
Aigaleo	A	0-0	Man Utd	A	0-3			
Portsmouth	H	1-1	Portsmouth	A	1-2			
Coventry	H	3-0	**Blackburn**	H	1-2			
Charlton	A	2-1	Bolton	A	0-1			
Lazio	H	2-0	**Grazer AK**	A	2-2			
Bolton	H	1-1	**Grazer AK**	H	2-1			
Liverpool	A	0-2	Charlton	H	2-2			
West Brom	A	2-1	Aston Villa	A	4-2			
Liverpool	H	2-0	Sp Lisbon	A	2-3			
Villarreal	A	0-2	Sp Lisbon	A	0-1			
Tottenham	A	0-2	**Southampton**	H	1-3			

STAR SIGNING

AYEGBENI YAKUBU

A powerhouse centre forward, brought into the Premier by the sharp eyes of Harry Redknapp at Portsmouth, Ayegbeni Yakubu was snapped up by Steve McClaren to add strength to the guile of Viduka and predatory instincts of Hasselbaink. He scored 17 goals last season.

NEWCASTLE UNITED

NEWCASTLE FACTS

MANAGER	CAPTAIN
GRAEME SOUNESS	ALAN SHEARER

ADDITIONS TO SQUAD 2005-06

▼ PLAYERS IN	▼ FROM	▼ COST
Michael Owen	Real Madrid	£16.5m
Nolberto Solana	Aston Villa	£1.5m
Albert Luque	Deportivo	£9.5m
Scott Parker	Chelsea	£6.5m
Emre Belezoglu	Inter Milan	£3.8m
Lee Clark	Fulham	Free
Craig Moore	Monchengladbach	Free
Tim Krul	Ado Den Haag	*

* Fee undisclosed

CLUB

Stadium: St James' Park
Capacity: 52,387
Pitch Size: 115 yds by 74.5 yds
Website: www.nufc.co.uk

RECORDS

Record Home Attendance: 68,386 v Chelsea (league) Sept.3, 1930
Record Victory: 13-0 v Newport County (league) Oct.5 1946
Record Defeat: 0-9 v Burton Wanderers (league) April 15, 1895
Most League Goals: Jackie Milburn (178)
Most League Apps: Jim Lawrence (432)
Most Capped Player: Alf McMichael, 40 (Northern Ireland)

HONOURS

Division One: 1905, 1907, 1909, 1927, *1993
Division Two: 1965
FA Cup: 1910, 1924, 1932, 1951, 1952, 1955
UEFA Cup: 1969 (as Fairs Cup)

THE STARS OF LAST SEASON

TEAM OF THE SEASON

Given (G)
Carr (D) · Bramble (D) · Boumsong (D) · Hughes (D)
Dyer (M) · Jenas (M) · Bowyer (M) · Robert (M)
Shearer (F) · Bellamy (F)

G STAR GOALKEEPER

SHAY GIVEN: Often inspired for the 'Toon' and the Republic of Ireland, Given follows Shearer as the second name on the team-sheet.

Average goals per game conceded by club	1.5
Goals per game conceded when player on pitch	1.44
Average number of League points per game	1.22
Minutes played 3240	Clean sheets 6

D STAR DEFENDER

STEPHEN CARR: The right-back had to fit in with an ever-changing line-up but still found time for his marauding raids up the wing.

Goals per game conceded when player on pitch	1.23
Average number of League points per game	1.23
Goals scored by player	1
Minutes played 2131	Clean sheets 4

M STAR MIDFIELDER

JERMAINE JENAS: This elegant England midfielder still needs to add consistency to his all-round game but Spurs pounced.

Goals per game conceded when player on pitch	1.55
Goals per game club scored when player on pitch	1.27
Goals scored by player	1
Minutes played 2539	Assists 3

F STAR FORWARD

CRAIG BELLAMY: Outspoken, out of position and finally just plain out! Bellamy's departure ensured Newcastle's season fizzled out too.

Average goals per game scored by club	1.24
Goals per game scored when player on pitch	1.53
% of club goals scored by player	14.9
Minutes played 1782	Assists 4

CURRENT SQUAD RECORD 2004-05

	CLUB				INTERNATIONAL			POSITIONAL RANKING		OVERALL RANKING
	Games	Goals	Mins per goal	% played	Country	Games	Goals	Domestic	World	All positions
GOALKEEPERS		CONCEDED					CONCEDED			
SHAY GIVEN	36	52	62	94	Rep. of Ire.	9	5	**13**	67	586
DEFENDERS		CONCEDED					CONCEDED			
STEPHEN CARR	26	32	66	62	Rep. of Ire.	6	3	**71**	333	1062
TITUS BRAMBLE	19	23	71	48	England	0	0	**77**	379	1199
JEAN-ALAIN BOUMSONG	14	16	77	36	France	9	2	**88**	460	1480
CRAIG MOORE *Monchenglad.*	3	14	75	31	Australia	0	0		494	1578
STEVEN TAYLOR	13	14	72	29	England	0	0	**99**	517	1633
ROBBIE ELLIOTT	17	26	51	38	England	0	0	**106**	550	1737
CELESTINE BABAYARO	7	8	78	18	Nigeria	0	0	**117**	584	1877
MIDFIELDERS		SCORED					SCORED			
NOLBERTO SOLANO *Villa*	36	8	349	81	Peru	0	0	**46**	256	677
LEE BOWYER	27	3	723	63	England	0	0	**67**	360	894
KIERON DYER	23	4	439	51	England	6	0	**84**	437	1109
EMRE BELOZOGLU	19	0	-	30	Turkey	8	0	**109**	604	1516
AMDY FAYE	9	0	-	20	Senegal	3	0	**137**	722	1842
CHARLES N'ZOGBIA	14	0	-	23	France	0	0	**145**	753	1929
SCOTT PARKER *Chelsea*	4	0	-	3	England	0	0	**160**	833	2104
FORWARDS		SCORED					SCORED			
MICHAEL OWEN *Real Madrid*	36	13	145	55	England	10	6	**14**	59	175
ALBERT LUQUE *Deportivo*	37	11	218	70	Spain	7	2	**19**	114	439
ALAN SHEARER	28	7	323	66	England	0	0	**33**	174	742
SHOLA AMEOBI	31	2	840	49	England	0	0	**63**	366	1645

KEY: Club stats are all for the 2004-05 season. Games = appearances in the league for club; Goals conceded = goals let in when the player is on the pitch; Goals scored = scored by the player; Mins per goal = number of minutes on average between each goal conceded or scored; % played = the percentage of the league season the player played; Domestic = player ranking by position in domestic league; World = player ranking by position in World; Overall Position = player ranking in world across all positions. * = player record from previous club

2004-05 SEASON REVIEW OF THE LEAGUE

■ Games won ■ Games lost ■ Games drawn — League position game by game

% of possible points won per month

Aug · Sep · Oct · Nov · Dec · Jan · Feb · Mar · Apr · May

2004-05 RESULTS ROUND-UP

□ Premiership □ League Cup □ FA Cup □ UEFA Cup □ Champions League

Middlesbrough	A	2-2	Chelsea	A	0-4	Portsmouth	A	1-1
Tottenham	H	0-1	**Portsmouth**	H	1-1	**Aston Villa**	H	0-3
Norwich	H	2-2	Sp Lisbon	H	1-1	Sp Lisbon	H	1-0
Aston Villa	A	2-4	Liverpool	A	1-3	Tottenham	A	0-1
Blackburn	H	3-0	Blackburn	A	2-2	Sp Lisbon	A	1-4
Bnei Sachnin	H	2-0	**Arsenal**	A	0-1	Man Utd	H	1-4
Southampton	A	2-1	Birmingham	H	2-1	Norwich	A	1-2
West Brom	H	3-1	West Brom	A	0-0	Man Utd	A	1-2
Bnei Sachnin	A	5-1	Yeading	A	2-0	**Middlesbrough**	H	0-0
Birmingham	A	2-2	**Southampton**	H	2-1	**Crystal Palace**	H	0-0
Charlton	A	1-1	Arsenal	A	0-1	Fulham	A	3-1
Panionios	A	1-0	**Coventry**	H	3-1	Everton	A	0-2
Man City	H	4-3	Man City	A	1-1	Chelsea	H	1-1
Norwich	H	2-1	**Charlton**	H	1-1			
Bolton	A	1-2	Heerenveen	A	2-1			
Dinamo Tbilisi	H	2-0	Chelsea	H	1-0			
Fulham	H	1-4	Heerenveen	H	2-1			
Chelsea	H	0-2	Bolton	H	2-1			
Man Utd	H	1-3	**Liverpool**	H	1-0			
Crystal Palace	A	2-0	Olympiakos	A	3-1			
Sochaux	A	4-0	**Tottenham**	H	1-0			
Everton	H	1-1	Olympiakos	H	4-0			

STAR SIGNING

MICHAEL OWEN

Belief flooded back to the tens of thousands of Newcastle fans who came out to cheer Owen, unveiled as first Shearer's partner, then successor, and key forward for both club and country. Madrid and Liverpool may yet regret their decisions.

PORTSMOUTH

PORTSMOUTH FACTS

MANAGER	CAPTAIN
ALAIN PERRIN	DEJAN STEFANOVIC

ADDITIONS TO SQUAD 2005-06

▼ PLAYERS IN	▼ FROM	▼ COST
Andy O'Brien	Portsmouth	£2m
John Viafara	Once Caldas	£1.5m
Laurent Robert	Newcastle	Loan
Azar Karadas	Benfica	Loan
Sander Westerveld	Real Mallorca	Free
Gregory Vignal	Liverpool	Free
Dario Silva	Seville	Free
Zvonimir Vukic	Shakhtar Donetsk	*

* Fee Undisclosed

CLUB

Stadium: Fratton Park
Capacity: 20,200
Pitch Size: 110 yds by 72 yds
Website: www.pompeyfc.co.uk

RECORDS

Record Home Attendance: 51,385 v Derby County (FA Cup) Feb.26, 1949
Record Victory: 9-1 v Notts County (league) April 9, 1927
Record Defeat: 0-10 v Leicester City (league) Oct.20, 1928
Most League Goals: Peter Harris (194)
Most League Apps: Jimmy Dickinson (764)
Most Capped Player: Jimmy Dickinson, 48 (England)

HONOURS

Division One: 1949, 1950, *2003
Division Three: 1962, 1983
Division Three South: 1924
FA Cup: 1939

CURRENT SQUAD RECORD 2004-05

	CLUB				INTERNATIONAL			POSITIONAL RANKING		OVERALL RANKING
	Games	Goals	Mins per goal	% played	Country	Games	Goals	Domestic	World	All positions
GOALKEEPERS		CONCEDED					CONCEDED			
SANDER WESTERVELD *Mallorca	6	8	67	15	Holland	0	0	25	135	1869
JAMIE ASHDOWN	16	25	57	42	England	0	0	22	108	1375
KONSTANTINOS CHALKIAS	5	11	40	13	Greece	0	0	31	160	2200
DEFENDERS		CONCEDED					CONCEDED			
LINVOY PRIMUS	35	46	62	83	England	0	0	54	232	784
DEJAN STEFANOVIC	32	53	54	84	Serb & Mont	0	0	65	282	940
ANDREW GRIFFIN	22	19	84	47	England	0	0	69	306	993
MATTHEW TAYLOR	32	44	49	63	England	0	0	82	425	1348
ANDY O'BRIEN *Newcastle	23	37	52	56	Rep of Ire.	8	4	91	476	1526
GREGORY VIGNAL *Rangers	30	15	167	73	France	0	0	2	-	-
MIDFIELDERS		SCORED					SCORED			
LAURENT ROBERT *Newcastle	31	3	634	55	France	0	0	77	418	1054
GARY O'NEIL	24	2	945	55	England	0	0	119	591	1478
RICHARD HUGHES	16	0	-	33	Scotland	3	0	123	599	1501
ALIOU CISSE	20	0	-	33	Senegal	0	0	129	662	1683
GIANNIS SKOPELITIS	13	0	-	23	Greece	0	0	149	773	1973
FORWARDS		SCORED					SCORED			
LOMANA LUALUA	25	6	288	50	Congo DR	0	0	41	193	878

KEY: Club stats are all for the 2004-05 season. Games = appearances in the league for club; Goals conceded = goals let in when the player is on the pitch; Goals scored = scored by the player; Mins per goal = number of minutes on average between each goal conceded or scored; % played = the percentage of the league season the player played; Domestic = player ranking by position in domestic league; World = player ranking by position in World; Overall Position = player ranking in world across all positions. * = player record from previous club

THE STARS OF LAST SEASON

TEAM OF THE SEASON

- G — Hislop
- D — Griffin
- D — De Zeeuw
- D — Stefanovic
- D — Primus
- M — Stone
- M — Quashie
- M — O'Neil
- M — Berger
- F — Yakuba
- F — LuaLua

G STAR GOALKEEPER

SHAKA HISLOP: Lost his position when Harry Redknapp left but his shot-stopping record was far better than his replacements.

Average goals per game conceded by club	1.55
Goals per game conceded when player on pitch	1.35
Points per game club won when player on pitch	1.12
Minutes played	1530	Clean sheets	3

D STAR DEFENDER

LINVOY PRIMUS: Along with the consistent Arjan De Zeeuw, Primus did enough to ensure Pompey battled clear of relegation.

Goals per game conceded when player on pitch	1.31
Points per game club won when player on pitch	1.03
Goals scored by player	1
Minutes played	2870	Clean sheets	5

M STAR MIDFIELDER

PATRIK BERGER: Shortlisted for goal-of-the-season with his stunning swooping volley and left Pompey fans with something to remember.

Goals per game conceded when player on pitch	1.45
Goals per game club scored when player on pitch	1.3
Goals scored by player	3
Minutes played	2496	Assists	5

F STAR FORWARD

AYEGBENI YAKUBU: This powerhouse was another of Pompey's stars of last season to have been sold despite scoring 17 goals.

Average goals per game scored by club	1.13
Goals per game scored when player on pitch	1.25
% of club goals scored by player	30.2
Minutes played	2458	Assists	3

2004-05 SEASON REVIEW OF THE LEAGUE

■ Games won ■ Games lost ■ Games drawn — League position game by game

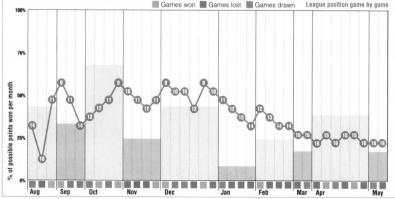

2004-05 RESULTS ROUND-UP

□ Premiership □ League Cup □ FA Cup □ UEFA Cup □ Champions League

Birmingham	H	1-1	Crystal Palace	A	1-0	Man Utd	A	1-2
Charlton	A	1-2	**Chelsea**	H	0-2	Arsenal	A	0-3
Fulham	H	4-3	**Norwich**	H	1-1	**Newcastle**	H	1-1
Crystal Palace	H	3-1	Everton	A	1-2	Fulham	A	1-3
Blackburn	A	0-1	**Gillingham**	H	1-0	**Charlton**	H	4-2
Tranmere	A	1-2	**Blackburn**	H	0-1	Birmingham	A	1-2
Everton	H	0-1	Chelsea	A	0-3	**Liverpool**	H	1-2
Norwich	A	2-2	Southampton	A	1-2	**Southampton**	H	4-1
Tottenham	H	1-0	**Middlesbrough**	H	2-1	Man City	A	0-2
Middlesbrough	A	1-1	Tottenham	A	1-3	**Bolton**	H	1-1
Leeds	H	2-1	**Aston Villa**	H	1-2	West Brom	A	0-2
Man Utd	H	2-0						
Aston Villa	A	0-3						
Cardiff	A	2-0						
Southampton	H	1-4						
Man City	H	1-3						
Bolton	A	0-0						
Watford	A	0-3						
West Brom	H	3-2						
Newcastle	A	1-1						
Liverpool	A	1-1						
Arsenal	H	0-1						

STAR SIGNING

AZAR KARADAS

A Norwegian described as an English style centre forward and signed from Benfica in Portugal. Pompey's new target man demonstrates the international nature of football. He is 1.9m tall and has Champions League experience with Rosenborg.

SUNDERLAND

SUNDERLAND FACTS

MANAGER	CAPTAIN
MICK McCARTHY	GARY BREEN

ADDITIONS TO SQUAD 2005-06

▼ PLAYERS IN	▼ FROM	▼ COST
Jonathan Stead	Blackburn	£1.8m
Kelvin Davis	Ipswich	£1.25m
Andy Gray	Sheffield United	£1.1m
Daryl Murphy	Waterford	£100,000
Alan Stubbs	Everton	Free
Joe Murphy	West Brom	Free
Nyron Nosworthy	Gillingham	Free
Tommy Miller	Ipswich	Free
Anthony Le Tallec	Liverpool	Loan

CLUB

Stadium: Stadium Of Light
Capacity: 48,353
Pitch Size: 115 yds by 75 yds
Website: www.safc.com

RECORDS

Record Home Attendance: 75,118 v Derby County (FA Cup) Mar.8, 1933
Record Victory: 11-1 v Fairfield (FA Cup) Feb.2, 1895
Record Defeat: 0-8 v Sheffield Wednesday (league) Oct.19, 1968; v Watford (league) Sept.25, 1982
Most League Goals: Charlie Buchan (209)
Most League Apps: Jim Montgomery (537)
Most Capped Player: Charlier Hurley, 38 (Rep. Of Ireland)

HONOURS

Championship:
2005

Division One:
1892, 1893, 1895, 1902, 1913, 1936, *1996, *1999

Division Two:
1976

Division Three:
1988

FA Cup: 1937, 1973

CURRENT SQUAD RECORD 2004-05

	LEAGUE RECORD				LAST SEASON		COUNTRY	POSITIONAL RANKING
	Games	Goals	Mins per goal	% played	Club	League		In division
GOALKEEPERS		CONCEDED						
KELVIN DAVIES	40	48	72	84	Ipswich	Champ'ship	England	17
DEFENDERS		CONCEDED						
ALAN STUBBS	25	24	102	71	Everton	Premiership	England	14
GARY BREEN	40	37	94	84	Sunderland	Champ'ship	Rep of Ire.	28
STEVEN CALDWELL	41	35	102	86	Sunderland	Champ'ship	Scotland	18
STEPHEN WRIGHT	39	35	99	84	Sunderland	Champ'ship	England	20
NYRON NOSWORTHY	37	49	66	78	Gillingham	Champ'ship	England	95
GEORGE McCARTNEY	36	30	107	77	Sunderland	Champ'ship	N. Ireland	12
MIDFIELDERS		SCORED						
JULIO ARCA	40	9	371	81	Sunderland	Champ'ship	Argentina	7
TOMMY MILLER	45	13	300	94	Ipswich	Champ'ship	Scotland	14
CARL ROBINSON	40	4	879	85	Sunderland	Champ'ship	Wales	4
LIAM LAWRENCE	32	7	275	46	Sunderland	Champ'ship	England	30
DEAN WHITEHEAD	42	5	690	83	Sunderland	Champ'ship	England	5
FORWARDS		SCORED						
ANTHONY LE TALLEC	4	0	-	6	Liverpool	Premiership	France	-
JOHN STEAD	15	2	893	52	Blackburn	Premiership	England	62
STEPHEN ELLIOTT	43	15	174	63	Sunderland	Champ'ship	Rep of Ire.	5
ANDY GRAY	43	15	235	85	Sheff. Utd	Champ'ship	Scotland	26

KEY: Club stats are all for the 2004-05 season. Games = appearances in the league for club; Goals conceded = goals let in when the player is on the pitch; Goals scored = scored by the player; Mins per goal = number of minutes on average between each goal conceded or scored; % played = the percentage of the league season the player played; Club = the club that the player was with last season; League = the league that the record was achieved in; Country = player's nationality; Positional Ranking (in division) = player ranking by position in the division

THE STARS OF LAST SEASON

TEAM OF THE SEASON

G Myhre
D Wright | **D** Breen | **D** Caldwell | **D** McCartney
M Whitley | **M** Arca | **M** Robinson | **M** Whitehead
F Elliot | **F** Stewart

G STAR GOALKEEPER

THOMAS MYHRE: Former Everton fave Myhre stepped into the Sunderland team when Mart Poom was injured, helping them to promotion.

Average goals per game conceded by club	0.89
Goals per game conceded when player on pitch	0.89
Points per game club won when player on pitch	2.17
Minutes played	2655	Clean sheets	11

D STAR DEFENDER

GEORGE McCARTNEY: McCartney joined Sunderland in 1998 and the 24-year-old was their best defender last season.

Goals per game conceded when player on pitch	0.84
Points per game club won when player on pitch	2.06
Goals scored by player	0
Minutes played	3198	Clean sheets	15

M STAR MIDFIELDER

CARL ROBINSON: Signed from Portsmouth, this versatile Welsh international starred in the champions' engine room

Goals per game conceded when player on pitch	0.84
Goals per game club scored when player on pitch	1.76
Goals scored by player	4
Minutes played	3515	Assists	–

F STAR FORWARD

STEPHEN ELLIOTT: 15 league goals at a strike rate of one every 174 minutes led The Black Cats assault on the Premiership.

Average goals per game scored by club	1.65
Goals per game scored when player on pitch	1.96
% of club goals scored by player	16.7
Minutes played	2438	Assists	–

2004-05 SEASON REVIEW OF THE LEAGUE

■ Games won ■ Games lost ■ Games drawn ● League position game by game

% of possible points won per month

Aug | Sep | Oct | Nov | Dec | Jan | Feb | Mar | Apr | May

2004-05 RESULTS ROUND-UP

□ Premiership □ League Cup ■ FA Cup ■ UEFA Cup ■ Champions League

Coventry	A	0-2	Stoke	A	1-0	Wigan	A	1-0
Crewe	H	3-1	**West Ham**	H	0-2	**Reading**	H	1-2
QPR	H	2-2	Cardiff	A	2-0	Ipswich	A	2-2
Plymouth	A	1-2	**Burnley**	H	2-1	**Leicester**	H	2-1
Chester	H	3-0	**Leeds**	H	2-3	West Ham	A	1-1
Wigan	H	1-1	Nottm Forest	A	2-1	**Stoke**	H	1-0
Reading	A	0-1	Preston	A	2-3			
Gillingham	A	4-0	**Gillingham**	H	1-1			
Nottm Forest	H	2-0	**Crystal Palace**	H	2-1			
Preston	H	3-1	Derby	A	2-0			
Crewe	A	2-4*	**Sheff Utd**	H	1-0			
Leeds	A	1-0	Everton	A	0-3			
Sheff Utd	A	0-1	Wolverhampton	A	1-1			
Derby	H	0-0	**Watford**	H	4-2			
Millwall	H	1-0	Brighton	A	1-2			
Watford	A	1-1	**Rotherham**	H	4-1			
Rotherham	A	1-0	**Cardiff**	H	1-0			
Brighton	H	2-0	Burnley	A	2-0			
Wolverhampton	H	3-1	Crewe	H	1-0			
Millwall	A	0-2	**Plymouth**	H	5-1			
Leicester	A	1-0	**Coventry**	H	1-0			
Ipswich	H	2-0	QPR	A	3-1			

TOTTENHAM HOTSPUR

SPURS FACTS

MANAGER	CAPTAIN
MARTIN JOL	LEDLEY KING

ADDITIONS TO SQUAD 2005-06

▼ PLAYERS IN	▼ FROM	▼ COST
Jermaine Jenas	Newcastle	£7m
Lee Young-Pyo	PSV	£2m
Tom Huddlestone	Derby	£2.5m
Grzegorz Rasiak	Derby	£2m
Wayne Routledge	Crystal Palace	*
Aaron Lennon	Leeds	*
Edgar Davids	Inter Milan	Free
Paul Stalteri	Werder Bremen	Free
Teemu Tainio	Auxerre	Free

* Fee Undisclosed

CLUB

Stadium: White Hart Lane
Capacity: 36,240
Pitch Size: 110 yds x 73 yds
Website: www.spurs.co.uk

RECORDS

Record Home Attendance: 75,038 v Sunderland (FA Cup) March 5, 1938
Record Victory: 13-2 v Crewe (FA Cup) Feb.3, 1960
Record Defeat: 0-8 v Cologne (Inter Totot Cup) July 22, 1995
Most League Goals: Jimmy Greaves 220
Most League Apps: Steve Perryman 655
Most Capped Player: Pat Jennings, 74 (N.Ireland)

HONOURS

Division One: 1951, 1961
Division Two: 1920, 1950
FA Cup: 1901, 1921, 1961, 1962, 1967, 1981, 1982, 1991
League Cup: 1971, 1973, 1999
UEFA Cup: 1972, 1984
European Cup Winners Cup: 1963

CURRENT SQUAD RECORD 2004-05

	CLUB				INTERNATIONAL			POSITIONAL RANKING		OVERALL RANKING
	Games	Goals	Mins per goal	% played	Country	Games	Goals	Domestic	World	All positions
GOALKEEPERS		CONCEDED					CONCEDED			
PAUL ROBINSON	36	40	80	93	England	9	2	6	20	129
RADEK CERNY	3	1	206	6	Czech Rep.	0	0	27	136	1886
DEFENDERS		CONCEDED					CONCEDED			
LEDLEY KING	38	41	83	100	England	7	3	15	37	139
PAUL STALTERI *W.Bremen	32	30	84	74	Canada	2	3	17	92	258
NOUREDDINE NAYBET	27	27	86	67	Morocco	5	4	32	113	427
STEPHEN KELLY	17	13	98	37	Rep. of Ire.	0	0	58	255	861
NOE PAMAROT	23	25	77	56	France	0	0	60	265	897
ANTHONY GARDNER	17	12	69	24	England	0	0	108	557	1760
PHILIP IFIL	2	1	180	5	England	0	0	111	568	1813
MICHAEL DAWSON	5	6	75	13	England	0	0	120	606	1962
MIDFIELDERS		SCORED					SCORED			
MICHAEL CARRICK	29	0	-	69	England	0	0	25	97	265
WAYNE ROUTLEDGE *Palace	38	1	3142	91	England	0	0	51	289	761
JERMAINE JENAS *Newcastle	27	1	2539	74	England	7	0	56	316	807
MICHAEL BROWN	24	1	1712	50	England	0	0	58	331	833
PEDRO MENDES	24	1	1947	56	Portugal	0	0	65	353	880
ANDREW REID	13	1	1072	31	Rep. of Ire.	8	2	91	467	1187
TEEMU TAINIO *Auxerre	27	2	827	48	Finland	4	1	72	496	1251
SEAN DAVIS	15	0	-	30	England	0	0	112	571	1439
EDGAR DAVIDS *Inter Milan	14	0	-	20	Holland	5	0	129	687	1753
JOHNNIE JACKSON	8	0	-	8	England	0	0	164	851	2146
FORWARDS		SCORED					SCORED			
JERMAIN DEFOE	35	13	194	73	England	11	1	7	48	138
ROBBIE KEANE	35	11	199	64	Rep. of Ire.	9	5	13	74	239

KEY: *Club stats are all for the 2004-05 season. Games = appearances in the league for club; Goals conceded = goals let in when the player is on the pitch; Goals scored = scored by the player; Mins per goal = number of minutes on average between each goal conceded or scored; % played = the percentage of the league season the player played; Domestic = player ranking by position in domestic league; World = player ranking by position in World; Overall Position = player ranking in world across all positions. * = player record from previous club*

THE STARS OF LAST SEASON

TEAM OF THE SEASON

G Robinson

D Kelly — D King — D Naybet — D Edman

M Mendes — M Carrick — M Brown — M Atouba

F Defoe — F Keane

G STAR GOALKEEPER

PAUL ROBINSON: Has cemented his place in the England team with eye-catching saves illuminating a season of secure keeping.

Average goals per game conceded by club	1.08
Goals per game conceded when player on pitch	1.11
Points per game club won when player on pitch	1.37
Minutes played 3214	Clean sheets 12

D STAR DEFENDER

LEDLEY KING: Came to everyone's attention deputising brilliantly for the banned Ferdinand in England's Euro 2004 team against France.

Goals per game conceded when player on pitch	1.08
Points per game club won when player on pitch	1.37
Goals scored by player	2
Minutes played 3420	Clean sheets 13

M STAR MIDFIELDER

MICHAEL CARRICK: Signed from West Ham and ignored by Jacques Santini before Martin Jol made him the hub of Spurs' midfield.

Goals per game conceded when player on pitch	1.06
Goals per game club scored when player on pitch	1.55
Goals scored by player	0
Minutes played 2374	Assists 5

F STAR FORWARD

JERMAIN DEFOE: 22 goals in all competitions led to eight caps for England and a reputation as one of the Premiership's best finishers.

Average goals per game scored by club	1.24
Goals per game scored when player on pitch	1.15
% of club goals scored by player	27.7
Minutes played 2525	Assists 2

2004-05 SEASON REVIEW OF THE LEAGUE

Games won ■ Games lost ■ Games drawn — League position game by game

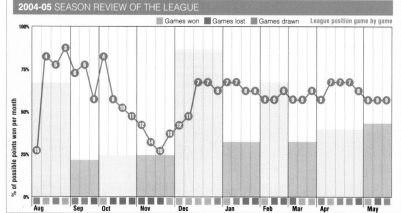

Aug Sep Oct Nov Dec Jan Feb Mar Apr May

2004-05 RESULTS ROUND-UP

□ Premiership □ League Cup □ FA Cup □ UEFA Cup □ Champions League

Liverpool	H	1-1	Norwich	A	2-0	Southampton	A	0-1
Newcastle	A	1-0	**Crystal Palace**	H	1-1	Newcastle	A	0-1
West Brom	A	1-1	**Everton**	H	5-2	Charlton	A	0-2
Birmingham	H	1-0	Man Utd	A	0-0	**Man City**	H	2-1
Norwich	H	0-0	**Brighton**	H	2-1	Birmingham	A	0-1
Chelsea	A	0-0	Chelsea	H	0-2	Newcastle	H	1-0
Oldham	A	6-0	Crystal Palace	A	0-3	Liverpool	A	2-2
Man Utd	H	0-1	**West Brom**	H	2-0	**West Brom**	H	1-1
Everton	A	1-0	Bolton	A	1-3	Arsenal	A	0-1
Portsmouth	A	1-0	**Portsmouth**	H	3-1	**Aston Villa**	H	0-0
Bolton	H	1-2	**West Brom**	H	3-1	Middlesbrough	A	0-1
Bolton	A	4-3	**Nottm Forest**	A	3-1	Blackburn	H	0-0
Fulham	A	0-2	Fulham	H	2-0	+Lost on penalties		
Charlton	H	2-3	Nottm Forest	A	3-0			
Burnley	A	3-0						
Arsenal	H	4-5						
Aston Villa	H	1-1						
Middlesbrough	H	2-0						
Liverpool	H	1-1+						
Blackburn	A	0-1						
Man City	A	1-1						
Southampton	H	5-1						

STAR SIGNING

EDGAR DAVIDS

A football colossus both playing in the Orange of Holland or in the black and white stripes of Juventus, Edgar Davids may be the signing to take Spurs into Europe. He has flirted with Barcelona and joins from Inter Milan where he had few games last season.

WEST BROMWICH ALBION

WEST BROM FACTS

MANAGER	CAPTAIN
BRYAN ROBSON	KEVIN CAMPBELL

ADDITIONS TO SQUAD 2005-06

▼ PLAYERS IN	▼ FROM	▼ COST
Nathan Ellington	Wigan	£3m
Curtis Davies	Luton	£3m
Diomansy Kamara	Modena	£1.5m
Darren Carter	Birmingham	£1.5m
Chris Kirkland	Liverpool	Loan
Steve Watson	Everton	Free

CLUB

Stadium: The Hawthorns
Capacity: 28,083
Pitch Size: 115 yds by 74 yds
Website: www.wba.co.uk

RECORDS

Record Home Attendance: 64,815 v Arsenal (FA Cup) Mar.6, 1937
Record Victory: 12-0 v Darwen (league) April 4, 1892
Record Defeat: 10-3 v Stoke City (league), Feb.4, 1937
Most League Goals: Tony Brown (218)
Most League Apps: Tony Brown (574)
Most Capped Player: Stuart Williams, 33 (Wales)

HONOURS

Division One: 1920
Division Two: 1902, 1911
FA Cup: 1888, 1892, 1931, 1954, 1968
League Cup: 1966

THE STARS OF LAST SEASON

TEAM OF THE SEASON

- G Hoult
- D Albrechtsen
- D Clement
- D Gaardsoe
- D Robinson
- M Gera
- M Wallwork
- M Richardson
- M Greening
- F Earnshaw
- F Horsfield

G STAR GOALKEEPER

RUSSELL HOULT: Only Norwich's Green conceded more goals in the Premier but a strong finish kept West Brom up.

Average goals per game conceded by club	1.61
Goals per game conceded when player on pitch	1.66
Points per game club won when player on pitch	0.83
Minutes played	3171	Clean sheets	6

D STAR DEFENDER

NEIL CLEMENT: Began the season scoring goals in midfield before dropping back to central defence and making 35 appearances.

Goals per game conceded when player on pitch	1.6
Points per game club won when player on pitch	0.88
Goals scored by player	3
Minutes played	3101	Clean sheets	6

M STAR MIDFIELDER

ZOLTAN GERA: The spring-heeled right midfielder who captains the Hungarian team, scored six vital goals from Baggies' midfield.

Goals per game conceded when player on pitch	1.58
Goals per game club scored when player on pitch	1.06
Goals scored by player	6
Minutes played	2374	Assists	5

F STAR FORWARD

ROBERT EARNSHAW: Often used as sub, he never complained and struck 11 goals, ending up with the division's second best strike-rate.

Average goals per game scored by club	0.95
Goals per game scored when player on pitch	1.05
% of club goals scored by player	30.1
Minutes played	1723	Assists	1

CURRENT SQUAD RECORD 2004-05

	CLUB				INTERNATIONAL			POSITIONAL RANKING		OVERALL RANKING
	Games	Goals	Mins per goal	% played	Country	Games	Goals	Domestic	World	All positions
GOALKEEPERS		CONCEDED					CONCEDED			
RUSSELL HOULT	35	60	52	92	England	0	0	15	70	650
TOMASZ KUSZCZAK	3	1	249	7	Poland	0	0	21	106	1304
CHRIS KIRKLAND *Liverpool	10	13	69	26	England	2	0	24	123	1667
DEFENDERS		CONCEDED					CONCEDED			
NEIL CLEMENT	34	56	55	90	England	0	0	45	208	712
MARTIN ALBRECHTSEN	18	21	84	51	Denmark	0	0	46	210	715
PAUL ROBINSON	26	39	63	72	England	9	2	47	212	720
THOMAS GAARDSOE	22	41	52	62	Denmark	1	1	73	359	1145
RICCARDO SCIMECA	26	55	45	72	England	0	0	80	405	1279
STEVE WATSON *Everton	25	0	-	35	England	0	0	87	457	1168
DARREN MOORE	10	20	49	28	England	0	0	112	570	1821
BERNT HAAS	6	15	50	22	Switzerland	5	4	121	619	2005
MIDFIELDERS		SCORED					SCORED			
ZOLTAN GERA	28	6	453	79	Hungary	5	4	42	229	604
JONATHAN GREENING	31	0	-	83	England	0	0	47	264	693
RONNIE WALLWORK	19	1	1726	50	England	0	0	62	337	848
STEVE WATSON	10	0	-	34	England	0	0	87	457	1162
ANDY JOHNSON	19	0	-	54	Wales	2	0	113	574	1448
RICHARD CHAPLOW	2	0	-	7	England	0	0	168	871	2191
FORWARDS		SCORED					SCORED			
ROBERT EARNSHAW	14	11	156	50	Wales	7	2	23	125	494
GEOFF HORSFIELD	14	3	540	47	England	0	0	44	228	1057
KEVIN CAMPBELL	13	3	434	38	England	0	0	46	244	1144
DIOMANSY MEHDI KAMARA	10	4	343	40	France	0	0	57	344	1558
NWANKWO KANU	19	2	963	56	Nigeria	3	1	60	354	1594
NATHAN ELLINGTON *Wigan	41	24	156	90	England	0	0	-	-	-

KEY: Club stats are all for the 2004-05 season. Games = appearances in the league for club; Goals conceded = goals let in when the player is on the pitch; Goals scored = scored by the player; Mins per goal = number of minutes on average between each goal conceded or scored; % played = the percentage of the league season the player played; Domestic = player ranking by position in domestic league; World = player ranking by position in World; Overall Position = player ranking in world across all positions. * = player record from previous club

2004-05 SEASON REVIEW OF THE LEAGUE

■ Games won ■ Games lost ■ Games drawn   League position game by game

% of possible points won per month — Aug, Sep, Oct, Nov, Dec, Jan, Feb, Mar, Apr, May

2004-05 RESULTS ROUND-UP

□ Premiership □ League Cup □ FA Cup □ UEFA Cup □ Champions League

Blackburn	A	1-1	Newcastle	H	0-0	Chelsea	A	0-1
Aston Villa	H	1-1	Preston	A	2-0	Charlton	A	4-1
Tottenham	H	1-1	Fulham	A	0-1	**Everton**	H	1-0
Everton	A	1-2	Man City	H	2-0	Aston Villa	A	1-1
Liverpool	A	0-3	**Tottenham**	H	1-1	Tottenham	A	1-1
Fulham	H	1-1	**Crystal Palace**	H	2-2	Middlesbrough	A	0-4
Colchester	A	1-2	Norwich	A	2-3	**Blackburn**	H	1-1
Newcastle	A	1-3	Tottenham	A	1-3	Arsenal	A	1-1
Bolton	H	2-1	**Southampton**	H	0-0	Man Utd	A	1-1
Norwich	H	0-0	**Birmingham**	H	2-0	**Portsmouth**	H	2-0
Crystal Palace	A	0-3						
Chelsea	H	1-4						
Southampton	A	2-2						
Middlesbrough	H	1-2						
Arsenal	A	1-1						
Man Utd	H	0-0						
Portsmouth	A	0-3						
Charlton	H	0-1						
Birmingham	A	0-4						
Liverpool	H	0-5						
Man City	A	1-1						
Bolton	A	1-1						

STAR SIGNING

NATHAN ELLINGTON

Nathan (Duke) Ellington is another forward to join the formidable group collected by Brian Robson. An elegant player, he has been scoring in the lower leagues for seasons and would have played in the Premiership with Wigan, his 24 goals having won them promotion.

WEST HAM UNITED

WEST HAM FACTS

MANAGER	CAPTAIN
ALAN PARDEW	CHRISTIAN DAILLY

ADDITIONS TO SQUAD 2005-06

▼ PLAYERS IN	▼ FROM	▼ COST
Yossi Benayoun	Santander	£2.5m
Paul Konchesky	Charlton	£1.5m
Clive Clarke	Stoke	£250,000
James Collins	Cardiff	*
Danny Gabbidon	Cardiff	*
Roy Carroll	Man. United	Free
Shaka Hislop	Portsmouth	Free
Petr Mikolanda	Viktoria Zizkow	Free

* Fee Undisclosed

HONOURS

Stadium: Boleyn Ground
Capacity: 35,595
Pitch Size: 112 yds by 72 yds
Website: www.whufc.com

RECORDS

Record Home Attendance: 42,322 v Tottenham (league) Oct.17, 1970

Record Victory: 10-0 v Bury (League Cup), Oct.25, 1983

Record Defeat: 2-8 v Blackburn Rovers Dec.26, 1963

Most League Goals: Vic Watson (298)

Most League Apps: Billy Bonds (663)

Most Capped Player: Bobby Moore, 108 (England)

HONOURS

Division Two: 1958, 1981
FA Cup: 1964, 1975, 1980
European Cup Winners Cup: 1965

CURRENT SQUAD RECORD 2004-05

	LEAGUE RECORD				LAST SEASON		COUNTRY	POSITIONAL RANKING
	Games	Goals	Mins per goal	% played	Club	League		In division
GOALKEEPERS			CONCEDED					
ROY CARROLL	26	16	146	68	Man Utd	Premiership	N. Ireland	2
SHAKA HISLOP	17	23	67	45	Portsmouth	Premiership	Trinidad & T.	20
DEFENDERS			CONCEDED					
DANIEL GABBIDON	45	48	84	98	Cardiff	Champ'ship	Wales	43
TOMAS REPKA	42	49	76	90	West Ham	Champ'ship	Czech Rep.	58
ANTON FERDINAND	29	28	79	53	West Ham	Champ'ship	England	52
CHRISTIAN DAILLY	3	1	181	4	West Ham	Champ'ship	Scotland	-
PAUL KONCHESKY	15	33	47	46	Charlton	Premiership	England	105
HAYDEN MULLINS	37	40	69	67	West Ham	Champ'ship	England	89
MIDFIELDERS			SCORED					
CLIVE CLARK	41	1	3562	86	Stoke	Champ'ship	Rep of Ire.	68
REO-COKER	39	3	1060	77	West Ham	Champ'ship	England	18
YOSSI BENAYOUN	35	8	373	87	R. Santander	Spanish Lge	Israel	43
MATTHEW ETHERINGTON	39	4	760	73	West Ham	Champ'ship	England	33
CARL FLETCHER	32	2	1199	58	West Ham	Champ'ship	England	53
FORWARDS			SCORED					
MARLON HAREWOOD	45	17	229	94	West Ham	Champ'ship	England	24
TEDDY SHERINGHAM	33	20	122	59	West Ham	Champ'ship	England	2
BOBBY ZAMORA	34	7	223	38	West Ham	Champ'ship	England	40

KEY: *Club stats are all for the 2004-05 season. Games = appearances in the league for club; Goals conceded = goals let in when the player is on the pitch; Goals scored = scored by the player; Mins per goal = number of minutes on average between each goal conceded or scored; % played = the percentage of the league season the player played; Club = the club that the player was with last season; League = the league that the record was achieved in; Country = player's nationality; Positional Ranking (in division) = player ranking by position in the division*

THE STARS OF LAST SEASON

TEAM OF THE SEASON

G Bywater

D Mullins — **D** Repka — **D** Ferdinand — **D** Powell

M Chadwick — **M** Reo-Coker — **M** Fletcher — **M** Etherington

F Sheringham — **F** Harewood

G STAR GOALKEEPER

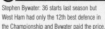

Stephen Bywater: 36 starts last season but West Ham had only the 12th best defence in the Championship and Bywater paid the price.

Average goals per game conceded by club	1.20
Goals per game conceded when player on pitch	1.19
Points per game club won when player on pitch	1.56
Minutes played	3240	Clean sheets	11

D STAR DEFENDER

Anton Ferdinand: brother of Rio, this Ferdinand can play centre or right back and was the Hammers' youngest and best defender

Goals per game conceded when player on pitch	0.97
Points per game club won when player on pitch	1.78
Goals scored by player	1
Minutes played	2199	Clean sheets	8

M STAR MIDFIELDER

Nigel Reo-Coker: came through the ranks and the bad times at Wimbledon and has skippered West Ham and the England Under 21 side.

Goals per game conceded when player on pitch	1.07
Goals per game club scored when player on pitch	1.48
Goals scored by player	3
Minutes played	3181	Assists	-

F STAR FORWARD

Teddy Sheringham: 40 this season, Teddy has won the Champions League, starred for England and still looks at the top of his game.

Average goals per game scored by club	1.43
Goals per game scored when player on pitch	1.64
% of club goals scored by player	30.3
Minutes played	2438	Assists	-

2004-05 SEASON REVIEW OF THE LEAGUE

■ Games won ■ Games lost ■ Games drawn — League position game by game

2004-05 RESULTS ROUND-UP

□ Premiership □ League Cup □ FA Cup □ UEFA Cup □ Champions League

Leicester	A	0-0	Millwall	A	0-1	Wigan	A	2-1
Reading	H	1-0	**Watford**	A	3-2	Burnley	A	1-0
Wigan	H	1-3	Sunderland	A	2-0	**Coventry**	H	3-0
Crewe	A	3-2	Leeds	H	1-1	Millwall	H	1-0
Southend	H	2-0	Preston	A	1-2	Stoke	A	1-0
Burnley	H	1-0	**Nottm Forest**	H	3-2	Brighton	A	2-2
Coventry	A	1-2	Rotherham	A	2-2	**Sunderland**	H	1-2
Sheff Utd	A	1-2	Ipswich	A	1-0	**Ipswich**	H	2-2
Rotherham	H	1-0	Sheff Utd	H	0-2	Ipswich	A	2-0
Ipswich	H	1-1	**Norwich**	H	1-0	**Preston**	N	1-0
Notts County	A	3-2	Wolverhampton	A	2-4			
Nottm Forest	A	1-2	Derby	H	1-2			
Derby	A	1-1	Sheff Utd	H	1-1			
Wolverhampton	H	1-0	Cardiff	H	1-0			
QPR	A	0-1	Sheff Utd	A	1-3*			
Stoke	H	2-0	Plymouth	H	5-0			
Gillingham	H	3-1	Gillingham	A	1-0			
Chelsea	A	0-1	Leeds	A	1-2			
Plymouth	A	1-1	**Preston**	A	2-1			
Cardiff	A	1-4	Reading	A	1-3			
QPR	H	2-1	Crewe	H	1-1			
Brighton	H	0-1	Leicester	H	2-2			

WIGAN ATHLETIC

WIGAN FACTS

MANAGER	CAPTAIN
PAUL JEWELL	ARJAN DE ZEEUW

ADDITIONS TO SQUAD 2005-06

▼ PLAYERS IN	▼ FROM	▼ COST
Henri Carama	Wolves	£3m
David Connolly	Leicester	£2m
Damien Francis	Norwich	£1.5m
Ryan Taylor	Tranmere	£750,000
Mike Pollitt	Rotherham	£200,000
Pascal Chimbonda	Bastia	*
Arjan de Zeeuw	Portsmouth	*
Stephane Henchoz	Celtic	Free

* Fee Undisclosed

HONOURS

Stadium: JJB Stadium
Capacity: 25,000
Pitch Size: 115 yds by 75 yds
Website: www.wiganlatics.co.uk

RECORDS

Record Home Attendance: 27,526 v
Hereford (league) Dec.12, 1953
Record Victory: 7-1 v Scarborough (league)
Mar.11, 1997
Record Defeat: 1-6 v Bristol Rovers (league)
Mar.3, 1990
Most League Goals: David Lowe (66)
Most League Apps: Kevin Langley (317)
Most Capped Player: Roy Carroll, 9
(N.Ireland)

HONOURS

Division Three: *1997

THE STARS OF LAST SEASON

TEAM OF THE SEASON

G — John Filan
D — Baines, Jackson, Breckin, Eaden
M — Mahon, McCulloch, Teale, Bullard
F — Ellington, Roberts

(G) STAR GOALKEEPER

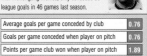

JOHN FILAN: The Australian who was once with Wollongong Wolves, only conceded 35 league goals in 46 games last season.

Average goals per game conceded by club	0.76
Goals per game conceded when player on pitch	0.76
Points per game club won when player on pitch	1.89
Minutes played	4140	Clean sheets	20

(D) STAR DEFENDER

MATT JACKSON: The 33-year-old spent five years at Everton but has been a defensive rock in Wigan's double promotion in three years.

Goals per game conceded when player on pitch	0.75
Points per game club won when player on pitch	1.85
Goals scored by player	0
Minutes played	3011	Clean sheets	15

(M) STAR MIDFIELDER

LEE McCULLOCH: With 14 goals, this Scot, who can also play in attack, was simply the best midfielder in the Championship.

Goals per game conceded when player on pitch	0.75
Goals per game club scored when player on pitch	1.88
Goals scored by player	14
Minutes played	3591	Assists	–

(F) STAR FORWARD

NATHAN ELLINGTON: Discovered playing non-league football, 'The Duke' hit 24 goals to earn Wigan promotion before joining West Brom.

Average goals per game scored by club	1.72
Goals per game scored when player on pitch	1.76
% of club goals scored by player	30.3
Minutes played	3744	Assists	–

CURRENT SQUAD RECORD 2004-05

	LEAGUE RECORD				LAST SEASON		COUNTRY	POSITIONAL RANKING
	Games	Goals	Mins per goal	% played	Club	League		In division
GOALKEEPERS			CONCEDED					
JOHN FILAN	46	35	118	100	Wigan	Champ'ship	Australia	1
MIKE POLLITT	45	67	60	98	Rotherham	Champ'ship	England	19
DEFENDERS			CONCEDED					
ARJAN DE ZEEUW	30	50	55	81	Portsmouth	Premiership	Holland	67
STEPHANE HENCHOZ	6	2	84	5	Celtic	Scottish Prem	Switzerland	-
MATT JACKSON	36	26	119	75	Wigan	Champ'ship	England	4
LEIGHTON BAINES	41	32	113	87	Wigan	Champ'ship	England	8
EMERSON THOME	15	5	200	24	Wigan	Champ'ship	Brazil	149
PASCAL CHIMBONDA	36	44	73	94	Bastia	French League	France	69
DAVID WRIGHT	31	20	93	45	Wigan	Champ'ship	England	32
RYAN TAYLOR	43	46	83	92	Tranmere	League 1	England	13
MIDFIELDERS			SCORED					
JIMMY BULLARD	46	3	1347	98	Wigan	Champ'ship	England	3
ALAN MAHON	27	7	272	46	Wigan	Champ'ship	Rep of Ire.	2
LEE McCULLOCH	42	14	257	87	Wigan	Champ'ship	Scotland	1
GARY TEALE	37	3	834	60	Wigan	Champ'ship	Scotland	6
DAMIEN FRANCIS	32	7	448	92	Norwich	Premiership	England	68
FORWARDS			SCORED					
HENRI CAMARA	12	3	273	24	Southampton	Premiership	Senegal	-
JASON ROBERTS	44	19	205	94	Wigan	Champ'ship	Grenada	18

Henri Camara and Stephane Henchoz didn't play enough games to get a ranking. KEY: Club stats are all for the 2004-05 season. Games = appearances in the league for club; Goals conceded = goals let in when the player is on the pitch; Goals scored = scored by the player; Mins per goal = number of minutes on average between each goal conceded or scored; % played = the percentage of the league season the player played; Club = the club that the player was with last season; League = the league that the record was achieved in; Country = player's nationality; Positional Ranking (in division) = player ranking by position in the division

2004-05 SEASON REVIEW OF THE LEAGUE

Games won ▢ Games lost ▢ Games drawn ▢ League position game by game

(Chart: % of possible points won per month, Aug–May)

2004-05 RESULTS ROUND-UP

▢ Premiership ▢ League Cup ▢ FA Cup ▢ UEFA Cup ▢ Champions League

Nottm Forest	H	1-1	Preston	H	5-0	
Millwall	A	2-0	Gillingham	H	2-0	Leicester A 2-0
West Ham	A	3-1	Ipswich	A	1-2	QPR H 0-0
Brighton	H	3-0	Derby	H	1-2	Preston A 1-1
Grimsby	A	0-1	Burnley	A	0-1	Reading H 3-1
Sunderland	A	1-1	Sheff Utd	A	2-0	
Cardiff	H	2-1	Wolverhampton	H	2-0	
Wolverhampton	A	3-3	Derby	A	1-2	
Burnley	H	0-0	Rotherham	A	2-0	
Sheff Utd	H	4-0	Watford	H	2-2	
Derby	A	1-1	Stoke	H	0-1	
Watford	A	0-0	Crewe	A	3-1	
Rotherham	H	2-0	Leeds	H	3-0	
Plymouth	A	2-1	Coventry	A	2-1	
Crewe	H	2-0	Gillingham	A	1-2	
Coventry	H	4-1	Ipswich	H	1-0	
Leeds	A	1-1	**Millwall**	H	2-0	
Stoke	A	1-0	Brighton	A	4-2	
Plymouth	H	0-2	Nottm Forest	H	1-2	
QPR	A	0-1	West Ham	H	1-2	
Leicester	H	0-0	Sunderland	H	0-1	
Reading	A	1-1	Cardiff	A	2-0	

There are four quiz pages in the 2006 MOTD Annual. Fill in the answers below to test your football knowledge against the experts from the world's best TV football programme!

QUIZ 1
FROM PAGE 23

ENGLAND WORD SEARCH

```
J A M E S N O R O O N E Y X E V D E D
O P Q R L M C O L E T U V Y L A E B C
H G H R A M S B E C K H A M T S F N C
N C A G A R R I C K N C O S G S O G A
S A R B U D E N E V I L L E S E E P R
O R G R E R D S N Q G B U T M L J E R
N S R F B H S O E F H E J E A L A F A
T O E G R E E N V J T O R T S K I N G
B N A U O S C O L A M P A R D I E S H
E L V A W A T O W E N A O Y A N G A E
A S E W N R I C K G A R D N E R D S R
T H S M I C A M P B E L L A J F D T D
T E R P L R I C H A R D S O N A U B I
I S B U T T F E Y O U I L A M E M V N
E K I N F E R D I N A N D G P J D A S
J E N T L R J O H S W R I G P E Y S M
E Y R O G R O U C H T E G P E N E T L
M E S B A Y O U N G A J E N F A R N T
Q V W R I G H T P H I L L I P S F E H
```

OUT OF 35 POINTS I SCORED	35

NAME THE YEAR

1	2004
2	1999
3	1992
4	2003
5	2001

1. 2004. 2. 1999. 3. 1992. 4. 2003. 5. 2001

2004-05 SEASON

1	Ash. Cole
2	Chelsea
3	Patr. Veira
4	
5	
6	
7	
8	
9	
10	
11	
12	

1. Ashley Cole (11) 2. Chelsea (112 subs). 3. Patrick Vieira. 4. Jurgen Klinsmann; 5. Southampton (30). 6. Andy Johnson (Palace). 11 pens scored. 7. PSV Eindhoven. 8. Fulham (8). 9. CSKA Moscow. 10. Jamie Carragher (Liverpool); Craig Fleming (Norwich). 11. Frank Lampard. 12. Cambridge United & Kidderminster; Lesley King (Tottenham).

NAME THE PUNDIT

1	Alan Hansel

1. Alan Hansen

WHO PLAYS WHERE

1	
2	
3	
4	
5	
6	
7	
8	

1. H; 2. C; 3. E; 4. A; 5. B; 6. G; 7. D; 8. F

SUMMER SIGNINGS

1	Inter milan
2	manchester city
3	Southampton
4	Newcastle
5	Real moralco
6	Aston villa

1. Inter Milan 2. Manchester City 3. Southampton 4. Newcastle; 5. Real Mallorca 6. Aston Villa

QUIZ 2
FROM PAGE 39

ENGLAND QUIZ

1	Scotland
2	USA
3	Bobby charlton
4	
5	
6	
7	
8	
9	
10	
11	
12	

1. Scotland. 2. USA. 3. Bobby Charlton. 4. Martin Peters. 5. Alf Ramsey. 6. Germany; 7. Alan Shearer. 8. Spain. 9. Michael Owen. 10. Peter Shilton. 11. Wayne Rooney. 12. Sol Campbell

CUP WINNERS

1	
2	
3	
4	
5	

1. Premiership. 2. UEFA Cup. 3. FA Cup. 4. European Cup. 5. Worthington League Cup

2004-05 SEASON

1	
2	
3	
4	
5	
6	
7	
8	
9	
10	
11	
12	

1. 4 goals. 2. Steve Wigley. 3. Celestine Babayaro. 4. City Of Manchester Stadium; 5. Marcus Stewart. 6. Gary Megson. 7. Brad Friedel. 8. John Terry. 9. West Ham; 10. Lyon. 11. Southampton. 12. Roy Carroll

NAME THE PUNDIT

1	

1. Gordon Strachan

WHO PLAYED WHERE

1	
2	
3	
4	
5	
6	
7	
8	

1. D; 2. A; 3. H; 4. G; 5. B; 6. C; 7. F; 8. E

MISSING PLAYERS

1	
2	
3	
4	

1. Jerzy Dudek. 2. Sami Hyypia. 3. Steven Gerrard. 4. Harry Kewell